I'

FORGET

IT WHEN

I DIE!

THE BISBEE
DEPORTATION
OF 1917

MITCHELL ABIDOR

I'll Forget It When I Die!: The Bisbee Deportation of 1917
© 2021 Mitchell Abidor
This edition © 2021 AK Press (Chico / Edinburgh)

ISBN: 978-1-84935-370-0
E-ISBN: 978-1-84935-371-7
Library of Congress Control Number: 2020946123

AK Press	AK Press
370 Ryan Ave. #100	33 Tower St.
Chico, CA 95973	Edinburgh EH6 7BN
USA	Scotland
www.akpress.org	www.akuk.com
akpress@akpress.org	akuk@akpress.org

Please contact us to request the latest AK Press distribution catalog, which features
books, pamphlets, zines, and stylish apparel published and/or distributed by AK Press.
Alternatively, visit our websites for the complete catalog, latest news, and secure ordering.

Cover design by T. L. Simons ~ tlsimons.com
Printed in the USA on acid-free paper

CONTENTS

Introduction

Heading east from Tombstone on Route 80, it is all but impossible not to be enchanted by the first glimpse of Bisbee. The refurbished miners' shacks spread across the hills, their colors all the brighter and clearer thanks to the city's elevation of almost six thousand feet and near-total lack of pollution, are, like almost everything else, cut off from Bisbee's history.

The once bustling town nearly died when the mines, which were its initial reason to exist, were shut in 1985. The town survived at first thanks to its administrative role as county seat of Cochise County and then thrived when young people, many of them artists, discovered Bisbee and its cheap housing.

Tourism is the heart of Bisbee's economy now, and on a recent trip there, an Airbnb flat in a converted miner's home, one with a koi pond but no central heating (and given its elevation Bisbee can be a cold place), cost as much as an apartment in London, one block from the British Museum.

Physically, little has changed since its heyday, and most of the buildings along the main shopping drag, Tombstone Canyon, have been there since the early twentieth century. They were all witnesses to one of the darkest, most shameful moments in American labor history: the Bisbee Deportation of 1917. On July 12, 1917, almost 1,200 men—most of them striking copper miners, but many others simply sympathizers with the cause of labor—were rounded up, marched at gunpoint to the town's ballpark, put in boxcars, and deported across the border to New Mexico. All of this was done without any legal justification and was organized by the mining companies and the town's sheriff in an effort to quell the supposed radical threat posed by the Industrial Workers of the World—more familiarly known as the IWW, the Wobblies, the Wobs, or the One Big Union—the main force behind a strike that had gone on for about two weeks.

So little has changed in Bisbee that if you sit in front of the Bisbee Coffee Company, located in the old mercantile exchange, and hold a picture of the miners being led down Tombstone Canyon, every building in the photo is still there. The deportation can be easily retraced and even reenacted, as it was in the recent film *Bisbee '17*.

History in Bisbee, though, like almost everywhere in America, is hidden from sight unless you know where to look for it. Longtime residents say they were told the deportation was something not to be discussed. Though the local history museum speaks of it, the ballpark, claimed to be in continuous use longer than any other in America, displays the logos of the Brooklyn Dodgers and Chicago Cubs, which once had farm teams in Bisbee, but bears no plaque commemorating the event or the stadium's role as a holding pen during it.

Though almost forgotten, talk of the deportation among families now living in Bisbee or those who have roots there is finally occurring. It's fitting, since the Bisbee Deportation is an expression of many dark currents in American history, currents that have maintained their hold on the American psyche. It happened because of a hatred of labor unions and radicals, because of racism and xenophobia, out of a sense of white American grievance against Mexicans and those not native-born. The fortitude and organizational skills of the men deported are inspiring; the fear and lies of those who carried out the deportation are all too familiar.

CHAPTER ONE

BISBEE'S BEGINNINGS

Labor troubles have never been known

In the beginning was copper. And Apaches. And a happy accident.

In 1877, a troop of US Cavalry from Fort Bowie—near what is today Willcox, Arizona—was pursuing a group of Apache in the Mule Mountains in the southeastern corner of the Arizona Territory. They set up camp at a watering hole named Iron Spring, but the water was so foul tasting that a scout named Jack Dunn was sent out to find another campsite. While searching, he stumbled upon a potentially lucrative iron and lead outcrop, and informed his unit's leader, named Lieutenant Anthony Rucker, and a friend about his find. Though on active duty, there was apparently nothing preventing the cavalrymen from filing mining claims, and they called their claim the Rucker.

This claim, which was made twenty years after mining began in southeastern Arizona, was filed the same year as that of Ed Schieffelin, whose claim led to the founding of Tombstone, twenty-five miles west of the future Bisbee. Though best known for the shootout at the O.K. Corral, the stand-in for all Western shootouts, Tombstone was first and foremost a mining town. The mines long gone, the town survives today on its tourist fakery, advertising itself as "The Town Too Tough to Die."

Filing the Rucker claim did the three men no immediate good, as they were still engaged in fighting the Apache, who refused to be dispossessed of their land. During this time, a man named George Warren, a former Apache prisoner, appeared in Fort Bowie, and the three partners financed Warren to work the claim for them while they were otherwise occupied. In this remote area of the Arizona Territory a claim was simply a claim with no actual effect in many cases: given the isolation and difficult location, many lay untouched and were taken over by other claimants. In a nice summation of the morality of the prospectors, Warren rounded up four other prospectors over the next couple of weeks and the new group filed twelve new claims. Warren's name was the one attached to these claims, and the area came to be called the Warren District.

The most promising claim in the district was the Copper Queen, which would later come to dominate the Warren District and become the jewel in the crown of the Phelps Dodge Mining Company.

George Warren managed to obtain a one-ninth share in the Copper Queen, which, had he held on to it, would have guaranteed his fortune for life. But in a story that seems almost too clichéd to be true, "fortified one day by too much frontier whiskey," Warren bet his share in the Cooper Queen on the assertion that he could run a hundred yards around a stake and return to the starting point faster than a man on horseback.[1] The bet was taken and the race was run in nearby Charleston, then a mining town only a few miles from the Clanton ranch, home of the opponents of the Earp brothers and Doc Holliday in the gunfight at the O.K. Corral, and by 1888 a ghost town. Unsurprisingly, Warren lost the race and the tens of millions of dollars the claim would have brought him.

Despite all the Western trappings, what followed this race demonstrates the extent to which the Wild West was nothing but a distant outpost of capitalist expansion.

Edward Reilly, a former lawyer, and Levi Zeckendorf, a Tucson shop owner, obtained an option on the Copper Queen mine. Reilly then went to San Francisco to convince two railroad contractors, John Ballard and William Martin, to finance the purchase of the mine. Advisers to the contractors directed them to put up the funds, as did their lawyer, DeWitt Bisbee. In honor of his role in the purchase, the lawyer's name was given to the city that would grow around the mine. It is thus not a grizzled prospector, or a miner, or a cavalryman, or an Indigenous leader whose name graces the city to this day: it is that of an out-of-town lawyer. The city eventually became the seat of Cochise County, replacing Tombstone, the original seat. The county itself was carved out of Pima County, in which Tucson is located, in 1881, bearing the name of the Chiricahua Apache chief who died in 1874 in the Dragoon Mountains.

The mine, which began with a capitalization of $2.5 million was in full operation in June 1880, and by August Bisbee had a population of five hundred, a post office, two saloons, a brewery, three boardinghouses, and a general store, the last owned in part by Joseph Goldwater, great-uncle of future presidential candidate and Arizona senator Barry Goldwater. Census reports give a far lower population, finding just fifteen men: ten Americans, one German, three Mexicans, and an Irishman.[2] As the Phelps Dodge company history put it, so rich was the mine that "the further the workings progressed, the further the limits of the ore body seemed to recede."[3]

It was in 1885 that the Copper Queen was purchased by the Phelps Dodge company, which would maintain its hold on the mine (and the town of Bisbee) until the mines were closed a century later. In 1900, when the smelter in Bisbee could no longer meet the needs of the company, a new one was built twenty miles east of Arizona in a new town, Douglas, which bears the name of James Douglas, the engineer who encouraged Phelps Dodge to expand its investments in Arizona.[4]

The Copper Queen was a resounding success, and between 1885 and 1908 it produced more than 730 million pounds of copper and paid dividends of $30 million. But according to the company history, there was more than just profit to be made. "It is said that the gruesome sight of the body of a Mexican desperado, left dangling by a self-appointed vigilance committee, brought home to Douglas, especially, the rough, lawless nature of Bisbee society in 1885 and the immediate need for establishing those cultural and ameliorating agencies which he believed the development of a self-respecting, law-abiding community required." Bisbee, thanks to Phelps Dodge, "soon had its church, hospital, company store, and recreation center."[5]

In these early days of mining in Bisbee, the bulk of the miners were men from Cornwall, England, and were familiarly known as "Cousin Jacks." Their presence would remain strong throughout the following decades, and they would constitute the core body of miners in the area who rejected union activity. By 1910, there were 1,500 English natives in Cochise County, mainly Bisbee, and another 500 with an English parent.[6]

As the nineteenth century ended, the Copper Queen faced competition, when the neighboring Irish Mag mine—named for a Bisbee prostitute—was purchased and became the heart of the Calumet and Arizona Mining Company (C&A). In 1904, Lemuel Shattuck organized a third company, which would shortly become the Shattuck-Denn Mining Company.

"As a result of the production of high-grade ores by the Copper Queen, Calumet and Arizona, and Shattuck-Denn, Bisbee became the most important mining city in Arizona and one of the most renowned copper centers in the world."[7] By 1905, the city had a population of between twelve thousand and fifteen thousand. By 1917, the Warren District had expanded and included—heading east down Tombstone Canyon—Bisbee. South of what is now the Lavender Pit (named not for its color but for a Phelps Dodge manager Horace Lavender), which opened in 1950 and closed in 1974, is Lowell, and north of it the Winwood Addition. Saginaw is east of the pit, and Warren lies southeast of it. The entire agglomeration had a population of nearly twenty-five thousand in 1917.

* * *

By 1917, Bisbee had churches. It had a thriving company store and would soon have a YMCA. It had bars, brothels, and breweries. What it didn't have were unions.

An undated article said that, "Labor troubles have never been known.... There is no miner's union and the men appear to want none. They have even placed themselves in opposition to the eight-hour bill that is pending in the Arizona legislature. Most of the men are married and own their own homes and consider themselves under employment for life. Many have been with the company for over twenty years and all appear well-satisfied with their lot. No Mexicans are employed underground, and the Mexican population is small, though the border is near."[8]

Opposition to an eight-hour day was short lived, if it ever truly existed. In March 1903, the territorial governor granted an eight-hour day to underground miners. The law, though, was toothless, and when workers in Morenci and Clifton, Arizona—who had no union—walked out, the companies convinced the governor to send in the Arizona Rangers. A few days later, President Roosevelt sent US troops from Forts Grant and Huachuca to Morenci. A court order finally put an end to the work action.[9]

Bisbee's first union was organized in February 1906, a local of the militant Western Federation of Miners (WFM). Not only was it opposed by the local business community, but it also received little support from the miners. In a vote that took place on March 1, 1906, 2,888 miners were opposed to the union versus 428 in favor. Four hundred of the men who voted for the union were fired by the copper companies, and a hundred more quit in solidarity.[10] However poor the turnout for the WFM, the reaction of the mine owners demonstrates their fear of union presence, a fear that would never leave them and would lead to the events of 1917.

There was a policy of employing Mexican workers only for undesirable aboveground tasks, like carrying goods up hills not serviceable by wagons. This policy was not to be varied from, and along with it, Mexicans were paid a lower wage, even when they worked at the same tasks as white workers. In 1917, these policies would feed into the strike and the deportations. The Presidential Mediation Commission that investigated the Bisbee Deportation in November 1917 was informed that the wage scale varied, depending on "whether they were Mexican or white men... Mexicans were paid at a lower rate."[11]

Anti-Mexican racism was not only a trait of the bosses. In April 1907, the WFM called a strike in Bisbee to protest firings at the mines, as well as to demand higher wages and stop the use of Mexican workers. Three thousand men walked off the job in support of these demands. The strike dragged on until December, but accomplished nothing.[12]

The restriction of Mexicans to certain jobs in the mines of the Warren District was part of the general tenor of life in the district, one that the official histories carefully elide. Bisbee and its environs were, from its beginning, a "white man's camp," and at times called an "American camp." The district had its own Chinese exclusion laws; Chinese were denied the right to live in the district, and at best were allowed to sell vegetables in town and then leave before sundown. An attempt to open a Chinese laundry resulted in the burning in effigy of the man bold enough to attempt to do so.[13]

There were few Black people, perhaps seventy in the early twentieth century, and they too were discriminated against in all facets of life. Strict segregation was the law of Arizona, and it was mercilessly applied: Bisbee's seven Black schoolchildren were forced to attend a separate school established just for them.

The definition of "Mexican" was an expansive one, not limited to those born in Mexico, and the definition of the "white man" who "rightfully" belonged in the camp was a narrow one. While immigrants from southern and eastern Europe had been kept out of other mining towns, like Cripple Creek, Colorado, they were allowed in Bisbee, but existed in a kind of racial limbo. Hundreds of immigrants from these parts of Europe were in Bisbee in 1917 and had their own neighborhoods, boardinghouses, and churches. Being allowed to work and live in Bisbee was one thing; being fully accepted was quite another. These European "white men" would be deported in large numbers and so discover that this "white man's camp" was not meant to include them.[14]

Phelps Dodge encouraged white workers with families to move to Bisbee, as the company offered a higher rate of pay for married men—the "family wage." Single white men also qualified for this wage, though married Mexican men didn't.[15] Despite the camp's "whiteness," and its discriminatory wages, Cochise County's Mexican population, largely if not exclusively Mexican-born, quadrupled in the first decade of the twentieth century, from 1,500 to 6,000.[16]

When referring to Mexican people and the conditions under which they worked and the way they were viewed, it is important to keep in mind that the characterization of someone as "Mexican" was not a national label, but rather, as Katherine Benton-Cohen points out, a "racial" one. Birthplace was not the determining element: someone of Mexican heritage but a resident for generations in the United States was still a Mexican, and would be treated as such, with all the disadvantages that entailed.[17]

Discriminatory wages were justified on the basis that Mexican residents and workers allegedly had lesser needs. For example, in 1906, the C&A Mining Company established a firm in order to build a suburb to lure American workers to the city, a company that would be taken over by Phelps Dodge in 1917. Mexicans were not part of this program, and the notion that they required less—their homes described as simple adobe huts with earth floors—meant their living costs were lower and could be used to undercut "white" wages.[18]

* * *

There was no requirement that Mexicans register at designated border crossings until 1919, so the border was fairly permeable. The permeability worked in both directions, for not only did Mexicans come north, but there was traffic headed south from Bisbee as well.

Cananea was a mining town in the northern Mexican state of Sonora, and this small outpost had turned into a city of twenty thousand by 1905. The mining company that ran the town was the American-owned Cananea Consolidated Copper Company (CCCC): the first thing that flowed south from Arizona was capital. The US Geological Survey engineer who issued the initial report on the potential wealth of Cananea site wrote of the town and the area: "Twenty years ago [Cananea was] as remote and inaccessible as Africa is today, now by the magic of the desert conquering railway, American enterprise, and mining exploration, there is not a mountain but what has been scanned; not an acre that has not been surveyed; hardly a stone that has not been scrutinized." Now connected to Arizona, with a railway built by the CCCC—without the assistance of Phelps Dodge, which had constructed its own railway in southern Arizona (the El Paso and Southwestern)—the town thrived. William C.

Greene, the company's American president, thrived even more, as he owned 30,000 acres in Arizona and 750,000 acres around Cananea.[19]

That the town was thriving didn't mean the residents were, at least not the Mexicans among them. "In terms of labor rights," a historian wrote, "Cananea was an abomination. Mexicans were second-class citizens in their own country." *Regeneración*, the newspaper of the left-wing Partido Liberal Mexicano, led by the revolutionary Ricardo Flores Magón, laid bare the situation for the natives of Mexico in the American-run town: "The people have to put up with the insolence of the three thousand Yankees who live in Cananea and with the disgusting filth of the two thousand Chinese there, part of whom have monopolized the grocery business, while the others give themselves to their parasitic and ignoble lives." Though Mexican wages in Cananea were half those of the Americans employed in the mines, they were still higher than wages in general in Porfirian Mexico, which led people with white-collar jobs, like teaching, to leave them to work in the mines.[20]

Along with capital, law enforcement also flowed in both directions. The Arizona Rangers, who were founded in 1901 and modeled on the Texas Rangers, during their eight years of existence developed a relationship with the Mexican gendarmes who were based in Sonora under the leadership of Russian émigré Emilio Kosterlitzky, and regularly crossed the border into Mexico to capture bandits. When a criminal was captured in Arizona and wanted in Mexico, extradition laws were circumvented by the Rangers, who simply dropped the outlaw at the Mexican border for pickup by the Mexican forces. And if the need arose to cross over into Mexico, the Arizonans would request a temporary leave from the American force and serve as auxiliaries to the Mexicans.[21]

This Old West solidarity in the war against horse thieves and rustlers and railroad robbers was only one element of cross-border activity. Cross-border work by Arizonans was also part of the labor scene.

On June 2, 1906, the Mexican miners at the Greene Consolidated Copper Company in Cananea went on strike, after only American workers were given raises. When the strikers marched through town (allegedly headed by a red flag) to meet with George McDonald, the American mine manager, George Metcalf, another American in the town and manager of the local lumberyard, fearful that the rumors were true that the miners were going to dynamite company property and kill the Americans working there, opened high-power hoses on the marchers. As the strikers' rage and confusion mounted, shots were fired and men on both sides were killed and wounded. George Metcalf was clubbed to death, and his brother Will was shot and killed. The telegram sent to their family informed them that the two brothers, "died bravely defending the lumber yards from striking Mexicans."[22]

As the situation spiraled out of control and the company lumberyard was set on fire—a fire that could be seen all the way into Arizona—the company bosses began deputizing American employees, and a second battle broke out in the center of town, with looting on one side and gunfire from the other.

An eyewitness account reported that the "revolutionists" had dynamited a pawnshop and taken a large number of arms and that the five thousand strikers "are very defiant and only awaiting the appearance of the anarchist flag to attack every Mexican and American in Cananea who will not join them." A more measured newspaper account stated that "Many exaggerated reports are being sent out of here."[23]

Word of the battle had reached Bisbee, and armed volunteers, under the leadership of Thomas Rynning of the Arizona Rangers, were gathered at the border to put an end to the troubles. The governor of Sonora initially denied the Americans' request to enter his country, but when told by William Greene, the American owner, that the strikers intended to blow the company up, the governor allowed the invading force to cross the border. The territorial governor of Arizona ordered the Americans not to do so, warning that if they crossed into Mexico they risked losing their American citizenship. But the Sonoran governor and the Arizona Ranger commander circumvented the order by having the Americans "break ranks and string across the line as civilians," at which point Sonoran governor Rafael Izábal made them Mexican volunteers. Rynning, who led the Americans across the border, claimed the telegram came too late to head them off. The Sonoran governor apparently ignored a telegram from his own government in Mexico City also banning the riders. According to the Ranger commander of the group, there were 275 men who served as a volunteer military to quell a labor dispute in a foreign country.[24]

They boarded a train for Cananea, where, officially under Mexican orders, they put down the riot. Many photos exist of this invasion, and in one particularly eloquent one, William Greene can be seen haranguing the strikers from his car, with armed Americans lined up behind him ensuring order is maintained.[25] A journalist circulated through the crowd while Greene spoke, making his case for a return to work, and the reporter, listening in on the conversation of the assembled Mexican workers, wrote that he heard one say, "Yes, all that is true, but why doesn't the company pay the Mexicans the same wages they pay the

Americans?"[26] Revolution was not in the air; a simple demand for equity was what was being made. To the Americans they were one and the same thing.

When the Bisbeeites arrived in Cananea on June 2, the shooting was fierce in both directions, and many deaths were reported, but reported numbers fluctuated wildly. On June 3, it was reported that three Americans had been killed after the Metcalf brothers, and that about fifteen Mexicans had been killed, the latter number described as a "conservative" estimate. Along with the Americans, the Mexican *rurales* were on the scene as well, and their commander, Emilio Kosterlitzky, was not best pleased to find the Arizonans in the town. Kosterlitzky had with him, by one account, thirty-five *rurales* and twenty-five soldiers, and their arrival brought about the end of the shooting, and the Americans were led back to a train that would take them home (another photo, of Americans and Mexicans on horseback, has written on the back that the men were there together "suppressing Cananea War").[27]

The *Douglas Daily International* reported the final mopping-up operation, where "no one was allowed on the streets, under penalty of death," a sentence the paper claimed was carried out against the town's adobe walls. Authorities supposedly buried bodies all night so no one would know how many victims there were.[28] Though it was admitted locally that the death toll was only an estimate, on June 3 the Mexican consul in El Paso reported a final death toll of two Americans and seven Mexicans.[29] The Bisbee volunteers were home by the morning of June 3, and they'd been told by Greene to relay the message that "everything is alright in Cananea. The mine and smelters will be running in Cananea tomorrow as usual."[30]

But the events in Cananea inspired a deep fear that was expressed in an editorial in the Bisbee paper. "There is no denying the fact that there is bad feeling among the ignorant Mexican laboring class at Cananea. The carrying of the red flag in the procession on Friday shows the source of the discontent."[31] Anti-Mexican feeling and fear of revolution were already brewing in Bisbee, and a decade later it would explode in broad daylight.

* * *

It wasn't only repression that crossed borders, though. The revolution that had been taking place in Mexico since 1910 had repercussions in southern Arizona as well, and its effects would also feed into the atmosphere in 1917 and the Bisbee Deportation.

In some instances, the revolutionary presence was fairly lighthearted. In November 1915, Pancho Villa, who was based just below the Mexico-Arizona border, threatened to seize Douglas, the Phelps Dodge smelter town east of Bisbee, if US troops interfered with his men. One day, John Slaughter, a former sheriff and the rancher of a large estate outside Douglas, sitting on his porch, "glared south to the Mexican side of his vast domain, watching for rebel soldiers." Slaughter saw Villa's forces killing his cattle, so he got on his horse and rode up to the Mexican leader, who knew the Arizonan. Slaughter addressed Villa, "You get into that saddle and vamoose pronto," he said. Villa supposedly returned with a saddlebag full of gold pieces in payment for his stolen and killed cattle. "That," we are told, "was the end of the stealing."[32]

In 1916, Pancho Villa led an incursion north to Columbus, New Mexico, and was pursued by US troops, under General Pershing. Later, Bisbee deportees would be exiled from their homes to Columbus.

The actions of Pancho Villa and his men were regularly featured in the Bisbee press in the year of the deportation. For example, a three-hour battle sixty miles south of the border received a write-up; in May 1917, his forces were defeated south of El Paso;[33] on June 23, thirty Villistas were killed in a battle in Ortiz.[34] Mexico was seen as a threat just miles from Bisbee, and Mexicans a threat living among them.

This perception was solidified in Arizona thanks to the presence of a more consequently revolutionary group, the previously mentioned Partido Liberal Mexicano (PLM). Far from being raiders into Arizona, like Pancho Villa, Ricardo Flores Magón and his comrades organized among the Mexicans in Arizona, Texas, and California with the goal of overthrowing the Mexican regime. The mobility of miners played an important role in the PLM's ability to spread its message and organization. The organization had supporters throughout Arizona's mining region, and, in 1906, its offices in Douglas were raided and documents seized.[35]

The party leadership fled, and on August 23, 1907, its principal leaders, Flores Magón, Antonio Villarreal, and Librado Rivera were arrested in Los Angeles. Either due to lack of sufficient evidence to support extradition to Mexico or because the Mexican government preferred to avoid negative press by demanding Flores Magón and his companions be returned to Mexico, it was decided to try the PLM members for violating neutrality laws by threatening a friendly government.

After nearly two years of legal wrangling, the men were sent to Tucson and then, seven weeks later, to Tombstone, then the county seat of Cochise County, for their trial.

The prosecuting attorneys feared that the discontent among native-born Americans, foreign-born men, and Mexicans would make it impossible to seat a jury fair to the defendants, while the defense attorneys claimed the jury was stacked with "thugs and gun men in the employ of the Copper Queen mining company who had been drawn especially to convict." In the end, the jury statistically resembled greater Cochise County.

The trial began on May 13, 1909, and, after the lengthy preliminaries, lasted only three days. Most of the evidence against the revolutionaries was documents seized by the Arizona Rangers without a warrant and at the behest of the Mexican vice-consul in Douglas. Though the evidence certainly pointed to plans for an "invasion" of Mexico, they indicated no acts having actually been committed.

Flores Magón and his men were defended by a local lawyer who, less than a decade later, would play a key role in the Bisbee Deportation and would himself be deported: labor lawyer William Cleary, who took the case when Clarence Darrow—the original choice for defense attorney—was unable. Though Cleary compared his clients to George Washington and Abraham Lincoln, they were found guilty, with the jury requesting leniency.

The case was another sign of cross-border activity, with revolutionaries on both sides of the border remaining in contact and the governments of both countries working in tandem to control and repress this activity. Even American-based private detective agencies surveilled the Magonistas. Bisbee sheriff Harry Wheeler, the animating force of the 1917 deportation, received a report dated June 5, 1916, from a certain Hopkins in the district who was forwarding information he'd received from his "informant" J.L.P., concerning "Mexican matters." The informant was confident that all was well among the Mexicans and that "there does not seem to be any plotting and organizing going on among them." In fact, far from engaging in any activity, "they are somewhat timid for fear that they might be molested by the Americans," a fear that would be amply justified a year later.

The Mexicans were presented as economic immigrants who "could not make a living or stay in Mexico and that all they want is to be protected with their families here."

Which is not to say that there were no political stirrings among them, as a certain Theodor Ballestaros had been inciting them to rise up in case of US intervention in Mexico, "but that he does not seem to get any following."

The Magonistas had an organization in the Warren District with about twenty members, and the informant was at a meeting on June 4, 1916, which was attended by ten people. No plots were discussed; nor was any anti-government movement mentioned. "In general things seem to be very satisfactory among the Mexicans in the District just at this time."[36]

That might have been the case, but when the deportation occurred, Mexicans would constitute the single largest nationality put on the train and sent into the desert.

* * *

By 1917, the Warren District had the third largest population in Arizona, and 4,718 men worked in the mines. As the deportation showed, there were many nationalities in the town, and most lived in specific enclaves. It was, still and forever, notoriously a "white man's camp"; the workers in the town supported the limitation of nonwhites. Despite the company's claims of the goodness of life in Bisbee, the most important historian of the events in Bisbee wrote that "management's belief in local autonomy and rugged individualism made the miner's life a nightmare of overwork, unsafe conditions and job insecurity."[37]

Business for the mines was, to put it mildly, booming. In 1916, the year before the strike and deportation, an industry journal reported that "new high record earnings and production have been established this year" by Phelps Dodge, the result being higher dividends than ever before. In the first three quarters of 1916, they had distributed $20 a share and were predicted to produce 170 million pounds of copper by year's end, compared to 140 million in 1915, with expected profits of $26,250,000.[38]

In the end, 1916 profits were $24,030,905, an enormous increase over 1915's $10,981,512. After paying dividends, the surplus on hand was $7,349,263, more than a tenfold increase over the previous year, which was $720,475.

A report issued in the first quarter of 1917, thus before the strike but also before US entry into World War I, which resulted in a massive increase in the need for and price of copper, Phelps Dodge was still distributing substantial regular and special dividends ($2.50 and $3.50 respectively) and was producing 15 million pounds of copper monthly, mainly from the Copper Queen and Detroit mines in Arizona and the Montezuma mine in Mexico.[39]

The miners, who put their lives on the line every day, began to ask whether some of that wealth shouldn't be shared. What they needed was a force that would guide the fight for the redistribution of the region's wealth.

CHAPTER TWO

THE INDUSTRIAL WORKERS OF THE WORLD

The working class and the employing class have nothing in common

In January 1905, twenty-three representatives of nine working-class organizations had a secret gathering that came to be known as the "January Conference," a conference that would lead to the founding of the Industrial Workers of the World a few months later. Miners played an important part in this first step along the road to the IWW, with the Western Federation of Miners sending its leaders, Charles Moyer and Bill Haywood, to the conference.

At its conclusion, those in attendance issued a manifesto that criticized the state of the existing union movement, particularly its craft organization, which in its separation of workers into discrete unions made scabbing all too easy. The manifesto said that the movement that was required "must consist of one great industrial union embracing all industries.... It must be founded on the class struggle ... and established as the economic organization of the working-class, without affiliation with any political party." The manifesto concluded by calling for those who shared these principles to meet in Chicago on June 27, 1905, "for the purpose of forming an economic organization of the working class along the lines marked out in this manifesto."[1]

On June 27, as proclaimed, 203 attendees gathered for what they would call the "Continental Congress of the Working Class." And continental it was, as a number of unions from Montreal, including the Wage Earners, Cloak Makers and Tailors, and Journeymen Tailors sent representatives. Indeed, the variety of unions is astounding; alongside the WFM were the American Labor Union; the Socialist Trade and Labor Alliance (ST&LA), the union of Daniel DeLeon's Socialist Labor Party; and representatives of locals like the International Musicians Union, Barbers Union No. 225 of

Sharon, Pennsylvania, and the Scandinavian Painters, Decorators, and Paper-hangers of Chicago.[2]

The attending delegates represented 142,000 workers, but only those representing slightly more than a third—50,000—were empowered to join the new movement, and these came from five organizations: the Western Federation of Miners (27,000), the American Labor Union (16,750), the United Metal Workers (3,000), the United Brotherhood of Railway Employees (2,087), and the Socialist Trade and Labor Alliance (1,450). Though the numbers of delegates varied widely (the WFM had only five while the ST&LA had fourteen), voting power was assigned based on the strength of the organization, so the WFM delegates each had 5,400 votes, and the ST&LA had 103.6.[3]

The conference was dominated by a handful of individuals, though debate was free and wide-ranging. Eugene Debs, the face and voice of American socialism, attended and spoke, as did Daniel DeLeon, with his mostly German Socialist Labor Party (SLP) and its union, the ST&LA, and, from the west, Bill Haywood, secretary-treasurer of the WFM—the most combative of unions and the most combative of union leaders, hated perhaps by the bosses more than any other labor leader in the country.

After praising in his speech the "sound" principles of the SLP, Debs added a demurral, saying that it doesn't "appeal to the American working-class in the right spirit." He credited it for its courage and pluck and was certain the ST&LA would be able to enter "into harmonious relations" with the WFM. Debs went on to say that "the supreme need of the hour is a sound, revolutionary working-class organization," in which all can set aside their differences, for "the great body of the working class in this country are prepared for just such an organization."[4] The hope that the IWW would be spared the fissiparous tendencies of the left was admirable but ultimately shattered by reality.

Bill Haywood, when he spoke, immediately set the IWW apart from virtually every organization of any kind in the US, asserting that it "recognized neither race, creed, color, sex or previous condition of servitude." In the America of Jim Crow and Chinese exclusion laws, where unions fought against rights for—and even the presence of—nonwhite workers, this was revolutionary, indeed. Haywood recognized the geographical differences in the trades and the ethnic makeup and wage scales of the working class across the broad continent, seeking to obliterate them. "We come out of the west to meet the textile worker of the east."[5]

Along with the founding of the organization itself, perhaps the most important result of the gathering was its constitution, more particularly, its preamble. It seems that nowhere in the history of the working-class movement anywhere in the world has a more direct, concise, and effective presentation of an organization's program been so perfectly phrased as it is in the first two of the four paragraphs of the preamble. In only ninety-six words the American working class had its credo:

> The working class and the employing class have nothing in common. There can be no peace so long as hunger and want are found among millions of working people and the few, who make up the employing class, have all the good things of life.
>
> Between these two classes a struggle must go on until all the toilers come together on the political field, as well as on the industrial field, and take and hold that which they produce by their labor through an economic organization of the working class without affiliation with any political party.[6]

As one delegate at the convention said during the debate on the wording of the preamble: "I have heard a good many Preambles read, and this is the first time I have seen a Preamble that has not got the ear marks of too many professors. The language sounds good to me. I believe we can go before the working class of this country with it and that they can understand the report without having to get dictionaries and find out what is meant. What we want is to go before the common people with a Preamble so plain that every honest Tom, Dick and Harry, including ourselves, can understand it. I am in favor of the entire Preamble as reported by the Committee."[7]

The mention of political parties would soon be cause for dispute and splits between those who believed in political action joined to their union activity and the "direct actionists," who abjured any form of political action. Even so, the preamble was widely accepted by the delegates in attendance when it was presented to them. A sign of what was to come, though, is demonstrated in the reaction of the ST&LA delegate and future head of the SLP faction of the IWW, Herman Richter, who was unimpressed by these stirring sentences. He dissented, saying the first paragraph "has no sense and is untrue," wanting to replace it with "Labor is necessary to satisfy the needs of society. Therefore, every able person should do some useful work for its maintenance."[8] The deadness of the language, so typical of the SLP, did not move the attendees, and the preamble stood, as it does today, only slightly revised, and is reprinted prominently in almost all IWW publications.

Nevertheless, as an early historian of the IWW wrote, contrasting the IWW to the American Federation of Labor (AF of L), "The latter body is craft conscious; the IWW is class conscious ... The idea of the class conflict was really the bottom notion or 'first cause' of the IWW. The industrial union type was adopted because it would make it possible to wage this class war under more favorable conditions."[9]

* * *

The IWW's early years were rife with internal dissension and stumbles, but also with striking successes and striking failures. Rival offices were set up, and leadership was overturned, as the fissiparous tendency of the left made itself felt. Fights about the direction of the union "erupted" in the summer of 1906, pitting industrial unionists and socialists on one side against anarchists and followers of the ever-disputatious Daniel DeLeon on the other. In August that year, sixteen locals called for the abolition of the office of president of the IWW, and at the IWW's Second Convention in October, this was implemented.[10]

Despite these internecine quarrels, the IWW managed to stake a vital place for itself on the labor scene, both in the East and the West.

On the East Coast the union made its presence most strongly felt among textile workers in cities like New Bedford, Lowell, and Lawrence, Massachusetts; and Paterson, New Jersey. Both Paterson and Lowell—the former in 1913, the latter in 1912—would be the sites of emblematic strikes of largely immigrant workers that would increase the notoriety and influence of the IWW.[11]

If in the East the union concentrated on the largely immigrant working class of the factories; in the West it organized miners (many of whom were immigrants, as we will see in Bisbee), lumbermen, and migratory workers. Shunning the ambient racism, they also organized Japanese and Chinese workers.

In its first decade, when the union grew in fame if not in stable membership, the IWW showed itself to be a master manipulator of public attention.

Lawrence was a town of about eighty-six thousand, of whom about sixty thousand—mainly immigrants—were employed in the textile mills. The IWW local, which was founded in 1906 and had straggled along with a membership of around three hundred, led a general strike in January 1912 to oppose a wage cut that was implemented when the state legislature ruled that children under the age of eighteen and women would have their work weeks reduced from fifty-six to fifty-four hours. The strike truly took off when strikers were met by militiamen who aimed water hoses at them. The strike had been on the brink of collapse, but the "shock of the icy water in subzero temperatures united the workers again and probably saved the strike from ignominious collapse."[12]

The largest contingent of immigrant strikers was Italians, but there were also Germans, Canadians (both French-speaking and Anglos), Poles, Lithuanians, Belgians, and Russians. The Wobs invested heavily in the strike, sending in some of their most important leaders and organizers, including Bill Haywood, Joseph Ettor, Arturo Giovannitti, and Elizabeth Gurley Flynn.

Clashes occurred between the militia and the strikers. A striker was killed, for which another *striker* was held on murder charges. Wobblies Ettor and Giovannitti were arrested as accessories—for advocating picketing. With representation that included Fred Moore—who would appear in Arizona in 1917 as lawyer for the deported strikers—and after a trial that lasted several weeks, the three were acquitted.

In the meanwhile, the workers held firm for ten weeks in the face of management's refusal to negotiate or even sit in the same room. The harsh conditions under which they were forced to live, deprived of wages as they were, forced the IWW toward a tactic that would turn out to be a masterful propaganda stroke. On February 17, the first group of 150 strikers' children was sent to New York and Vermont to stay with the families of supporters, a move coordinated by a committee headed by Margaret Sanger.[13]

The authorities played into the hands of the Wobblies when, a week later, the mothers of forty children about to be sent out of Lawrence were arrested by club-wielding police for "neglect" and "improper guardianship." The outrage was nearly universal, and on March 1, the bosses capitulated and the textile workers were granted raises of between 5 and 20 percent, as well as better overtime rates.[14]

The strike resulted in a massive increase in new IWW members, the local branch claiming fourteen thousand members by 1912. But, as was often the case throughout Wobbly history, an immediate success didn't lead to a sustained increase in membership, and by 1914 membership in Lawrence had sunk back to four hundred members.

The IWW's next moment of glory and renown also took place in a textile town—in this case, Paterson, New Jersey. The silk mills there had long been a target of Wobbly organizers, who were met with little success. This changed in 1912, when the factory owners imposed a new order, requiring weavers to tend four instead of two looms, while also cutting wages. Anger mounted among the largely immigrant workforce.[15]

A strike led by Daniel DeLeon's splinter group, the Detroit IWW, achieved some short-term victories but was ultimately crushed. The situation in Paterson moved to front stage with the settling of the Lawrence strike, and the IWW went into action when the largest mill in Paterson—Doherty and Co.—adopted the four-loom system. On February 25, 1913, the IWW told the workers, "It is far better to starve fighting than to starve working," and throughout the city workers in the silk mills walked off the job. Ultimately, twenty-five thousand went out on strike with two main demands: the eight-hour day and a minimum weekly wage.[16]

As in Lawrence, the strike was largely an immigrant affair, with the American workers standing aside and ultimately contributing mightily to the strike's failure. In the left-wing magazine the *Masses*, John Reed wrote of the strike, "There's war in Paterson. But it's a curious kind of war. All the violence is the work of one side—the Mill Owners. Their servants, the Police, club unresisting men and women and ride down law abiding crowds on horseback." And he made it clear who was striking. A "young Jew, pallid and sick-looking from insufficient food," told him that "'t'ree great nations stick togedder like dis.' He made a fist. 'But how about the Americans?' They all shrugged their shoulders and grinned with humorous scorn. 'English people not go on picket line,' one said softly. ''Mericans no lika fight.'"[17]

The IWW again sent its heavy hitters to run the strike, among them Big Bill Haywood, Elizabeth Gurley Flynn, and Carlo Tresca (who would be assassinated on a Manhattan street corner by mafiosi in the pay of Mussolini). The IWW benefited immediately from the strike, its membership leaping from a mere nine hundred to ten thousand. Despite this massive force, the bosses refused to negotiate and even encouraged the AF of L to come to town and set up a counterforce to the Wobblies.[18]

As the strike dragged on, the IWW realized they needed to draw attention to the strike and the strikers, in the same way the kindertransport did in Lawrence. Mabel Dodge Luhan, hosting a gathering of organizers and intellectuals at her New York home, had a sudden inspiration: "Why don't you bring the strike to New York and *show* it to the workers?" Bill Haywood enthusiastically backed the idea but wondered how it would go down and where it could be staged. A young man "burst out: 'I'll do it. My name is Reed.... We'll make a pageant of the strike. The first in the world.'" Bill Haywood conveyed the idea to the workers, and the Paterson Pageant was born.

The pageant was written and designed by the cream of New York's left-wing intelligentsia and performed by the strikers, who had crossed the Hudson from Paterson and marched en masse to the venue, Madison Square Garden, which had been decorated for a week with a giant sign in red lights saying "I.W.W."[19]

* * *

The pageant was performed in six episodes, with titles like "The Mills Alive–The Workers Dead" and "The Workers Begin to Think" and "The Mills Dead–The Workers Alive." "The Pageant," the program explained, "represents a battle between the working class and the capitalist class conducted by the Industrial Workers of the world (I.W.W.), making use of the General Strike as the chief weapon. It is a conflict between two social forces—the force of labor and the force of capital."[20]

The pageant came to a rousing finish with the band striking up "The Marseillaise" and "The Internationale."

Despite its success as a spectacle, it brought in only $150 after expenses.[21] It did, however, give the IWW something of long-lasting value: the image that appeared on Wobbly publications, of a worker rising from a factory first appeared on the pageant's program.

But the financial failure of the pageant disheartened the workers, and their unity was soon shattered. More skilled workers split off from the less skilled and accepted the bosses' offers, as did English-speaking socialists on July 18, 1913. Two days later, the strikers returned to work, and, as Melvyn Dubofsky wrote, "Nobody had obtained much of an improvement in either wages or working conditions."[22]

Dubofsky's summary of the two major East Coast strikes summed up the IWW situation accurately, and not just in the East. For the strikers, "the IWW was never a home, never a true belief, never the kind of cause that merited absolute sacrifice. For a time, the IWW had simply offered Paterson's workers hope for an immediate improvement in their wretched lives. Then the unyielding structure of American society and capitalism ... made it impossible for the IWW, which promised the immigrants so much, to give them anything at all."[23]

* * *

In the West, the IWW presence was strongly felt in the mines, where its militancy served as a contrast and alternative to the now more compliant Western Federation of Miners, which had seceded from the IWW in 1907. But its presence was also felt outside the mines, among lumberjacks in the Northwest and itinerant laborers in the fields, not to mention the ephemeral union of Bronco Busters and Range Riders.

The IWW's originality was demonstrated by the union's free-speech fights during a period that ran from 1907 to 1916. In these battles—the first of which was fought in Missoula, Montana, in 1907, and perhaps the most famous of which was in Spokane the following year—the IWW insisted on its members' right to make speeches and recruit on city streets, a right denied them specifically by local ordinances throughout the West. Their tactic was a simple one: a Wob would climb onto a soapbox, make a speech, and be arrested by the police. Once he was taken away, another would climb onto the soapbox, speak, and be arrested in turn. Wobbly organizer Frank Little, who would be lynched in Montana in 1917, was arrested in Spokane for reading the Declaration of Independence. The trouble and expense of housing hundreds of free-speech fighters would lead local authorities, in most cases, to release those held and rescind the ban on speech and negotiate the pending issues.[24]

But not in all cases. On November 5, 1916, in Everett, Washington, two ships carrying Wobblies from Seattle to support striking shingle workers were shot at by the sheriff and two hundred armed vigilantes; the IWWs fired back. Five Wobs were killed and thirty-one wounded, while two vigilantes were killed and nineteen wounded. Seventy-four of the Wobs were arrested and charged with murder, the trials beginning with that of Tom Tracy. After a two-month trial, Tracy was found not guilty and the remainder of the Wobs were released. But as historian Joyce Kornbluh writes, "The Tracy trial was won in the courts but lost in the press." In words that do much to explain what would happen in Bisbee, Kornbluh continues, "The news of the trial swept the fear of internal violence onto the doorsteps of many American communities and presented an image of a domestic enemy attacking American values of industrial peace and property."[25]

Miners in Butte, Montana, went on strike at approximately the same time as Bisbee in 1917, and so both cities are considered exemplary of the situation for the Wobs and radical unionism in general.

The WFM local there—Local 1—fell under the control of a pro-boss leadership, a leadership so supine that it did nothing when between two and three hundred socialist Finnish miners were fired, while internal dissent was handled brutally and expeditiously. "Any miner or union member who complained about company influence was apt to be labeled a Socialist, a Wobbly, or an anarchist, and thrown out the window of the union's hall."[26]

Matters reached a head on June 13, 1914—Miners' Union Day—when the overwhelming majority of miners refused to participate in the march and instead charged the Local 1 headquarters, trashing everything in the building, until, as a federal investigator said, "there was not a whole article left in the place." Matters did not improve when WFM head Charles Moyer came to Butte to speak to the disgruntled workers. Gunfire broke out, killing a miner outside the hall, and the dissidents again attacked the hall, forcing Moyer and his allies to flee via a rear fire escape. At that point, the miners placed dynamite around the building and blew it up.[27]

Moyer and AF of L head Samuel Gompers blamed the IWW for the violence, but there were only about two hundred Wobblies in Butte, so though they would certainly have acted as agitators, they were agitating a populace that was ready for it.

When the dust finally settled in and after 1914, all that was left of unionism in Butte was a new independent union and an IWW local, the two collaborating closely given their shared hostility toward the WFM. Moyer's misreading and mishandling of the situation there, a historian wrote, "opened the Western nonferrous mining industry to IWW influence and penetration, which would reach its peak in the war years."[28]

WFM had little hold in Arizona, and so dire was their situation in the state that the local union secretary in Humboldt quit when the union couldn't pay him $214 in back salary.

In 1915, a strike in Clifton and Morenci of mainly Mexican mine workers was met with threats of violence by the owners, and it was only the intervention of pro-labor governor George W. P. Hunt that preserved the peace and prevented violence being inflicted on the strikers. The strike did little to help the WFM and increased the mine owners' hatred for Governor Hunt, leading to their circulating a petition to recall him. Hunt would survive the recall threat only to be narrowly defeated in the 1916 gubernatorial election. So narrow was his defeat (thirty votes separated the major party candidates on the first count) that he refused to vacate his office, and both he and his opponent,

Thomas Campbell, were sworn into office by competing judges. It took over a year for Hunt to be declared the winner, after all, and in the interim he played an essential role in the Bisbee events, always on the side of the miners.[29]

But as David R. Berman, a historian of Western radicalism writes, "the WFM came out of the 1915 experience in Clifton-Morenci in a weakened position." Union members were unhappy with the "heavy assessments levied on them" by the union's leadership, and it was clear that overall they had made little headway in organizing the industry. It was at this point that the union, in order to free itself of the WFM's negative image, changed its name to the International Union of Mine, Mill, and Smelter Workers.[30] But the discontent with the union under whatever name (and with continued leadership of Charles Moyer), left an opening for a union with a record of combat. The arrival of Grover Perry in Arizona in early 1917 was the beginning of the rise of the IWW, both through boring within old WFM locals and the establishment of IWW locals.[31]

Perry arrived in Phoenix on February 1, 1917, and almost immediately met J. L. Donnelly, the president of the state Federation of Labor and a former mine union member. The nature of the relations between the IWW and the AF of L are exemplified by the game of cat and mouse the two men played. Perry wrote to Bill Haywood that Donnelly attempted to get information about "what so many Wobblies were doing in Arizona." Going further, Donnelly attempted to convince Perry that "everything would turn out lovely" if the Wobs would support Moyer, their sworn enemy. He also said that "there is no future for the IWW either here or elsewhere." Having been fully aware that Donnelly was trying to "pump" him for information, Perry told Haywood that "I reversed the pump and got quite a lot of information out of him." Secrecy was the key: "No one knows what I am here for. Will keep them in the dark as long as possible."

The rival union, Arizona, and the whole country would learn soon enough what was in the works.[32]

* * *

As the organizing drive among miners heated up, two important questions had to be confronted: sabotage and the position on the war. Both involved key questions of principle and tactics.

On April 28, 1916, a year before US entry into the European conflict, a letter from the general secretary-treasurer, Bill Haywood, to A. C. Christ in Detroit, suggested that, though the IWW was on record for its opposition to the war, "it might be a good thing at this hour to reiterate our position in a brief definite statement." The letter went on to specify what this meant: "Not a declaration for a general strike, but a statement of what a general strike would mean in the event of a war, and the fact that we advocate the general strike as one of the weapons to be used against the capitalist class."[33]

Organizer Frank Little, who was one of the loudest voices in support of militant activity against militarism, both before and after American entry into the European conflict, expressed his uncompromising stand against the war in the statement he sent the IWW offices for wages and expenses for the week ending April 14, 1917, just after the US joined the Allies. He described the conditions he was confronting in his organizing trips around Arizona. Organizing, he felt, was going well, and delegates were taking in members in all the mining camps. The International Union of Mine, Mill, and Smelter Workers (IUMMSW), the heir of the WFM and enemy of the IWW, was in cahoots with the mine owners, Little said, in blocking access to halls for meetings. The war, for its part, was having an especial effect on the foreign-born workers, "as they are afraid they will be arrested if they join." But Little was optimistic that a revolutionary stance would be the best one. "In all places one can hear them backing the stand of the IWW in it's [sic] stand on the WAR, and denounceing [sic] the A.F.L." He moved from this to his general point, one he maintained throughout this period: "The IWW is a Revolutionary Organization and must stand up on [sic] a Revolutionary Principal [sic], we are opposed to WAR and must fight with all our power the efforts of the Capitalist Class to force in to [sic] the army. Even to the limet [sic] that some of us is lined against the Dead wall and shot. The fight is on. On with the fight to the end."[34]

The IWW's position on capitalist war had long been one of clear opposition, and any Wob joining the army automatically lost his membership. Ralph Chaplin, Wobbly organizer, songwriter, and poet, whose position we will see became somewhat equivocal, wrote a poem in 1914—that, slightly revised, made it into the *Little Red Songbook*—called "The Red Feast," which presented the early Wob position:

> Go fight, you fools! Tear up the earth with strife
> And spill each other's guts upon the field,

Serve unto death the men you served in life
So that their wide dominions may not yield.
…
But whether in the fray to fall or kill
You must not pause to question why nor where.
You see the tiny crosses on that hill?
It took all those to make one millionaire.[35]

Frank Little played a prominent part in the internal debates about the war. Like Bill Haywood, he had only one eye and had been a member of the Wobs since 1906, a veteran of countless battles, and by 1916 was a member of the General Executive Committee. He was a fierce opponent of capitalist war, and in the time until his lynching in August 1917, he fought indefatigably against working-class participation in the capitalist slaughter.

This was the official IWW position as well, but the union's practice was less unequivocal. The leadership was split over correct practice in the matter: Did they not risk running ahead of their membership, much of which supported the war effort, by maintaining a strict antiwar position, which called for the ejection from the union of anyone who donned a uniform? When the Wobbly leadership was arrested and put on trial in 1918, Bill Haywood testified that Little maintained that "the IWW is opposed to all wars, and we must use all our power to prevent the workers from joining the army."[36]

In January 1917, Haywood received a letter from John Pancner, a Wobbly in Detroit, who wrote that "militarism will be the downfall of Capitalism," speculating that the "armed Proletariat will rise and mutiny." Haywood, in response, insisted that "education along Industrial Union lines is the best anti-military propaganda that I know of."[37]

In March 24, 1917, shortly before US entry into the war, there appeared on the front page of the IWW's paper, *Solidarity*, an antiwar tract along the lines advocated by Little. It was called "The Deadly Parallel" and contrasted the antimilitarism of the IWW with the pro-war posture of the AF of L. The article was uncompromising, declaring, "We condemn all wars, and, for the prevention of such, we proclaim the anti-militarist propaganda in time of peace, thus promoting class solidarity among the workers of the entire world, and, in time of war, the general strike in all industries." Propaganda of this sort would not continue for long, and in fact, Bill Haywood later testified at his trial that "'The Deadly Parallel' was never circulated from headquarters after war was declared."[38] A week later, on April 1, Little continued to hammer away at the need to fight the war, sending a telegram from Jerome, Arizona, to Haywood in Chicago recommending that they call a conference of "all radical organizations ... to prepare to fight compulsory enlistment[,] to prepare for and advocate the general strike of all industries[,] to strike for industrial freedom of the working class[.] must act at once."[39]

Richard Brazier, West Coast organizer and a new member of the General Executive Committee, called on Wobblies to declare themselves to be conscientious objectors and prepared an open letter to President Wilson in which he admonished the leader: "We hope you will realize that in the name of liberty you are destroying every vestige of liberty the American people ever had."[40]

Liberty was being chipped away in ways big and small. In Globe, Arizona, a city ordinance was passed requiring that every house fly an American flag. The Wobs were having none of this, and on April 20, Perry informed Haywood that "up to date our boys have not complied with the ordinance and it is raising some little commotion." In the same letter, Perry warned Haywood that J. L. Donnelly, the head of the state Labor Federation, whom he had met the day after his arrival in Phoenix, had been appointed chairman of the subcommittee of labor of the National Defense Council. "I have no doubt but that Donnelly will use this position to get in a few digs at us."[41]

Ralph Chaplin, Wob militant and author of one of the greatest Wob songs, "Solidarity Forever," wrote in his memoirs that the spring of 1917 was a time of growth for the IWW but that their antiwar writings "attracted more and more adverse attention throughout the nation." Members weren't sure of the union's stance and what course they should take: Should they resist the draft or serve? They asked union leadership for guidance.

But no decision had been taken, so a meeting of the General Executive Committee was called in late July. After meeting for three days, this too failed to reach an agreement. Richard Brazier, according to Chaplin, opposed coming out against serving, saying, "If we oppose the draft, they'll run us out of business." Frank Little answered prophetically, "They'll run us out of business anyhow." His prophesying continued: "Better to go out in a blaze of glory than to give in. Either we're for this capitalistic slaughterfest, or we're against it. I'm ready to face a firing squad rather than compromise." He was only a week from being hung in Montana.

Chaplin proposed a compromise in which IWW members would register for the draft but sign as "IWW opposed to war." The board rejected this proposal, but Haywood told Chaplin to run it in *Solidarity*, where it appeared on July 28. Chaplin registered for the draft in just that fashion.[42]

In the end, Haywood and the IWW leadership left the decision to individual conscience; the union, according to West Coast militant James Rowan, refused to take "foolish chances."

Individual choice ultimately led to approximately 95 percent of eligible Wobs registering, most of whom served when called. Rowan wrote to a fellow worker that "if we do not have the economic power, it is of little use to raise a ruction about it." The war would give the working-class and the Wobs an opportunity to exercise their muscle, for if war was usually a time when industry thrives, this time the IWW would be there to see that the wealth would be shared. Their attempts to do so, as in Bisbee, would rile businessmen and the authorities and bring the hounds of hell down on the union. A lumber worker organizer wrote in 1917 that "the masters are undoubtedly looking for an opportunity to close down some of our halls, and if we do give them an excuse we should be sure to give them a damn good one." This, as historian Melvyn Dubofsky writes, was just what the IWW intended to do: the IWW, if it would face repression, would do so not by "squandering precious resources" fighting the war effort; rather, it would make the fight about improved wages and working conditions. If they'd go down, they'd go down fighting for concrete advantages, not a matter of principle that interested few of its members. "The IWW intended to use all its strength to fight what Haywood labelled America's 'industrial oligarchy.'"[43] And go down they did.

* * *

"Violence" was a word much attached to the Wobblies during their heyday, and it continues to be part of their historical image. They certainly viewed violence as part of the class struggle, but it is impossible to deny that, in almost all cases, the Wobblies were the victims of violence, not its perpetrators. If in Centralia, Washington, in 1919 members of the American Legion were killed by IWWs, it was as a result of an attack by the Legionnaires on the town's IWW headquarters. This pattern is replicated everywhere, when indeed there is any basis that the IWW engaged in violence. No plot was too far-fetched to impute to the Wobs, in almost every case an attribution that was entirely fictitious. Setting fire to crops, poisoning reservoirs—nothing was beyond the IWW in the press, but none of it was real. But that did not prevent the press from spreading these baseless tales, which led to the growth of the Wobs' reputation for violence, which in turn was used as a pretext for events like the Bisbee Deportation, executed to forestall the feared depredations of the strikers.

In the history of social movements, it is not rare that fighting against a wrong, even peacefully, earns the protester a reputation for violence. The Wobbly free-speech fights, contesting laws that aimed to prevent Wobs from making public speeches in cities throughout the Pacific Northwest, were all peaceful. They were, in fact, a model for nonviolent protest, with people knowingly violating the law and then peacefully going to jail and gumming up the legal system with their presence. Despite their nonviolence, opponents could see the protesters as potentially violent rebels, as was the case a half century later with the civil rights movement.

Wobbly *opposition* to violence was actually part of the essence of the organization. The Wobbly goal was not an uprising at the barricades; victory would be achieved by a general strike of the entire working class, which, by downing its tools as one, would force the ruling class to cede, at which point the workers' commonwealth would be a fait accompli. In 1920, the IWW executive board openly expressed its position against violence, saying, "Such methods destroy the constructive impulse which it is the purpose of this organization to foster and develop in order that the workers may fit themselves to assume their place in the new society."[44]

This statement was issued relatively late in IWW history, when its decline was well under way, but it shouldn't be thought of as a new position, the fruit of weakness. After all, two of the most important strikes in Wobbly history, those in Lawrence, Massachusetts, in 1912 and Paterson, New Jersey, in 1913, are not known for their violence but are famous in the first case for giving us the phrase that summed up the strikers' demands, "Bread and Roses," and in the latter case for the pageant organized by John Reed at Madison Square Garden. The violence in the Lawrence strike, particularly the killing of a picket, was attributed to the Wobs, and two IWW leaders, Arturo Giovannitti and Joseph Ettor, were charged with the murder, for which they were acquitted. Another typical example of the IWW's real relationship with violence in Lawrence was the false claim that the union's leadership had purchased and planted dynamite, which was in fact the work of locals attempting to have the explosions imputed to the IWW.

It is common—and to an extent accurate—to view the IWW as two unions within one: an East Coast, largely immigrant and less violent union, and a Western, more American-born, rougher crowd in the mines and fields. Easterners, as a rule, had families and varied social affiliations in their towns and cities; the westerners were younger, more footloose, going wherever the work was, either in the fields or the mines.[45]

This, of course, was a result of the marriage within the IWW of the various socialist groupings in the East with the WFM, the largest union to join the IWW at its founding. The WFM had been a predominantly Anglo-Saxon organization, and its leadership had reflected that since its beginnings. Bill Haywood would write of his background in the opening line of his autobiography that "my father was of an old American family, so American that if traced back it would probably run to the Puritan bigots or the cavalier pirates." The men who headed the union were veterans of the mines; Charles Moyer, a president of the WFM who later split with Bill Haywood, was a smelter before he was president, and Bill Haywood, who would be the face of the IWW and was the best-known WFM leader, worked in the mines in the mountain west from the time he was a teenager until he was elected secretary-treasurer of the WFM.[46]

Even so, violence initiated by the IWW is all but unheard of, even among miners. This was the case in Butte, Montana, throughout Arizona mining country, and in the industrial areas of Pennsylvania—as for example in McKees Rocks, Pennsylvania, where a violent strike was reduced to a peaceful demonstration of force by the workers when the IWW entered the fight.

As one scholar phrased it, not only did the IWW not bring about violence, but it also "stemmed it in the face of the workers' frustration, the employers' provocations, and the militia's irresponsibility."[47]

* * *

The IWW was also constantly accused of engaging in or threatening to engage in sabotage. Sabotage, and the IWW definition of it, is a matter of some debate, but that it was a method taken very seriously by the union is unquestionable. A letter from General Secretary-Treasurer Haywood to member Hugh Gallagher in July 1915 complained of an account he'd received from his correspondent since "I should have liked ... to have a story of some instance of sabotage where you have known it to be applied. I know there must be some way by which stingers and pick handlers can throw the hooks into the railway companies when they are not looking."[48]

A report sent to Grover Perry, Arizona statewide organizer for the IWW based in Phoenix, from Roger Culver in the mining town of Globe, Arizona, gives a good indication of Wobbly organizing and of sabotage's role in it. Pamphlets in Spanish, Italian, and an unidentifiable Slavic language (the book on hand is simply called *Strajk*) were among the stock at Wob offices in Globe. Wob history and theory were also present, as was a substantial stock of copies of the Wobbly songbook and packages of Wobbly stickers. Not one but two pamphlets on sabotage were available, though only one of Émile Pouget's classic accounts of it was on hand. There were also 149 dues books in Culver's possession, and since he didn't request more, we can extrapolate the extent to which he expected the Globe membership to grow.[49]

And yet ...

A 1913 report by the Ohio legislative committee investigating rubber strikes in Akron stated that "very few of the striking employees... testified that they believed in the doctrine of sabotage." They were attracted to the IWW not because of its alleged bent toward this tactic but because "they hoped, through collective action, to increase their wages and improve their conditions of employment."[50]

In fact, for all the allegations of actual or potential acts of sabotage, and however omnipresent the black cat that symbolized it was in Wob propaganda, lawyers at the Department of Justice—hardly people who could be suspected of IWW sympathies—wrote, in August 1917, that though there was a certain amount of advocacy of "the turning out of worthless products at the factories, the impeding of factory output... and the practice of 'sabotage,'" they found that what was meant by the word was "not altogether clear or well defined."[51] The mystery of the meaning of the Sab Cat was clearly explained by Ralph Chaplin, the man who drew it, who wrote that the "'Sab Cat' was supposed to symbolize the 'slow down' as a means of 'striking on the job.'"[52]

Joseph Conlin, in his study of the IWW, examines the matter closely, insisting that the IWW's meaning of "sabotage" was not the same as that of the average American, who considered it to be the damaging of machinery. Violence, to be sure, was one form of sabotage, but more frequently it was a matter of adopting the Scottish labor movement's tactic of "ca'canny," "to go easy," and engage in an unofficial work slowdown. The connection to sabots, wooden shoes, might mean to throw them into machinery, but Conlin insists that it actually meant to walk as if one were wearing them.[53] Elizabeth Gurley Flynn, in her pamphlet on sabotage, stocked by the Wobs in their offices, provided a definition that matched Conlin's: "Sabotage means either to slacken up and interfere with the quantity, or to botch in your skill and interfere with the quality of capitalist production so as to give poor service." She stressed that, whatever the common misconception might be, sabotage is "not physical violence [but]... is an internal industrial process."[54]

Another form of sabotage was to simply follow all rules to the letter, a method employed even today, and which serves to bring work and production to a halt. Another form utilized in France was to reveal to customers the flaws in the products they were purchasing. That tactic was used successfully by the IWW in a waiters' strike in New York when workers threatened to publicize a list of hotels with unsanitary kitchens and that served spoiled food. Another French method was to benefit the customer at the expense of the employer by, for example, recommending cheaper varieties of prescribed drugs in pharmacies.[55]

It was not only Flynn who wrote of nonviolent means of sabotage. Arturo Giovannitti, who would be accused (and acquitted) of murder in 1912 and who translated Émile Pouget's classic exposition *Le Sabotage* for the Charles H. Kerr Publishing Company in Chicago, was reported in a magazine story saying that when he spoke of "an eye for an eye" he meant the Scottish "a dishonest day's work for a dishonest day's pay."[56]

Conlin concludes his discussion of the topic by pointing out that the examples cited by Wobs when they called for sabotage were in almost all instances drawn from Europe. But even more, things like performing a work task poorly, rulebook slowdowns, and siding with customers over the bosses are all practices that predate the Wobblies and that workers still do today. John Spargo, a critic of the IWW, wrote of sabotage that it was a practice that "corresponded with an almost universal instinct of oppressed workers."[57]

Even so, the accusation that they were saboteurs who threw spanners in the works in factories and fields across the nation played a role in the anti-IWW campaign that went on for years. This, like their reputation for violence, fed into the hysteria that led to the Bisbee Deportation and served to justify the massive, nationwide raids on IWW offices in September 1917, in which documents were seized, and thousands of Wobblies, including the bulk of the leadership, were arrested, tried, and ultimately convicted.[58] The alleged Wobbly penchant for violence and sabotage played a large role in the main Chicago trial and the guilty verdicts rendered. The government argued the classical reading of sabotage was what was meant in the IWW's documents—though they could not prove it had ever been applied in that way—and as defendant Ralph Chaplin wrote, "Thanks to our own careless use of the word, the prosecution's case seemed plausible to the jury and the public."[59]

That the accusation that the IWW were saboteurs and perpetrators of violence stuck was not surprising, though. The fine points noted above were buried beneath the avalanche of stickers of black cats, the IWW's symbol for sabotage, distributed wherever Wobs could be found. A past history of accusations of violence against various IWWs, like Bill Haywood, who had been accused of murder in Idaho, made accusations of violent tendencies plausible. We will see the ceaseless and merciless propaganda circulated by the bourgeois press against the IWW, and a lie repeated often enough takes on an aura of truth. Enemies even within the working-class movement, like the Socialist Party and the AF of L, added to the IWW's violent reputation, and agents provocateurs should not be left out of the equation. Even so, Eldridge Foster Dowell's 1939 *A History of Criminal Syndicalism Legislation in the United States* came to the almost shocking conclusion that there was "no case of an IWW saboteur caught practicing sabotage or convicted of its practice."[60]

It is not the least of the oddities of IWW history that the Supreme Court should have found, in the 1924 Fiske decision, that the IWW was absolved of the charge of advocating force or violence as a means of political or industrial change.[61]

The defendant in the case, Harold Fiske, was an organizer for the IWW's Agricultural Workers Industrial Union No. 110. He had suffered two arrests prior to being locked up in Kansas—once in Oklahoma for vagrancy and a second time in Missouri "for being an IWW." On July 2, 1924, just three days after arriving in Geneseo, Kansas, he was arrested carrying massive quantities of Wobbly literature.

At his trial, Fiske and his lawyers denied he advocated violence as a means of changing the government, though he also testified that he understood the teachings of the IWW and stated that the IWW would someday "overpower the capitalists of the United States." It took the jury two hours to find him guilty of violating the criminal syndicalism statute.

Fiske appealed to the Kansas Supreme Court, which upheld the conviction on November 8, 1924, but the only evidence of Fiske's advocacy of violence was the preamble to the constitution of the IWW, then nearly twenty years old, and which made no mention of violence, focusing instead on the industrial organization of the working class. Even the Kansas Supreme Court accepted that the preamble didn't advocate violence, but conjectured that he would have elaborated on the preamble when discussing it.

The case was then appealed to the US Supreme Court, which unanimously overturned the verdict, stating that its own examination of the preamble revealed it to be lacking in any calls to violence. In its decision, the Supreme Court wrote that the Criminal Syndicalism Act was applied to Fiske "without any charge or evidence that the organization in which he secured members advocated any crime, violence, or other unlawful acts or methods as a means of effecting industrial or political change or revolution." The Criminal Syndicalism Act was simply a means of suppressing free speech.

The case Kansas made against Fiske was a foolish one, but if even the Supreme Court of the US—which in 1925 affirmed the conviction of communist (and future anticommunist informer) Benjamin Gitlow for violation of New York's Criminal Anarchy Act—found that Wobbly propaganda did not form the basis for affirming that Fiske was guilty of wanting to overthrow the government, then it is clear that the Wobblies' reputation as a bunch of violent hotheads was unjustified and unfair. But it served the purpose for which it was concocted: to destroy the IWW's threat to the existing order.

CHAPTER THREE

THE STRIKE

We will not sign peace terms ...

As was the case throughout the mining West, the history of labor in Arizona is a turbulent one. The first strike in a mining town was in Globe in 1884, and martial law was declared in the same town in 1896, when miners struck after a wage cut and in protest against the employment of Mexicans. Ironically, during that strike, the WFM local warned the mine owners that they either meet the workers' demands or—reversing what would later be the fate of miners in Jerome and Bisbee—they would be escorted out of town.

However difficult the conditions, in 1903, while Arizona was still a territory, an eight-hour bill was signed for underground miners, though in Morenci and Clifton, two towns where miners had no unions, the mine owners cut wages to go along with the cut in hours. When Morenci's workers walked out, the governor sent Arizona Rangers, and President Roosevelt sent in the cavalry. A court order ultimately forced the miners back to work.[1]

Though one historian of the era states that relations between labor and management in Bisbee were amiable in the first decades of the town, he admitted that, as mining techniques developed and skilled labor became less prized and necessary, the relationship deteriorated. But he also describes working conditions that lead one to wonder how accurate his characterization of the earlier relationship was. "From the beginning, working conditions in Bisbee had been treacherous and miserable. The miners worked in wet stopes and drifts often in water up over their shoe tops. They breathed wet, foul air."[2] Drilling resulted in dust floating in the air, causing pneumoconiosis. Though Bisbee's altitude prevents the town itself from reaching the unbearable temperatures experienced in places like Tucson and Phoenix, the temperature in the mines nevertheless reached 100 degrees. Conditions were such that, in February 1906, the first union, a local of the Western Federation of Miners, was secretly founded in Bisbee.[3]

The situation in the mines of the Warren District was apparently a cause of concern to the bosses and the authorities well before any of the events of the summer of 1917 occurred, or at least among the Mexicans there during this period of revolution in their homeland.

That the Wobs were acutely aware of the importance of organizing Mexican workers is demonstrated by the fact that, at the inaugural session of the first convention of the Metal Mine Workers' Industrial Union, held from June 15 to 17, 1917, it was decided that the Spanish-language paper *El Rebelde* "be made an official organ of [Local] 800 and moved to Salt lake." It was also a Mexican delegate, listed only as Rodriguez, who reported that conditions were ripe for action in Tombstone, though this motion was referred to committee and never acted on.[4]

The *Bisbee Daily Review* played an important role in whipping up anti-IWW sentiment and exaggerating the threat the union posed, which was quite natural, given that the paper was controlled by Phelps Dodge (the paper's general manger was also hired to do public relations work for the mining giant). Nevertheless, they seemed to be taken by surprise when the strike broke out in Bisbee on June 27.[5] Perhaps sensing what was in the air, the *Review* had been giving regular progress reports on a strike in Butte, which started on June 12, four days after one of the worst disasters in western mining—the mine disaster at Butte's Speculator Mine. This strike, nearly thirteen hundred miles away, was to be one of the catalysts for the one in Bisbee.

* * *

It was at midnight on Saturday, June 8, when a fire broke out in Butte's Speculator Mine, 2,400 feet below ground. The blaze began when a lead-covered cable that was being lowered got twisted and the lead coating was stripped from the insulated wires. A miner's carbide lamp touched the flammable matter, igniting the fire. Air coming down the shaft provided a draft, and as the flames rose, the men lost any possibility of escape. The *Butte Daily Post* reported that the flames were so intense that the faces of men 1,600 feet from the fire, 700 and 800 feet below ground, were burned. Rescue efforts continued for days, and though some survivors were miraculously found, in many cases those killed were buried without a name, burned beyond recognition.[6] The Wobblies saw those killed in the fire as victims "sacrificed to the Gods of Profit," and repeated a claim by miners that the company had flooded the lower levels of the mine while workers were still trying to escape.[7]

On June 12, the *Butte Daily Post* announced that "IWW agitators plan to involve the city in serious labor troubles," as the Wobblies circulated flyers calling for the organization of a union and improved working conditions in the aftermath of the fire. The circular read: "On this June evening the miners at two of the largest mines in this district will walk out, followed in regular order by miners employed in every mine (except those engaged in rescue work at the Speculator) in retaliation for the refusal of the mining companies to give so called 'rustling cards' to hundreds of miners whose only offense is their determination to stand unflinchingly for those rights guaranteed us by the constitution of the United States."[8]

It went on to call for the end of the rustling card system, the observance of state law, the firing of the state mine inspector, the respect for their right to speak and meet, for hiring put in the hands of a union committee, and a wage raise. The workers were called on to walk out and stay out until the demands were met. Experienced Wobblies were behind this nascent movement. The Butte strike had begun.[9]

The "rustling cards" spoken of by the miners was a central element in life in the mining camps and were described by Montana congresswoman Jeannette Rankin in the socialist weekly the *Appeal to Reason*. Mining companies, she wrote, have "an employment bureau to which every miner must apply if he wishes a job. Here his record is investigated, and if it is found that he has never complained of his working conditions, if he has a clean record as to unions (that is, if he is not what they call an agitator), or if he has voted the right political ticket, he is given a 'rustling card.' This card, is in effect, a permit, as we say in the west, 'to rustle' for a job. The man who applies for work at any mine is first asked to show his 'rustling card.' If he cannot produce one, he is not hired."[10] The *Bisbee Daily Review* reported almost daily that the walkout in Butte was a failure. But, on June 24, it was forced to report that Butte mines would be closing because other unions and trades had joined the Wob local in its action. A couple of days later, it reported that the Anaconda Mining Company in Butte was refusing to negotiate with Metal Mine Workers' Industrial Union Local 800, "which the company charges is controlled by the Industrial Workers of the World."[11] Which, indeed, it was. It was Wobbly control that allowed the strikes in the mines of such distant states as Montana and Arizona to be coordinated.

* * *

All of this was cause for optimism among the Wobbly hierarchy. From Phoenix on June 25, Grover Perry, the chief organizer in all of Arizona, sent an inspiring telegram to Bill Haywood in Chicago: "On verge state wide strike could you come wire answer."[12]

* * *

On June 26, local IWW leader A. S. Embree wrote to Perry to lay out the situation in Bisbee. The demands of the workers were presented to the mine owners at an afternoon meeting. Gerald Sherman, manager of the Copper Queen, "refused to hear anything from the committee" and tore up the list of demands, tossing the shreds into a wastebasket. The delegation from the IWW had been unable to locate the management of Calumet and Arizona, leaving the demands with company head W. B. Gohring's secretary, adding that if a positive response wasn't received by 5:00 they would assume he had refused the demands, while Lemuel Shattuck expressed the hope that he would be able to come to an agreement with his employees individually, and that "he would have nothing to do with the IWW."[13]

Following their visits to the companies, the executive committee made a report to the branch, at which their actions were approved, and a meeting was called for that evening at 7:00 at City Park.

Embree described that evening's meeting as "a success beyond our best expectations," the speakers all being "mud diggers who got up at a minute's notice and rivalled [local labor lawyer] Bill Cleary at his best."

At the meeting, where attendees seemed solidly behind the IWW, speakers made the point that it was necessary that they go out on strike while Globe, Miami, and Butte were also out.

From a recruitment point of view, the meeting was a huge success, with over a hundred men joining the IWW. At a meeting at the union hall that followed, pickets were assigned to "take charge of the shafts and urge men to keep away from work." Though some of the men who volunteered for this task wanted to take up their strike duties immediately and pull the night shift out, it was decided they'd wait, "as we were not organized for it, and we were afraid if we tried and did not make a good job of it, it would have a bad effect on our work in the morning."

Wob organizers went to all the Copper Queen shafts that night to talk to the men about the strike, talks that were obviously successful, since the only work being done was "stulling"—constructing props and platforms to protect miners from falling objects—and the cleaning and removal of tools. They were confident the Mexican workers would be supportive, as they'd found and put on the payroll "a good man for organizer" among the Mexicans, and were asking for a minimum wage for the topmen of $5.50 an hour.

Embree also discussed bootleggers with Perry. Bootleggers are seldom brought up when discussing the Wobs, but they were an important issue, one that recurred during the strike and after. The Bisbee branch had contacted Sheriff Wheeler "to take care of the bootleggers and told him we would give him all the information we could so as to put them out of business."[14] The Wobblies would soon be handling the presence of bootleggers by themselves, without the intervention of the sheriff.

* * *

Sheriff Harry Wheeler would emerge as the single most important figure involved in the strike and deportation. If some figures from the mining companies, like Phelps Dodge head Walter Douglas, worked in the shadows, Wheeler was the man who, during the strike and deportation and in its aftermath, was the face of repression.

Wheeler was the Florida-born son of a West Point graduate. Though he served in the US Cavalry at the time of Spanish-American War, he was not, as many sources claim, one of Teddy Roosevelt's Rough Riders, nor did he ever serve in Cuba.

Wheeler settled in Arizona after his military service and served in the Arizona Rangers from 1903 to 1907, when the organization was disbanded.

The sheriff was forty-one in 1917 and had a reputation for being fair and open-minded: Mother Jones met Wheeler in 1907 and described him as "a pretty fine fellow." There was even some doubt as to whether Wheeler would participate in the roundup; on June 29, just five days into the strike, Walter Douglas wrote to a friend that "the sheriff has completely lost his nerve." Given how unbending Wheeler was during the strike, this accusation says more about the insensate rage of the mine owners than it does about Wheeler's dependability as an enemy of the strikers. As we will see, Wheeler, far from having "lost his nerve," had, by this time, deputized hundreds of men for further action against the strikers.

It would seem that it was not (or not mainly) anti-union sentiment that was Wheeler's prime motivation in the events: he had shown himself to be neutral during the 1907 strike in Bisbee. What swayed him and led him to take so active a part in the strike and roundup was his conviction that the strike was the work of German agents. And not just German agents: German agents allied with Mexico in the aftermath of the Zimmermann Telegram, in which the Germans promised Mexico the return of Arizona, New Mexico, and Texas if it would attack the US.

Finally, making Bisbee an "American camp" played no small part in Wheeler's actions. As he said, "We will make this an American camp, where American men may enjoy life, liberty and the pursuit of happiness unmolested by any alien enemies of whatever breed."[15]

* * *

In 1917, there were more than 4,500 strikes. On June 27, a strike was called in the Warren District.[16] Seven demands were officially submitted to the mine operators, who refused to acknowledge them the previous day. The demands were:

1. Abolition of the physical examination…. Often able-bodied, husky men are turned down by the so-called "doctors," while the unfit are often accepted. Nothing but a blacklist in disguise. No real man likes to be stripped and handled like a mule at an auction sale when he applies for work.

2. Two men to work on machines. The machines used today, operated by one man, are much heavier than the machines formerly run by two men.

3. Two men to work together in all raises…. How can the companies follow their own advice, "Safety First," without considering this demand?

4. To discontinue all blasting during shift…. Blasting during the shift and at dinner time is part of the speed-up system and we intend to do away

with it. Also we have enough powder smoke from the previous shift, without continually eating smoke and being subject to severe headaches and sickness from this cause.

5. The abolition of all bonus and contract work.... The men are working hard enough now at day's pay. Under the bonus and contract system, the men are setting a pace that the men on day's pay must eventually follow.

6. To abolish the sliding scale. All men under ground a flat rate of $6 per shift. Top men $5.50 per shift.... Under the sliding scale the men have no protection whatever. When the scale slides down and the cost of living stays up, we don't intend to be the goats.

7. No discrimination to be shown against members of any organization.[17]

* * *

The mining companies "took no cognizance of the demands," though they did issue statements of their positions, which would not vary from the start of the strike until the deportation and well after. Phelps Dodge said it "will never negotiate with an organization founded on principles Inimical to good government in times of peace, and treasonable in times of war." The IWW "can not represent the sentiment of our men who are loyal American citizens ready to stand by their country at this critical time." The company warned that "any demands by their organization will be refused, even though such refusal may result in shutting down the mines for an indefinite period."

The Calumet and Arizona Mining Company also issued a statement explaining its refusal to deal with the IWW and its "impossible demands." Insisting that Bisbee was the "highest paid camp in the world," the C&A continued that the IWW, in its eyes, was "apparently engaged in a nation-wide conspiracy to close down the copper mines of the United States which would cripple and greatly imperil the government of the United States in the great war upon which it is entered."

The third company in the district, the Shattuck-Denn dismissed the IWW as the "floating population of the district [and they] have not expressed the sentiment of the mine employees of the Warren District." The demands presented were "unreasonable and are the plans of a nation-wide conspiracy by enemies of the United States government to restrict or cut off the copper output required to prosecute the war."

The companies' battle lines were drawn with these statements, and they would not be varied from, ever. But, as if already aware that everything hinged upon the actions of Sheriff Wheeler, the local paper featured a box high on the front page, dead center, with his statement concerning the strike, which was almost too eerily prescient. Questioning the patriotism of the copper strikers, he issued a warning: "I beg those interested to take notice that I will, in case of any disorder calculated to injure or harm the interests of this community, or of the United States of America, call upon and deputize, if necessary, every able-bodied loyal American in Cochise County to assist me in preserving peace and order, and, should necessity exist therefore, I shall not hesitate to demand aid and assistance from both the state and federal governments."

That evening, a meeting was held at City Park, which would be the center of public union gatherings until access was banned on July 11. Six Wob speakers addressed the crowd. The mine owners' paper said there was "little enthusiasm ... evinced" by those in attendance, most of whom were attracted by "idle curiosity." Attempting to paint the union leaders as outside agitators come to Bisbee to stir up trouble, the paper noted that a "peculiar feature of the meeting was the fact that hardly one of the speakers was known to the crowd."

Though Wheeler's statement said he intended "to protect all men in their constitutional rights as citizens ... and all aliens in peaceful pursuit of their daily labor or vocations," as well as "all private and public property," that first night was reported to be a quiet one. "The streets were as quiet as usual last evening," the *Review* reported the next day. "They appeared calm and gave no evidence of any untoward events, pending or otherwise."

"Prominent local miners" speculated—correctly as it turned out—that the unleashing of the strike in the Warren District was part of a statewide plan to pull out copper miners everywhere in Arizona, with Globe, Miami, and Morenci also likely to go out. And they did, in the case of Globe, with disastrous consequences.[18]

* * *

The copper strikes in the West were part of the IWW's national strategy, evidence of which can be found in the minutes of the convention of Metal Mine

Workers' Industrial Union 800, which, at its June 17, 1917, session, spoke of a motion made and carried that "we advocate strike to embrace whole industry instead of one locality wherever possible."[19] The strategy was fully outlined in an article that appeared in the Chicago-based *International Socialist Review* by John MacDonald, a Wobbly organizer who would soon be a defendant in the massive trial of IWW leaders. The title of the piece explained the program, "From Butte to Bisbee."[20]

For MacDonald, the fifty thousand miners engaged in strikes from Butte, Montana, to Bisbee were fighting "for the right to organize into one big union," which would take in the five hundred thousand unorganized workers in the metal mining industry.

The strike had first carried along the fourteen thousand miners in Butte. The miners in Bisbee, Globe, Miami, Clifton, Morenci, Jerome, and Golconda, Arizona, had all joined in "refusing to scab on the miners of Butte."

The strike, MacDonald wrote, rather than a series of unrelated events, was "a big industrial walkout. All for one and one for all," with activities coordinated by IWW Local 800 headquarters in Salt Lake City.

The Wobs, as we saw with their publishing of the Spanish-language *El Rebelde*, took especial pride in their willingness to fight the usual division between Americans and foreigners. MacDonald reported that "the boss is the only foreigner in the eyes of the workers here. All nationalities are together. Out of three hundred and fifty Mexicans who were working on top at the mines, only eighteen are scabbing."

In fact, Mexicans were the most unified group supporting the strike, as one manager said, having quit "practically in a body at the first announcement of a strike." In one mine, 300 of the 350 Mexican workers walked off the job. The Wobs were bearing the fruit of their longtime support of Mexican workers, of their closeness to the Flores Magón brothers, of the presence of organizers working specifically among Mexican workers, and most obviously, for their fight against the wage differential between white and Mexican laborers.[21]

According to MacDonald, contrary to the statements of the bosses, "Ninety per cent of the five thousand who work in the mining industries in Bisbee are out.... Over three thousand eight hundred have already joined the One Big Union."

Solidarity, one of the main IWW papers, also connected the strikes in Bisbee and Butte to those elsewhere. According to that paper, "the miners of the West are in revolt," and the strike was the fruit of the One Big Union idea: the miners in Arizona, in Bisbee, Globe, Miami, Swansea, and Jerome, "refuse to scab on their fellow-workers now striking in Butte." It wasn't local demands that *Solidarity* spoke of. Rather, the Arizonans had "decreed that not a drill shall move, that not a bucket of ore shall be hoisted till the Copper Trust shall come through with Butte demands." And so, twelve thousand men were out in Butte, and twenty-five thousand in Arizona. All of them asking the same question: "War prices for Copper—Why not for labor?"[22] The organizers in Bisbee spoke of offers of assistance from the IWW's Agricultural Workers Organization, which controlled the harvest fields, though there is no indication this ever materialized.[23] Interestingly, a letter sent to the Bisbee Executive Committee by IWW secretary-treasurer Bill Haywood two days before the roundup noted that the "convention on Bisbee" never mentioned using the Butte demands in Bisbee, and that the IWW "considered that it would have been better if they [the Bisbee miners] had waited a few weeks" before going out.[24]

It was not just the left that recognized the connection between the strikes in Bisbee and Butte. The Butte strike received extensive coverage in the *Bisbee Review*, and was front-page news on June 20, with a report that only one shift was worked in the mine because of concern "for the safety of the men who desired to work but who were intimidated by the Metal Mine Workers' Union."[25] The next day it was again front-page news, when it was announced that "80 percent of miners at Butte walk out."[26]

In an article published immediately after the deportation, and alleging an IWW attempt at establishing a "reign of terror"—part of a campaign that the article said was well financed "from sources unknown even to those well versed in the working of the union"—the *New York Times* cataloged the IWW's activities in the West, and the list was impressive. Along with Bisbee, strike activity was underway in Arizona in Globe-Miami, Clifton-Morenci, and Jerome; in Mexico, labor was active in Cananea, El Tigre, and Nacozari; in El Paso, three Wobs had been arrested on suspicion of plotting to blow up a bridge, and organizing among Mexican smelter workers was underway; in Oregon, a lumber strike was called in field and there were allegedly threats to destroy crops in the eastern part of the state; in Washington, timber workers were striking east of the Cascade Mountains, and five hundred IWWs passed through Seattle for the lumber camps, where they "seek to stir up trouble," and loggers were on strike in the Upper Yakima; and lumber camps were shut down in northern Idaho.[27]

Within days, the Department of Justice released the results of an investigation into German activity in the West. It revealed that no German funding had gone to the IWW, and that the "percentage of German sympathizers found in the [IWW] was believed to be no higher than that in any other organization."[28]

The US had just entered into World War I, and copper was an essential element in the construction of weaponry. Since the Arizona copper fields accounted for 28 percent of the total US production of the mineral, according to federal figures, and provided the operators with huge profits, a strike there would not only support the Butte miners, but it would also be the perfect time to improve the wages and lives of the miners in the newly minted forty-eighth state.[29]

This solidarity with Butte would later become a weapon wielded in defense of the vigilantes in the trial of Harry Wooton—the only trial of a Bisbee Deportation kidnapper. For his defense, one of his lawyers adopted a strategy of putting the IWW on trial. He read from correspondence by Wob leader A. S. Embree, which stated that the strike in Bisbee was in solidarity with the men in Butte. Wooton's attorneys claimed that this proved that what went on in Bisbee was not "a labor strike but ... a part of a revolutionary movement," and so no one who participated should be shown any sympathy as they were open to whatever fate might befall them.[30]

* * *

The number of Wobs in the Bisbee mines when the strike broke out is all but impossible to determine, but Arizona state senator Fred Sutter, representative of Cochise County, would say a year later that the Wobblies came to Bisbee and at first worked in secret, until by May "their membership exceeded that of the IUMMSW. Having obtained a majority of membership the IWWs took possession of the hall occupied by the legally constituted Miner's Union and the Warren District Trades Assembly."[31] Though a tribute to the organizing abilities of the Wobs, Sutter's statements must be taken with a grain of salt. His goal in this speech was to prove the illegitimacy of the strike and the danger the Wobs presented. Exaggerating their numbers was thus very much in his interest.

Some indication of their membership can be gleaned from the vote in the local's executive committee on June 23. Five hundred and three votes were cast for those elected as either members of the Executive or alternates.[32]

Charles Ward, a blacksmith in Bisbee, later said that he was a member of two unions, the IWW and the International Brotherhood of Blacksmiths and Helpers. He was a member of the Wobs for about a month. Asked by a member of the Presidential Mediation Commission why he joined the IWW, he replied that, "Well, the miners wanted me to take out a card with them and I was in a mining camp." Asked if he believed in the organization's principles, he likely spoke for more than himself when he said, "I didn't get a chance to know much about them in a month, you know."[33]

The IWW's strength did not lie in its ideology, but in its fighting ability. Frank Vaughan, president of the non-IWW painter's union, was certain the strikers did not belong to the IWW out of conviction. "When the strike was called," he told the Presidential Mediation Commission later in 1917, "they came out, and there was no other organization to belong to." For Vaughan, people joined the union as a way "to help out the boys who were carrying on the strike," and became members by handing in their WFM cards in exchange for "the Red Card, as we call it here, the IWW card."

His vision of how the IWW secured its hold was less than positive. "They had been here over a year, and they gradually worked their way in ... and they were very active, and I suppose, you all know that any active member can push himself up and finally grab all the offices."[34]

The extent to which the miners were members from conviction is difficult to answer. Fred Brown, also of the AF of L, estimated that three hundred men held cards in both the WFM and the IWW, and he later said that perhaps twenty-five were IWW members out of conviction, understanding the philosophy of the movement. His description of the rise of the IWW resembled that of Vaughan; Brown told the Mediation Commission that, a year before the events, there were about 1,700–1,800 members of the WFM, but shortly after Labor Day 1916 that union went into decline, while the IWW, which arrived about that time, was on the rise. He said that the WFM was soon down to a hundred members, which contradicts the other figures he would give, and attributed the decline to dissatisfaction with union head Moyer and the union's general inability to change conditions the men found unacceptable.[35] The AF of L would later allege that the IWW was funded by the mine owners in an effort to "disrupt duly organized labor."[36] In fact, the men were ripe for a more militant union.

Grover Perry, state IWW organizer, arrived in Bisbee on February 1, 1917, and his sights were set high. He wrote to Bill Haywood that he'd come with a supply of three thousand membership cards (specifying to the union leader that "they cost me 9.75 for the first thousand and 4.50 for each additional thousand."). Initiation fees for new members were $2, and monthly dues were

50¢. He met the president of the state Federation of Labor, who was curious what so many Wobs were doing in Arizona, and told Perry there was no future for them there.

* * *

Organizer Embree was more than pleased with the results of the strike's first day, calling it "a great success." Pickets had succeeded in turning back men on the morning shift; picket captains kept count of the men working, and according to them, of the 2,700 men who normally worked, only 740 had reported to the mines. Even better results were expected from the night shift, since they had "been drilling them all day and had a splendid meeting again at one o'clock in the park."[37]

Cornishman Fred Watson arrived in Bisbee in 1914, having hopped a boxcar from Tucson to Bisbee, where he worked as a tool nipper. In 1977, he was interviewed by a professor from the University of Arizona, giving us an important account of the events. Watson told of how he was working on the night shift when the strike was called. A fellow miner asked him, "What shift are you on?" and he replied, "I bet I ain't on any ...I bet I ain't on any shift." His friend replied: "No," he said, "you ain't. They called a strike at midnight last night."[38]

The mine owners questioned the legitimacy of the strike, saying it was imposed by the IWW, and Fred Brown, the local AF of L organizer, admitted he wasn't sure how a strike vote was done, able only to say that there was "a meeting of some kind." He had heard widely varying numbers of participants in this meeting, maybe two hundred, or one thousand, or very few. Whatever the case, he felt safe in saying 80 percent of the miners honored the call.[39]

* * *

In a sense, the strike couldn't have begun on a worse day. The main headline of the *Review* was "First contingent of American army reaches France," so the stage was set to present the strikers as shirking, draft-dodging, antiwar, anti-Americans. The businessmen of Bisbee didn't miss their chance and issued a statement condemning the "untimely demands of the strikers," imputing the trouble to "a small number of irresponsible men who have recently drifted into this camp for the avowed purpose of causing trouble and embarrassment to our government by tieing up a large unit of its much needed copper output." The men, the members of the Citizens' Protective League insisted, were not employed in Warren, "unless by an alien enemy," and resolved that the strike was "treason to our government."

All of this sounds odd when placed alongside the account of day one, where there was "no disturbances and little excitement" at the strike called by the Bisbee branch of the IWW. The mine owners' organ said that 50 percent of the miners remained at work in the Warren District, though the Shattuck-Denn mine was shut down, as were the Higgins Mine and all the surface leasers in the town.

As was the case throughout the strike, pickets were placed at the most heavily trafficked spots of Bisbee, specifically the post office and the depot, and wherever else they were likely to encounter fellow workers. The bosses attempted to provoke the miners in odd ways. For example, striker Fred Watson told of how a flag had been hung over the door of the post office—one of the main picketing spots—covering its full length, forcing anyone who entered the building to push it aside. (The flag can be seen hanging in just this fashion in photos of strikers being marched through the town on the day of the deportation.) "They were waiting for us to go there and tear it down," he later wrote. "We never touched it."[40]

In November 1917, Felix Frankfurter of the Presidential Mediation Commission would ask state mining inspector Edward Massey what conditions were like in Bisbee during the strike, and his opinion mirrored that of the strikers. "The only thing I saw was the pickets here at the depot and also up front of the Copper Queen store, just milling back and forth." Frankfurter pressed him about the question of disorderly conduct by the pickets, and Massey didn't hesitate to talk about how peaceful it all was: "Yes, sir, I went through the line one morning, and some fellows told them who I was and the pickets said to me, "'Make it safe for them scalies over there.'"[41]

Bisbee's representative in the state legislature, Rosa McKay, an unflinching supporter of the working class, later wrote that the unions claimed that 80 percent of the workers followed the strike order, while the mine owners insisted it was only 30 percent. "However, that matters but little; the fact is that the companies were crippled, one shutting down entirely, and the production of copper was curtailed to a great extent."[42]

By the second day of the strike, Sheriff Wheeler had already lost patience with the strikers (always defined by Wheeler and the press as IWW) and appointed two hundred additional deputies when the IWW broke its "promises" to not place pickets on company property. The sheriff issued a trespassing order and appointed the deputies to enforce it, confident that these added forces would encourage workers to ignore the strike—workers who "promised to return to work ... if protected."[43]

Both the lists of deputies and the appointment cards for the individual deputies demonstrate the ethnic element of the fight in Bisbee. Looking at a random file, we find under "C," the names Cunningham, Cook, Carver, Campbell, Connelly, Colson, Corcoran, Carver, Clark, Clampitt, Compton.... All of Anglo assonance. Though a Slavic name like Kolowski or Milutinovich occasionally appears in the file, it is a rarity.[44] The drive for an "American camp" would be carried out by the stereotypical image of an American as a white Anglo-Saxon.

At a rally that second day, a Wobbly speaker said the strike was only an opener, "but that it would be followed by continued efforts until they finally got what they wanted—the mining properties—and put the mine owners where they belonged, earning their living with their shovels underground."

The alarm was repeatedly sounded, falsely, that strikers were intimidating nonstrikers, and "delegated 'Wobblies'" were said to have gone to people's homes to threaten workers, wives, and children. But it is important to note that while the *Daily Review* and the authorities were insisting that workers were being intimidated and prevented from returning to work, the actual speeches of Wobs were being reported, and they wildly contradicted what was being alleged in them.

Contrary to the claims of union lawlessness, at a rally on the evening of June 28, pickets were told by the strike leaders to "regard the authority of the sheriff," though dodging it if possible, "by moving to points where there might be no deputies." The sheriff had ordered they stay off company property, and the Wob leadership told them to post themselves at as many road crossings as possible "*off the company property*" (emphasis added) and also to "deal with the men quietly and without offense."

Of course, the presence of foreigners was stressed in the press, as a "large percentage of men in the picket lines yesterday were foreigners." For once, German agents were not the sole issue, but instead, "among the speakers last night was a Mexican who addressed those of his race in their own language." On the other hand, nothing could be more American than the Copper Queen baseball team and the band, and both of them had joined the strikers.[45]

* * *

The mine owners were not about to leave the fate of their holdings solely in the hands of the police and constituted authorities, and so, as was the case in all major strikes, they resorted to informants. The papers of former Arizona governor George Hunt contain an unsigned "List of Undesirables, from Globe," apparently prepared September 1, 1917, which gives us an indication of what would have been occurring in Bisbee as well.

The list includes thirteen men, nine of whom are described as "American," one as "American-Italian" (despite his Irish name, Frank Dougherty), one Mexican, one Swede, and one "Austrian and French." The American nature of the western IWW, which we know to be a historical fact, was already known and ignored at the time.

The anonymous informant was nothing if not thorough. Heights are given to the half inch, and we get an idea of the size of the militants: seven were shorter than five foot nine, and eight weighed less than 160 pounds: they were not a stocky crowd.

The informant reports the men's misdeeds, indicating that they were all dedicated fighters for their class and their union.

B. H. Cain, a thirty-five-year-old "agitator" and organizer for the IWW, was overheard telling a woman that he was going to "get" someone at the Miami mine. "He is on the job for the IWW all the time."

J. O. Cain (no mention of a relation to B. H.) was in jail on a rioting charge, while Frank Dougherty of the IUMMSW "is strong in keeping the men from going back to work at the O D [Old Dominion] mine."

M. P. Guyer, a member of both the IWW and the IUMMSW, was "a man who ought to be watched," not least because he went to Clifton with a letter of recommendation from the operators' *bête noire*, Governor George Hunt. The Italian-American Dan Dougherty, also a member of the two miner's unions, "of broken speech," was considered to be a plant for the union officials who would bring up questions "they say are all right." Though a miner, he had organized newsboys and was sent to jail for doing so. He was a "bad man to deal with."

W. W. Smith, yet another member of both the IWW and the IUMMSW, was also a socialist. An engineer and pumpman, thus part of a trade that ordinarily did not strike with the miners, he was "quite a talker and tries to preach Socialism to all who he meets." If that wasn't enough, he also "hates Phelps

Dodge." Like the abovementioned Guyer, he was tainted by having contact with Governor Hunt, who stood bail for him along with the president of a bank when he was arrested as a picket in Globe.

Will Jefferson, also a socialist and member of the two unions, was a "strong Socialist [who] talks against government and conscription," but was "rather a coward." He also stood in the way of a return to work, according to the informant, by preventing workers from talking about voting for such a return.

Charles Powers, yet another member of both unions, was described by the informant as a "good looking, Mexican organizer and agitator who tries to run the Mexicans," a man who'd been arrested for rioting and who either raised bond or "skipped," leaving his family behind to be maintained by the union. And Bob Capps was described as simply active in the union, though unknown to the bosses he was a member of both.

Victor Mackley, a Swede, and Will Evans were members of only the IWW, and they were not men to be trifled with: Evans was a "heavy drinker, foul mouth, don't care what happens," while Mackley was possibly a "Sab Cat"— that is, a Wob who engaged in sabotage.

Sam Ford was the vice president of the IUMMSW local "and does all he can to keep the men from going back to work [at the Old Dominion mine] until all demands are granted." Austrian Frenchman Charles Patrick was a "strong IWW man," in jail for rioting.[46]

* * *

The campaign against the Arizona strikes was a national issue, and in Washington on June 28, Colorado senator Thomas laid correspondence before the Senate charging the IWW with working with German agents "to cripple smelters and industries in the west," particularly the mines in Arizona.[47]

On June 30, the strike was only days old and the owners' newspaper was already reporting fantastically that 65 percent of the miners had reported for work the day before, up from 50 percent the previous day, and that the skilled workers—the electricians, engineers, machinists, blacksmiths, boilermakers, carpenters, surface mechanics, and pumpmen—voted on June 29 not to strike at the Copper Queen and the Calumet and Arizona mines.

The strike itself was described as "arbitrary," called without the support or approval of any recognized union, and a "farce ... very near to collapse." And Governor Campbell once again asserted that the strike was the work of German agents, more specifically, that "reports have been made to me that activities of a sinister German character have been discovered at work in the district."

The denial of agency to the miners was a constant refrain. The crowd of a thousand who gathered at City Park was said to have "come out under imperative command," cheered when signaled to do so, "and its composition was so largely foreign and so plainly dominated by the few hundred imported IWW strikers who have provided the backbone of the entire movement." Somehow, the *Daily Review* was privy to conversations among the leadership of the strike, who, though allegedly aware the strike could not succeed, were nevertheless satisfied that they had accomplished what they set out to do: "The stirring up of trouble and the decreasing of efficiency."

The forces of order were beefed up, as the Protective Association was given fifty deputy sheriffs by the sheriff "who thus raised his force of deputies to over 300." It was ominous for the future that City Marshal Allison claimed he had a list prepared of other men ready and willing to be deputized should the need arise. Rumors that Sheriff Wheeler had asked for federal assistance from El Paso were dismissed by the sheriff, who "feels that the situation is well in hand and that the force he has sworn in, and additional men who are quickly available for swearing in, should emergency arise, will be abundantly equal to any service that may be required in the district under the wildest remote possibilities."[48]

Despite having deputized hundreds of additional men, despite the absence of any signs of trouble, despite the claims that the strike was already fizzling out, Sheriff Wheeler decided, on June 30, to escalate the fight against the strike, sending an alarming telegram to Governor Campbell that, in its brevity, managed to summarize the entire case of the mining companies and the authorities: "The strike here is most serious and I anticipate great property loss and bloodshed. Majority strikers seem foreign the whole thing appears pro German and anti American [sic]. I earnestly request you use your influence to have the U.S. troops sent here to take charge of the situation and prevent bloodshed and the closing of this great copper industry now so valuable to the United States Government."[49]

That there was little chance of bloodshed was later confirmed by lifelong Bisbee resident and deputy US Marshal J. F. McDonald. Bisbee, he felt, was "more peaceful than ordinary." This extraordinary peacefulness was a result of a campaign consistently carried out by the IWW throughout this period and which, as noted above, was already a concern prior to the strike: a war on bootleggers. As they would later do in Columbus, New Mexico, the IWW "had instructed the bootleggers whom they knew not to sell any liquor to the men or they would turn them in to the sheriff." This was good enough, and liquor all but disappeared from the district during the strike.[50]

* * *

The strikers held two mass meetings in City Park on July 2, one in the afternoon and one in the evening. "Raising their sights ... the IWW in Bisbee have decided that, in the words of one of last night's speakers at the City Park, 'We will not sign peace terms until every other company which now has labor trouble on its hands accedes to the demands of the strikers in every part of the country.'" This action followed a similar announcement made by the Butte, Montana, Wobbly organization. The strike movement was continuing to spread in Arizona as well, as the IWW office in Miami, already on strike, received word that the miners in Jerome would be going out in sympathy with them.

The Bisbee paper reported the day "was very quiet in every respect," with no arrests made and only one "Slavonian" worker threatened should he continue to work. The number of workers returning to the pits was described as "substantial," though the mining companies could provide no figures. In an account headlined "IWW Admit Effort to Cripple U.S.," the paper reported that one Wob speaker said that "the kind of Liberty Bond you fellows want is the little red card. It only costs $2.50."

In an effort to split the miners, Governor Campbell released a telegram from Charles Moyer of the IUMMSW, which said that "his organization of the American Federation of Labor has no authority for calling a strike at Bisbee and assumes no authority therewith."[51] This disavowal by the AF of L union did little to hinder the strike or persuade the strikers, even those members of both the IUMMSW and the IWW, who lived the seeming contradiction quite easily.

In Washington, Secretary of Labor William B. Wilson decided the time had come for him to get involved as the area was vital to American war interests. On July 2, he telegrammed once and future governor George P. Hunt: "I have been very much concerned to hear of the possible serious misunderstanding between the miners and the operators in the Copper Mines and I would deem it a very great service on your part if you would be generous enough to do what you could to act as mediator and conciliator. I know how confidently I can appeal to your public spirit." Hunt immediately accepted.[52]

Hunt would subsequently be granted travel authorization to Bisbee, compensation of $10, a per diem for incidental expenses of $4, and instructions on how to expense the trip and his time in Bisbee.[53]

* * *

On July 3, it was again reported that the number of workers returning to the mines had increased, with more expected for Thursday, after the Fourth of July, and "with the city officers clearing the streets during the afternoon, July 3 passed quietly and orderly in this walk-out ridden camp."

At a rally of the Workmen's Loyalty League, attended by six hundred men, Sheriff Walker "asked the crowd how many of them would be loyal to the American government and support him in maintaining law and order in the Warren District. He asked those who would be with him to stand and hold up their hands. Inspiring in the extreme was the sight. The six hundred and more miners, mechanics, muckers—American all—sprang to their feet, with their hands in the air and rent the air with their approval of the little man, with big thoughts and big actions, who stood on the stand addressing them."[54]

Police court judge Frank Thomas later told the Presidential Mediation Commission that the Loyalty League was "controlled exclusively by the companies."[55] Loyalty League leader M. W. Merrill told the commissioners that his organization was founded to combat the Villista threat, and had forty captains, ten majors, and sixty to seventy men in the ranks. Little training of any kind was given the men, despite the appearance later given by the smoothness of the roundup. "When the thing took place it automatically worked itself out."[56]

Elsewhere in Arizona, the mine owners were organizing in ways remarkably similar to those in Bisbee. "Not to be outdone in loyalty to her country in this world war," the Citizens' and Property Holders' Protective Association was founded at a meeting on July 3, in the Ajo mining district in Pima County, west of Bisbee, and quickly signed up 143 members. Two days later, a strike began in Jerome, Arizona, and a Workmen's Loyalty League was also founded, which soon was said to have 350 members, 60 percent of the payroll in the mines there.

In Ajo, the organizations were established expressly to forestall any IWW activity, though the Workmen's Loyalty League claimed it was not opposed to unionism and was supposedly composed of a large group of union members. But it was "opposed to disloyalty and to anything savoring of lack of

Patriotism, and is opposed to action by a small minority that would bind the majority in that which they did not desire."[57] It is doubtless not coincidental that the owner of the New Cornelia mine and manager of the Calumet and Arizona mine in Ajo was John Greenway, who would be one of the leading forces of the deportation in Bisbee.

In a report of July Fourth activities, locals were informed by the press of the "fall" of "wobbly stock" as "many miners prepare to return to work." The *Daily Review*'s front page aimed at undercutting the IWW by reporting on strikes around the nation.

An article from Scranton, Pennsylvania—a region that had recently seen a dozen strikes—reported that the arrest, under the Alien Enemies Act, of James Graber, a Wobbly organizer charged with "being a spy in the employ of the German government," had satisfied federal authorities that "the recent strikes of the Industrial Workers of the World in coal districts had been stirred up by Germans in the hope of lessening the power of the United States by decreasing coal production." The assistant US District Attorney asserted that "information in our hands ... proves the connection between the organizers and leaders of the IWW and the German government." The assistant DA was categorical: it was German money that was behind the strikes.

Closer to home, Wobbly "disloyalty" was addressed by a punch in the face at the Bisbee Fourth of July parade—organized by the Copper Queen Corporation. A "wob" refused to take an American flag offered by another spectator, saying, "I don't associate with such trash." When he refused to take off his hat for the "Star Spangled Banner," "Bing! The marcher struck hard and right on the point of the jaw." He was then rushed by other spectators. "Only the interference of Sheriff Wheeler and deputies saved the man from violence." This was the first verifiable act of violence during the strike, and was front-page news. "But it is not to be expected that red-blooded Americans will march in a parade and submit to insult to their flag and their national hymn."[58]

As Wheeler praised the Americanness of his audience from the Loyalty League, the only arrest of the day was that of an "Albianian [*sic*] Turk by the name of James Cocoves." The "Albianian" was punched for saying that "we will do to the American government what was done to that of Russia," and was saved by "the prompt work of city and county officers." Held on federal charges, "he is said to be an alien."[59]

For M. W. Merrill of the Loyalty League, the disloyalty of the strikers manifested itself in many ways. He claimed to have heard strikers say that the

Red [IWW membership] Card was better protection than the American flag, that the IWW button the members wore was "above Liberty Bonds." And nothing could be more culpable than something said by a man who worked with Merrill in the mines: "This is nothing more or less than a capitalistic war, these poor devils are going to get killed, so why should we buy a Liberty Bond."[60]

The Bisbee press committee of the IWW, likely A. S. Embree, dismissed the Independence Day parade in Bisbee, noting that it only had "680 (business) men and a few scabs" in attendance.[61] Filling out the crowd were children and residents of Douglas and Tombstone.

On the union side, Wob organizer Stanley Clark (who would soon be leaving Bisbee for Globe) spoke at a rally attended by over three thousand people on the evening of July 4. The IWW reported that the strike was thus far a huge success, with production reduced by half a million pounds per day and all the Mexican topmen out on strike. The press committee boasted that there was "no disorder and no boot leg booze," two matters of great concern to the Wobs, and because the situation was so orderly they were confident they could defeat the copper companies, since "they can find no excuse to use violence."[62] Even a hardheaded group like the Wobs was subject to illusions.

A Bisbee resident wrote to Governor Hunt after the roundup and deportation to tell him precisely how peaceful a town Bisbee was during the strike, with "no fighting or bootlegging." Using Fourth of July festivities as his benchmark, he wrote that on July 4, 1916, there had been twenty-seven arrests for drunk and disorderly conduct, while on the same date in 1917 there had been only two.[63]

Sheriff Wheeler, in explaining the trouble he expected from the strikers because of their "anti-American" nature, later said that around this time, a week before the deportation, whenever he saw a group made up mainly of Germans, Austrians, and Mexicans he would approach them and appeal to "patriotic motives and reasons." He would usually be rebuffed, the men asking, "What do the companies care for us; we care for ourselves." Now, fearing bloodshed was imminent, he "began to really fear that something should be done." Requests for assistance from federal forces had been denied, the army feeling the situation did not warrant the sending of troops. Wheeler would use this as the justification for what would ensue.[64]

* * *

Escalating the war between the Wobblies and the AF of L miners' union, and acting on the "grounds of treachery to the principles," on July 5, Charles Moyer, president of the International Union of Mine, Mill, and Smelter Workers, telegraphed the secretary of the Bisbee local, revoking its charter.

"I do this to protect our union," Moyer said. "We have not authorized any action on the part of our Bisbee local."

Moyer's telegram to Charles Tannehill, secretary of the local, was unequivocal: "This is to officially advise you that, acting under the power vested in me by the constitution of the International Union of Mine, Mill and Smelter Workers, I have and do hereby revoke the charter of Bisbee local no. 106 on the grounds of violation of the constitution on the part of said local and satisfactory proof of treachery on the part of said local to the principles of the International."

Enjoying what it assumed would be the discomfiture of the strikers, the *Review*, questioned the strength of the walkout—as it had every day of the strike, and as it would continue until it was forcibly ended. "With public sentiment increasing on all sides against the strike leaders, and with the statement of Charles H. Moyer that the local branch of the International Union of Mine Mill and Smelter workers would lose its charter for allowing the IWW to gain control of its organization, the strike agitators' outlaw union certainly presented a wobbly appearance last night."

The mine owners showed a particular solicitude for the IUMMSW. Since it opposed the strike it was considered "the only real union organization of miners in the district," and their hope and expectation was that the "real union" would be saved "from the clutches of the labor outlaws."[65]

The hatred and disdain of the IUMMSW for the IWW was expressed openly in an article in that union's journal on July 6. Stating that "practically all workmen except a few Mexican surface workers and the professional I.W.W. pickets returned to work today," the organ of the IUMMSW went on that "the strike here is virtually at an end today."

Referring to the "so-called Industrial Workers of the World" as "buzzards," looking to pluck members from among their estimated eight hundred members, the IUMMSW accused the Wobblies of using their "usual tactics of misrepresentation" and of "poisoning the minds of the members of [IUMMSW Local] 106 to the extent that men were placed in office who were well known to be active IWWs. The result being that they secured control of the local and used it in advancing their own interests." In all of this, Moyer found his pretext for revoking the charter of the Bisbee local of his union.

The IUMMSW's limited vision of unionism was in stark contrast to the IWW's insistence on industry-wide actions versus simple local activity in their statement that "the wrecking crew has moved to Jerome...regardless of the fact that as a result of a strike settlement there a short time ago the men received a substantial increase in wages and recognition of their grievance committee." Even more, the organ of the IUMMSW found it "significant" that the names of the unions organizing the strikes in Bisbee and Butte were the same. "The conditions calling the strike were very similar; Butte came first, followed by Bisbee. The story has been written in Bisbee, and let us see what effect it will have on Butte."[66] What was a point of pride for the IWW—the national character of their strikes—was a cause for censure for the IUMMSW.

Another enemy was entering the field, though, at least in the eyes of the bosses: former governor George Hunt, known for his sympathy for the cause of labor, was to be named mediator of the Arizona strikes by President Wilson. The strikers were said to be "wild with joy" at this announcement, and were certain ("offering bets of five to one") that all their demands would be met if Hunt took the post.[67]

* * *

It's strange that, in the mining towns of Arizona, among strikes and deportations, the IWW was viewed as the devil incarnate, as traitors, slackers, agents of the Kaiser, violent saboteurs, and enemies of the nation, but the individual who was a demon in the eyes of the mine owners, their supporters, and their press, was, of all people, Arizona's first state governor, a politician who would serve seven terms in that office, and who was only temporarily out of office in 1917: George W. P. Hunt. Hard as it is to imagine today, it was a governor of Arizona who was among the best representatives of progressive state government in the United States. Certainly he had personal and political flaws, but if you can know a man by his enemies, George Hunt had all the right enemies.

Hunt was born in 1859 in Huntsville, Missouri, a slaveholding part of the state settled by many, like Hunt, whose families came from the South. His family fought for the Confederacy and were enslavers.

The future governor received limited education in Missouri, going only as far as the eighth grade, which left huge gaps in his learning and poor mastery of grammar and spelling, for which he would be mocked later in life by fellow politicians and the press. When Hunt said during his campaign to be

Arizona's first governor that the first thing he'd do was write a message to the legislature telling them to put judicial recall on the ballot, the *Arizona Republican* wrote, "Of course, Mr. Hunt will get someone else to write that message. The writing of messages, or anything else for that matter, that requires proper spelling and the arrangement of words into sentences, is not Mr. Hunt's strong point." In later years, he'd admit to not being all that educated, "but then Abe Lincoln and Andrew Johnson didn't go through any universities either." His home situation was a bad one; his parents didn't get along, and neither did he and his father. Hunt left the family home when he was eighteen, only returning to Huntsville once, twenty-two years later, when he was a William Jennings Bryan delegate to the 1900 Democratic convention in Kansas City.[68]

After three years of roaming the West, Hunt made Arizona home, settling in the mining town of Globe. He spent two and a half years as a waiter and was active in the waiters' union before moving on to work as a mucker in the Old Dominion Mine, the most important one in Globe. When the mine closed, he left Arizona for California, but was back in Globe in 1897, where he worked raising cattle.

Busy on what passed for the social scene in Globe, Hunt spent much of the 1890s in the territorial legislature representing the town, elected for the first time in 1892. In 1896, a bitter strike broke out at the Old Dominion Mine over an issue that would haunt the mines and mining camps in the West for years. The mine owners decided to cut the wages of the mainly Irish and Anglo miners and replace the "white" miners with Mexicans and Chinese workers. The strike, fought on strictly racist terms, was won, and Globe became a white man's camp. It was also a stronghold of the radical Western Federation of Miners and the Populist and Socialist Parties. Hunt firmed up his reputation as a supporter of labor at this time, though he had become a relatively wealthy man, as in 1900 he became president of the Old Dominion Commercial Company. He would later write that "through study and close contact with the men who toil in the mines and smelters" he developed his views on "the economic situation."

Though a Democrat, he opposed many policies of President Cleveland, particularly the latter's sending in of federal forces to break up the Pullman workers' strike of 1894, led by Eugene V. Debs. It was as a result of this strike that he introduced bills in the territorial legislature taxing the sleeping car companies and banning blacklisting of workers, as had happened after the strike. Hunt was and remained part of the Bryan wing of the Democratic Party, supporting his stands on the monetary standard and labor. All of his political life, Hunt supported popular initiatives, referenda, and recall, and was on the popular, if not populist, wing of the party.

As statehood neared, Hunt's legislative focus was on issues like the outlawing of gambling and raising taxes on saloons to make drinking more difficult. More importantly, he fought strongly to increase the taxes paid by the mines and to cut freight and passenger rates on the railroads, earning him the hatred of these two powerful industries. When a legislator in neighboring New Mexico, also waiting for statehood, suggested Hunt take it easy on big business because his acts would scare off investment, Hunt stood firm. The capitalists, he said, "represent but one class, and that a very small class of our citizenship," noting that they had "never been marked by a noticeable sympathy for the right or the welfare of others." He then laid out what would be his guiding principle as governor: "Those who have or may hereafter invest their millions here will have to content themselves as well as they can afford to with status molded with an eye single to the welfare of the whole people."[69]

Whenever a piece of pro-labor legislation came up, Hunt was one of its main backers. He helped extend the eight-hour day, set up a commission to write a mine safety code, and worked to have the Arizona Rangers, modeled on the Texas Rangers but often used for union busting, shut down. Among those who were Rangers was his future nemesis, deportation leader Sheriff Wheeler.

Hunt hoped to become governor when Arizona achieved statehood, but he first had himself elected president of the constitutional convention, where he pushed to write a constitution enshrining progressive principles, like the notoriously radical Oklahoma constitution of 1907. Included in the constitution was a commission regulating the railroads and other public utilities, which also had oversight over the mining companies. The eight-hour day, an end to blacklisting, workers' compensation, and judicial recall were also part of the new pact. Hunt's pet project, initiative, referendum, and recall were all included, as was short terms for legislators—the governor included—of only two years. The constitution was overwhelmingly approved by the voters in February 1911, once judicial recall was removed from the constitution—President Taft having said he'd veto statehood if it remained.

Late 1911 also saw Hunt campaigning for governor of the Arizona territory. During the campaign he stressed his progressive bona fides, working to win over the not-insignificant socialist vote, with his Republican opponents going so far as to claim he had been a charter member of the Globe socialist club. In fact, he would later write in his diary that he was curious about IWW ideas and wanted to discuss them with IWW members. Hunt narrowly defeated his opponent, and was sworn in as governor on February 14, 1912, when Arizona became the forty-eighth state.

As governor, Hunt followed through on his promise to make the corporations pay their share. A tax commission created by the legislature and backed by Hunt increased the assessment roll by $255 million. For the mines, that increased from $19 million to $45 million between 1911 and 1912, and in 1913 it soared to $131 million—37 percent of the state's tax revenues. Hunt also saw to it that the railroads were placed under stricter control, giving the Corporation Commission the power to look into and reduce passenger rates. There was hardly a large interest whose depredations Hunt didn't attempt to block, as he prevented cattle companies, business interests, and speculators from purchasing public lands at low rates. A measure that failed to pass, but that would certainly have been enlightening in Arizona, was one that would have forced all newspapers to prominently identify the people behind the newspaper. In Bisbee, where the *Daily Review* was owned by the Phelps Dodge Mining Company, and was its propaganda organ during the labor troubles there, this would have been a valuable measure.

Hunt was a lifelong campaigner for prison reform and against the death penalty, going so far in the former case as to have himself locked in a state prison to see what conditions were, while also implementing a liberal system allowing prisoners to temporarily leave the prison on giving their word of honor they would return. When the abolition of the death penalty was reversed in a referendum, Hunt planned a "hanging bee": a mass execution to which he would invite the leaders of the major firms in Arizona, who had worked to overturn the ban. If they supported the death penalty so strongly, he felt, they should be made to witness a mass of them at once, and even be made to spring the trap. He backed off at the request of the state prison's warden, but among those he wanted to embarrass was Walter Douglas, head of Phelps Dodge in Bisbee. The enmity between the two men was building and would soon explode.

George Hunt was not a plaster saint, and the southerner in him came out in this early period and throughout his political career in matters of race and ethnicity. Hunt signed a law forbidding members of racial groups—in this event, Chinese and Latinos—from obtaining citizenship or purchasing land. In 1915, he would rise in anger against a federal court ruling voiding a law that restricted the number of aliens who could be hired, a measure also backed by the AF of L, which called for 80 percent of all workers hired by any company with five or more employees to be qualified electors or native-born citizens of the United States. Hunt claimed that such a measure was needed to protect American workers from "the wholesale importation of aliens." Hunt's racism was ecumenical, and he was behind a strict segregation law, banning Black people and white people from being in the same classrooms together and even attending the same schools. The matter no longer became optional: if there was one Black student, a new school was needed. In Bisbee, this meant a separate school for its eight Black schoolchildren.

His attacks on the mines, of course, infuriated the mine owners, and their rancor would be long lasting. The railroads went so far as to threaten to cease construction in Arizona. Despite Hunt's racism, his biographer, David R. Berman, wrote of his speeches in the early years of his governorship that "it was difficult to distinguish him from a socialist orator."[70]

When the Western Federation of Miners sent organizers into Arizona in 1915 and a strike broke out over the lowering of wages in the Clifton-Morenci mining district, Hunt went to the area and gave a speech to the striking miners, telling them that he was not going to intervene on the side of the mine owners and praised the workers' restraint. He took a novel tack, however: he threatened to have both the strikers and the owners rounded up by the state militia so that they could talk matters over while in custody.

In the end, he sided at all points with the miners, particularly the Mexican miners—the lowest paid and most exploited of an exploited group—and when the mine owners fled the area for New Mexico, claiming their lives were in danger, Hunt would have none of it. In order to forestall federal intervention, which would almost certainly side with the owners, Hunt sent in a small contingent of state militia, which also served to block the importation of strikebreakers. Hunt refused to be budged, even when the mine owners said that his speeches and his taking sides with the miners had made the district unsafe.

The mine owners refused to negotiate with the WFM for the entire five months of the strike, and a compromise was reached when the Arizona State Federation of Labor intervened and served as the negotiation partner of the workers. The strikers won almost all their demands. If his actions won him the praise of such labor stalwarts as Mother Jones, with whom he had friendly relations, it also, Hunt wrote, "greatly increased the desire of the mining companies for my elimination as a political factor in Arizona."[71]

Hunt survived a recall campaign in 1915, a hotly contested election in 1916 that resulted in Arizona temporarily having two men claiming to be governor, and a ceaseless campaign of vilification on the part of the mining companies ultimately serve seven terms as governor.

* * *

The rage of the mine owners at Hunt's appointment as strike mediator was not something they hid: as a group, the general managers of Phelps Dodge, the Arizona Copper Company, and the Shannon Copper Company in Clifton wrote directly to labor secretary William Wilson, and not in measured tones.

Their lengthy telegram condemned the appointment of Hunt because of his "well known animosity ... towards the mining companies operating in this district [which] was manifested unreservedly in a speech to the strikers the greater part of whom were Mexicans and other foreigners in the labor troubles in this district in nineteen fifteen and in our opinion was one of the main causes of violence and destruction of property at that time."

Hunt's presence would bring nothing but trouble: "His past record in this district has been such that his appearance would be taken by certain lawless element [sic] as a signal for defiance of the present constituted authorities of the state in their efforts to maintain peace, thus contributing to bringing about violence and disorder rather than lead to conciliation."[72]

The violence of the strikers was invoked over and over again, and Bassett Watkins, a shift boss in the mines, who had been a deputy for a year and had also once been chief of police, provided testimony about violence during the strike. He claimed there were assaults carried out by strikers and was asked by presidential commission member Felix Frankfurter how many. Watkins could only reply, "I never seen any myself." Pressed by Frankfurter about how many he'd heard of, he could be no more precise than "I heard of several, I remember, but the number I could not tell you." It was always thus in the allegations of striker violence.[73]

Sheriff Wheeler could be no more precise about strikers' violence. He later defended the deportation by saying that nonstrikers were being beaten up by strikers, that lunch pails were being stolen, that "foreigners" were visiting women at their homes when their husbands were out and threatening to blow the houses up.

The starkest coloration was given to every utterance of any striker or strike leader. When Mayor Jacob Erickson told A. S. Embree and other IWW leaders that use of the "public square" would be denied them because they were obstructing circulation and people were complaining of "unpatriotic speeches made at the park," Sheriff Wheeler alleged that Embree heatedly responded that he could no longer be responsible for the actions of his men.[74] For Wheeler, this was a threat requiring the deportation of 1,200 men.

* * *

One incident in particular demonstrates the ways events could be twisted to justify the deportation, and also speaks volumes about the attitude towards and fears of Mexicans in Bisbee in 1917.

In his testimony before the Presidential Mediation Commission, county and state deputy engineer J. C. Ryan described events that had occurred at the laundry in Warren. He reported that "every industry was assailed, private concerns, auto drivers, restaurants, boarding houses, and finally the poor women and girls who worked in the Warren laundry. They were so terrorized by visitations of a committee of Mexicans, after threats of dynamite, etc., that the women one day left in a body in abject terror. Think of white women in an American town so terrorized by foreigners that they were compelled to quit work in terror for their lives."[75]

Sheriff Harry Wheeler saw things differently, saying the white women were more "nervy" and that it was the Mexican women who were terrorized and fled from the laundry.[76] Indeed, Wheeler's account of this event, which he used as proof of the violence the deportation forestalled, is a farrago of racist tropes and illogical statements that baffled the commissioners. One of the latter was so lost by Wheeler's account of the threat that he could only draw the conclusion that the laundry was threatened with bombing while laundry workers, deputies, and menacing Mexicans were all gathered in the same location and so risked being blown up together.[77]

Sheriff Wheeler testified that the laundry workers had been threatened, and yet, when asked if he'd made an attempt to arrest the men who made the threats, he said, "I could not prove they made them."

Wheeler's version thoroughly confounded the commissioners, and one of them wondered, if the threat was made and the women were made to abandon the laundry at noon when the place would be dynamited, why wasn't protection put in place? Wheeler then insisted protection was put in place and, as the questioning continued, he reverted to racism: "You don't understand the situation. You never lived in this country and you don't know Mexicans." Commissioner Walker readily admitted this was true and Wheeler continued: "You must understand that in that laundry a portion of the women were Mexicans and a portion were white women... The Mexicans got these girls together down here somewhere and put this up to them down here at a meeting. See? And threatened them at that meeting... and at the appointed hour these Mexicans who had threatened them marched past the laundry and the girls thought sure they had come to keep their word, and they all rushed out and went home. Do you begin to understand?" They didn't.

Marching Mexicans would appear regularly in Wheeler's accounts. He would testify that four hundred to five hundred Mexicans, who supposedly had Villista rifles hidden away, would parade in the streets of Bisbee. He was unable to arrest any of them because none could be identified. "How could you separate one Mexican from another?," Wheeler wondered. And the solidarity among the Mexicans was unbreakable. "No Mexican, hardly, will testify against another. Even if one is dying, stabbed by another, when you get there and ask who hurt him, he will tell you he does not know."

The existence of the Villista rifles was not revealed by the Mexican strikers, and none were seen by Wheeler; rather, a Mexican deputy, now conveniently dead and so unable to testify, allegedly overheard a conversation among chambermaids about them! Equally vague was Wheeler's knowledge of the "leader" of the Mexicans, who, he said, was a bootlegger now in Agua Prieta, across the border from Douglas. This same leader was also, Wheeler said, "guilty of the murder of a white man." The commissioners were told that this Mexican killer / bootlegger / labor leader said that "at the opportune time he and his Mexicans, and his white friends, will return and punish Bisbee for what they did to him."[78]

Wheeler's tales of guns and laundry bombing, reported four months after the event, can be checked against a contemporary account in the normally alarmist *Bisbee Daily Review*. The paper, which never missed an opportunity to paint the strikers in the most dangerous of hues, covered the event on its front page on July 7, and their reporting contradicts both Wheeler's and Ryan's accounts. In it, we read about "an attempt on the part of the IWW leaders to cripple the two laundries in the Warren District. On Thursday some Mexican agitators induced a number of women ... to leave their work. Yesterday morning from twenty-five to fifty pickets of the IWW appeared before the same institution and endeavored to draw all of the force out. This effort was unsuccessful."

According to the paper, similar attempts on the laundry were made in Bisbee in Brewery Gulch, and "not one of the women quit her employment."[79]

The story was also, and perhaps primarily, a holdover from the fears generated by two local events with international ramifications: the Villista revolt, which was occurring just south of Bisbee, and which would lead to a Villista incursion into Columbus, New Mexico, the future site of the encampment of the deportees. Reports of the activities of Pancho Villa and his men featured regularly and prominently in the Bisbee press. Every bit as important were the strikes in the mines of Cananea, Mexico, which though they occurred in a foreign country, were in many ways a Bisbee event. Indeed, Wheeler claimed that many of the Mexicans in Bisbee were newly arrived there after fighting alongside Pancho Villa's forces, and had also participated in running the Americans out of Cananea.[80]

* * *

Despite all the claims that the strike was dying out, that the "healthy element" of the working class was rejecting Wobblyism, the fear and rage that gripped the bosses was clear in their activities on July 6. If the gloves were ever on, they were now off, and the smell of repression was in the air.

The central office of the IWW was anxious to join the fray, writing to local organizers in a July 6 telegram that the "entire organization [is] back of you." Frank Little and Bill Haywood wrote local leader A. D. Kimball that they "will drop all plans and be with you." Little would make it to Bisbee; Haywood wouldn't.[81]

As if in response, at a meeting of "five hundred residents of the copper district" at the federal building on July 6, resolutions were passed "declaring the IWW to be a public enemy of the United States." The unconstitutional events that were now less than a week away were prefigured at this gathering. That much of what would occur was already in the planning stages, or at least was being contemplated, is clear from the fact that so much of it appears in the resolutions passed.

> That terrorism in this community must and shall cease.
> That all public meetings of the IWW as well as all other meetings where treasonable, incendiary or threatening speeches are made shall be suppressed.
> That we hold the IWW to be a public enemy of the United States.

That we absolutely oppose any mediation between the IWW and the mine owners of this district.

That after settlement of the strike we are opposed to the employment of any IWW in this district.

That all citizens who have been deputized be retained until peace is restored in this district.

Though there was never any doubt as to the view of the IWW held by the mine owners, their attitude was neatly summarized on July 6 in a front-page cartoon in the *Daily Review*, which pictured a miner being tied up by a man labeled "agitator" with ropes bearing the words "treasonable propaganda," "German plots," and "IWW influence." The cartoon was headed, "These bonds, tied by treason, can be cut by patriotism."

More alarming still, and indicative of the state of mind of the vigilantes toward radicals and people of color, was expressed in a short piece in a cartouche on page 1 on July 7, which quoted a certain C. L. Carpary in the *El Paso Herald*. After saying that El Paso needed to organize "a vigilance committee of 500 to take care of any such troubles as are now harassing the people of Arizona's mining camps," Carpary cited two historical precedents: "The Ku Klux, to which I belonged, saved the south from humiliation in the days of reconstruction, and it could be used with profit to our country today." This example was not limited to the mining camps of the southwest, though. Vigilantes "would make good Americans out of traitors, as our western pioneers made good Indians. The government should not hesitate to use machine guns on our enemies at home."[82]

The next day, the stark choice between the IWW and right-thinking Americanism was again displayed on the front page of the local paper, this time in the form of the Joe Hill Memorial Edition of the IWW Songbook, the cover described as "red—blood red." The headline reads, "Do you want this domination in Bisbee?" The paper printed the words to the Wobbly song "Christians at War" by John Kendrick. Sung to the tune of "Onward, Christian Soldiers," the song calls on good Christians to "slay your Christian neighbors, or by them be slain."

The brief squib asks: "Can You Brook an Organization which Tolerates Such Sentiments in this Community?"[83]

* * *

Buried in all the coverage of the weakness and weakening of the strike was the fact that the Shattuck mine had closed as a result of the strike call on June 27. It thus comes as something of a surprise to read a congratulatory notice that it had *reopened* on July 9. This, readers were assured, was "a good omen for the Warren district ... a certain sign that the backbone of the Bisbee lockout is gone and only the remnants of the affair remain."

Another surprise was the news that on July 8 "the first real trouble of the strike" had taken place, when G. M. Jones, a Copper Queen miner, was accosted by five men when leaving his shift. The men asked him where he worked, and after he told them "he was attacked from the rear. He was badly beaten up and left nearly unconscious. *Though severely bruised and hurt Jones is not seriously injured*" (emphasis added). Jones could not identify the men, so Sheriff Wheeler was unable to make any arrests, but the "assailants were foreigners, not being able to speak English with any fluency."

Foreigners were also monitored at the funeral over the weekend of an IWW member, and "an actual count" was made of those in the procession. The members were "320 Mexicans and 198 other foreigners, and presumably, Americans." This crowd of over five hundred people at a simple funeral somehow struck the editors of the newspaper as "small."

Five pickets were arrested on July 8 on a charge of blocking circulation at the usual picket lines at the post office and the depot. They were supposedly arrested at the behest of "certain citizens of the city," on behalf of whom city ordinances gave the police the right to make the arrests. The goal was baldly stated: "To eject all pickets and eliminate all picketing from the streets of the city of Bisbee." The hearing was scheduled for July 10, and police court judge Frank A. Thomas later testified about the events to the Mediation Commission. He spoke of the five arrests, the only ones of the entire strike, and denied that the arrests were strike related. "You could not really say they were by reason of the strike; they just merely wanted to test certain features of the City ordinance." Asked how he disposed of the case, Thomas said that "the case was bitterly fought ... and there was an exciting time in the courtroom. We had to open all the doors to let the crowd in, and they argued it very fully." He explained that he took the case "under advisement," continuing it until July 12 at three o'clock, but when he went to the courthouse on that day none of the defendants were present.[84] All of them were on boxcars headed for New Mexico.[85] Deportee Fred Watson, one of the five arrested strikers, wrote years later that the trial was still pending.[86]

The strike was now two weeks old. On July 10, the IWW central office wrote to the Bisbee executive committee to address the issue of the demands placed before the mine owners. Given the statewide nature of the strike—indeed, the industry-wide nature of it—Bill Haywood wanted the workers' demands to be modified, in particular that the six-hour day now become a central demand in Bisbee, as it already was in Jerome. It was the hope of the central IWW offices that this would be the key demand everywhere. Bisbee leader Embree had told the IWW that they would be making the demand formal in a day or so, but that it would immediately do so if Globe or Miami or any of the other striking camps were to do so.

The Bisbeeites were told that "there is no time like the present to demand the six hour day in all mining camps. The Bisbee demands means nothing to most mining camps if we leave the six hour day program out." Some of the Bisbee demands simply did not apply everywhere, since it was one of the few camps to have mandatory physical examinations, and it was only in Arizona that wages were on a sliding scale. The six-hour day was the way to go.

"The six hour day is the real move and it was the six hour rallying cry in Globe, Miami, Jerome, Golconda, and elsewhere that made the great state wide strike in Arizona possible. It is the six hour day program that is going to make possible camps in Utah going out. Also it is the six hour program that is going to prove the greatest factor in swinging men from the W.F. of M. into the IWW."[87] Events would cut this short.

* * *

Walter Douglas, president of Phelps Dodge, who was confronting strikes all over Arizona, was reaching his wits' end. When asked about a possible compromise with strikers in Globe he responded that "there will be no compromises because you cannot compromise with a rattlesnake." And he claimed these rattlesnakes had foreign backers. Germans, no doubt. He dubiously claimed that "these men had no money yet they are rich with it now." He hinted at a grudging belief in the intelligence with which the strike was being managed, for it required the presence of someone with "brains far bigger and more capable than Big Bill Haywood." Haywood was too obviously American to play the role of the head of a foreign-led conspiracy, and so he was dismissed as "the only American I know mixed up in the IWW business."

Douglas was sure that things were improving in Bisbee, but things were deadlocked in Clifton where there was also a strike, also supposedly foreign-led, but this time from a different corner of the world: it was "Spaniards from the anarchical provinces of Spain [who] controlled and led the way for the IWW organization."

In Bisbee it was reported that all signs point to "a steady resumption of work," and though pickets continued to gather at their regular assembly points the number was alleged to be shrinking, those few still out "strangers in the district who were not working when the strike was called."[88]

Workmen's Loyalty League head M. W. Merrill later asserted that, as the strike dragged on, word got around that the companies were giving the men until July 13 or 14 to return to work, and that those who did would "not be considered strikers, and those who didn't [were] to get their clothes and belongings from each locker and take them off the job." Merrill added yet another rumor to this one, which though groundless, would reflect poorly on the strikers and injected the proper element of fear into the proceedings. Merrill continued that "there was a movement on foot that the men were to avail themselves of that opportunity of going on the companies' grounds at that time and would run the men off the job that was working, and things began to look very serious."[89]

What was the source of these reports and rumors that provided a pretext for the roundup? Merrill told the commissioners that they had started circulating on July 10, and their sources were difficult to define. "Why, we had different, they weren't agents. We had men who were out on the streets....Men inside, practically two or three at different times ... they didn't belong to any agency.... They weren't hired; they were just men working there." There is no doubt that there would have been miners providing information to the companies: the Cousin Jacks, the Cornish miners, were notoriously anti-strike. But that private agencies were on the scene—as they were whenever there was a strike—is even more certain. Merrill, later in his testimony, would contradict himself, and when pressed by Felix Frankfurter about how many "secret service men" there were, he said they paid "sometimes three or four, or maybe ten."[90]

A deputy marshal later spoke of a man named John Foster, whom he described as an "information gatherer or detective" employed by the banks and the mining companies. Foster's presence and activities were a matter of general knowledge, and he advised the Mediation Commission members to "just speak of him—that is the general matter about town."[91]

Since the brief scuffle of Sunday, no trouble had been reported anywhere in Bisbee.[92]

* * *

Things were different elsewhere, though, and three hundred miles north of Bisbee, in Jerome—midway between Phoenix and Flagstaff—a dress rehearsal for the Bisbee Deportation was taking place.

Those miners, either members or supporters of the IWW, had gone on strike on July 5, without the support—indeed with the condemnation—of the local branch of the IUMMSW, which had voted overwhelmingly against the work stoppage.

As in Bisbee, the strikers were alleged to have threatened to use dynamite against the mines, to have intimidated strikebreakers, to have called them names (IUMMSW boss Moyer responded that it was a compliment to be called a "scab" by the Wobs). The mine owners organized a Loyalty League.

A fight broke out between IWWs and nonstrikers on July 9 at the picket line at the United Verde mine in Jerome, and "citizens" discussed the possibility of driving the IWW from the town. Nonstrikers asked for forty-eight hours, saying they were capable of handling the situation, but it was decided to put an end to the strike and rid the town of the Wobbly presence. At a meeting at the local high school, which was attended by a hundred people the night of July 9, "there was no need to discuss what was to be done. The only question before the house was ways and means."

The vigilantes would be divided into four groups that would go to four places where strikers were known to assemble or live. The vigilantes—as was the case in Bisbee—would all have white handkerchiefs tied around their arms for identification. Though a hundred men were expected to show up at 6:00 a.m. at their city hall gathering place, 250 men arrived to carry out the roundup. As the local newspaper wrote, "The big hunt was on."

When no Wobs could be found at the United Verde mine, one of the four locations the vigilantes had designated as an object of attack, it was feared that the IWW had learned of the planned roundup, but in the end the vigilantes caught everyone they'd planned to capture.

The *Verde Copper News* described the flow of events:

> There was no yelling, no boisterousness no loud threats. Determined citizens went grimly but cheerfully about the work of ridding their town of the wobbly pests. They marched through the halls of the rooming houses, knocking on each door and requiring each occupant to present himself. Usually there

was someone in the party who recognized the occupant as a decent citizen or wobbly. Whenever an innocent sleeper was aroused the vigilantes apologized and passed on. Most of those disturbed took the matter good-naturedly and many directed the searchers to places where Wobblies could be found.

After half an hour, only fifteen men had been rounded up and taken to jail. In one boardinghouse notorious for its IWW residents, no strikers were found; however, a list of IWW members was discovered, and this increased the rate of arrest. Fifty were in custody by 8:30. Wobbly weapons were a cause of much fear in Jerome and led the vigilantes to believe they would be facing "desperate resistance," and a search of the seized men came up with two revolvers, one long knife, and one pair of brass knuckles. Included among the prisoners were B. "Wobbly" Brown, the IWWs main organizer in Jerome; "Red" Thompson, "a Wobbly spellbinder and organizer of evil reputation" who had been active in other Wob actions, including Everett, Washington; and Jack Gillette and Tom Ford, local activists.

Sixty-seven of the hundred men picked up were accompanied by fifty guards, and led to the train station. They were thought to be headed for Jerome Junction at 10:30 that morning.

The Wobbly hunt delayed mine operations in Jerome that day, and only one mine functioned for the day shift, though "it is expected the excitement will die down tonight and that full crews will report at 4 o'clock."[93]

"Every available member of the IWW to be found in Jerome," was loaded onto two cattle cars. Accompanied by armed guards, they began their voyage.[94]

As with the Bisbee deportees, the roundup went smoothly, but little else did.

The train reached Jerome Junction, twenty miles from Prescott, Arizona, where ten squads of the Prescott Home Guard, "called to actual service for the first time," as the local paper reported, met the train and surrounded it with men armed with high-powered rifles. The men were gathered together between two boxcars and held until the full contingent of Home Guards, twenty automobiles in all, arrived.

The deportees were examined, and nine of the most important "agitators" among them were removed from the bunch and taken to jail. It is a typical sign of the times that, though they had been forcibly removed from their homes, transported across Arizona, and were now in jail, *no charges were filed against any strikers or their leaders.* The plan was to hold them "pending a decision by the citizens whether or not they want to declare martial law and make the constitutional guarantees subservient to the public need." The remaining men—sixty-three, according to the papers—were ordered to get back on board and the train sent on westward toward California.[95]

The next day, it was leaked that the supposed ringleaders held in the Prescott jail, still with no charges against them, might be charged with treason by the federal government, in the hope "that by placing the wobblies on trial [the authorities] will secure evidence to prove that German money has been advanced to the agitators who have partially succeeded in shutting down the copper mines of Arizona."[96] It was reported a few days later that the grip of Wobbly "spellbinder" "Red" Thompson was found to contain two boxes of dynamite caps along with correspondence detailing the supposed IWW plot to shut down the copper industry in Arizona. Details of the contents of the correspondence weren't revealed, but the letters were supposedly in the hands of federal authorities, to be used as evidence against Thompson in the event he would be charged with treason. That nothing was revealed about the contents of the correspondence didn't prevent the mine owners' organ of Jerome from speculating that it might "bare secrets of the wobbly organization and methods which will result in the stamping out of the IWW by the iron hand of authority." It also felt free to broadcast the "news" that German rioters among the Wobs in Arizona and Montana had been reported to the Department of Justice by federal authorities and then arrested "unofficially" as participants in German plots. Preventive arrest was also planned, as it was said IWW members arrested in the future would be held as "anarchists" until "some connection can be established between the central organization behind IWW trouble and German-paid propaganda." The constitution was being shredded daily in the forty-eighth state.[97]

Their train stopped in Kingman, Arizona, which "was most unwilling to host the wobblies," who, for the moment, were held in the county courthouse. The number of men involved becomes confused in the accounts, as it was reported the day after the roundup that two hundred men, more than were rounded up, had taken "French leave." Happy to be shed of the out-of-town strikers, local officers in Kingman "are not losing any sleep holding the others," though they didn't want any of them to remain in their county.

The train crossed into California and reached Needles, where it was turned back to Kingman, having been told that California "won't be made the dumping ground for Arizona's undesirables."[98]

The men were returned to Kingman, and on July 11, the day after their expulsion from Jerome, Governor Campbell wired the sheriff of Mohave County, where Kingman is located, that the men could not be held unless charges were placed against them. Judge John Ellis addressed the men and told them they would be released if they promised not to engage in agitation. The men promised and were set free. Some left for Los Angeles, some for Needles, and some returned to Jerome and their families. The *Prescott Journal Miner* reported that the men's spirits were "broken" and that "they probably will cause no further trouble."

Tempers were rising in Arizona, as the IWW warned Governor Campbell that he would be held responsible for the Wobblies deported from Jerome, which Campbell considered a threat and an infringement on his prerogatives as governor, and he would hold responsible those who made it. At the same time, in Globe, hope for the settlement of their strike had waned.[99]

With the strike crushed and the strikers shipped out of town, fear remained. Days later an anonymous letter signed "One of your readers" was received at the offices of the *Verde Copper News*, which said that a dozen Wobblies had returned to town. In fact, three Wobs who were able to establish that they had funds and were not going to "cause trouble" had been allowed back into town by the acting marshal. The letter was dismissed as "over-anxious and suspicious."[100]

Events in Jerome and Globe would be quickly eclipsed.

* * *

On July 11, the eve of the roundup in Bisbee, Mayor Jacob Erickson decided the time had come for him to throw a major roadblock in the path of the strikers. Arresting strikers at gathering places was no longer enough, and on July 11 he banned any further meetings at City Park, which the Wobs had made "their ground for the dissemination of anathema and sedition." Erickson claimed his closure was the result of an investigation that revealed that "the grounds were being diverted from the use to which they were dedicated." Rosa McKay condemned the ban, saying that the park "was built with money contributed by the public and dedicated to the use of the public.... There were many among [the strikers] that had contributed. That being the only place where they could hold their public meetings, it hurt, of course, but they took it calmly and good naturedly and many remarked that it was perhaps for the best."[101]

The head of the Workmen's Loyalty League, the miner M. W. Merrill, provided the Presidential Mediation Commission with details as to why access to the park was denied the strikers, though he admitted he was never there during any of the strikers' gatherings. The city council had met, he said, on either July 10 or 11, where it was decided the strikers could no longer gather at the park without the written permission of the mayor. A. S. Embree, "took exception to that and said he would not be able to restrain his men any longer, nor would he try." Merrill also claimed to have seen a letter sent to the mayor, though he admitted he couldn't quote it correctly, which said, "Who in Hell is the Mayor, and we will see who is running this City," and signed "IWW."[102]

No longer able to gather at the park, the strikers packed the sidewalks in nearby Brewery Gulch. As events were building to their tragic climax, it is again worthy of note that, despite the alleged sedition cooked up at the park, no one attempted to violate the mayor's order and "no trouble of any kind occurred."

Similarly, Lowell, some three miles from the heart of Bisbee, was crowded with Wobs, "the streets ... lined day and night with men who are out of work and who desire to keep others from going to work." Again, though, order reigned, credited to Sheriff Wheeler, but more accurately the result of the calm maintained by the strikers throughout the walkout.

Yet another funeral was held in Bisbee on July 11, and the Wobs used it to show their strength. Counts of those in the procession varied widely, from 915 to 1,054, but the *Review*—despite these large numbers—somehow determined that the crowd included only one Serbian and one Montenegrin. "All of the others were either Austrians or professional 'Wobblies.'"[103]

Workers were reported to be returning to work in numbers that were "not large, but consistent," and those still out were warned that "all employees who do not report for work this morning or this evening will be obliged to go through the regular routine in order to secure employment." In fact, by the time this notice appeared in the daily paper, those who were out on strike no longer were able to return to work.

Fred Watson, who'd be deported on July 12, wrote in an affidavit a half century after the event that the night before the deportation, he was out with the woman with whom he was "keeping company" and would eventually marry. She was employed at the Phelps Dodge store and told Watson that the previous day she had received a list of men who were to receive guns from the company without charge. She offered him a copy of it, but not knowing or suspecting the use to which the weapons would be put, Watson refused the list. The warning signs were clear.[104]

* * *

The night of July 11, a large meeting was held, with forty to fifty attendees according to participant Bassett Watkins, or a hundred according to another attendee, George Kellogg. All of them were the organizers and motive forces behind the roundup.[105] Chaired by Sheriff Wheeler, the meeting shored up and detailed the plan to expel the town's dissident residents. Though there is a mass of evidence that there was discussion of the roundup deportation prior to this date, vigilante M. W. Merrill assured the federal commissioners in November that he had never heard any suggestions of a deportation until July 11, "when they presumed to be fact that they were going to run the men off." Far from there being a formal meeting, Merrill implausibly claimed, "Sheriff Wheeler came and said, 'There must be something done,' and we got together and talked over what was best to do.'"[106]

Deputy Bassett Watkins gave a slightly different account, saying he heard about the roundup, "The night before.... Along in the afternoon."[107]

At the Mediation Commission hearings, Felix Frankfurter was dubious. The drive was organized, he said, "with great efficiency," and he suggested the organizing had gone on for two weeks. Merrill refused to concede the point, saying that nothing was "done at all in that line until after the fourth of July." The Fourth of July, in any event, was still eight days before the roundup and deportation.[108]

It is inconceivable that a roundup of this magnitude was the work of one night, that when the leaders met on July 11 everything was decided and organized on the spot. That a meeting took place the night before the roundup is certain. It is no less certain that it was carried out as successfully as it was because it was the fruit of weeks of preparation. Clarence Wittig, a town resident, later said of the roundup and deportation that "the planning of this deportation was fantastic."[109]

In a typescript, "History of the Bisbee Deportation," Bisbee resident William Beeman gave a detailed account of all that led up to the deportation, which he claimed to have been at the heart of and, in fact, the brains behind. It presents clear evidence that the roundup was considered and in the works well before the eve of the deportation.[110]

Beeman claims that it was only two or three days after the strike began when he ran into Gene Whitely, the assistant superintendent of the C&A mine. Beeman suggested that, given the "belligerent attitude" of the strikers, it would be best to round up the ringleaders and send them across the Mexican border, while "placing guards at the line to prevent their return to Bisbee." Though he gives no details, it should be remembered that Bisbee is on the border, so this would not be a complex maneuver, though certainly illegal.

Whitely liked the idea and sent Beeman to the Warren home of John Greenway, the general manager of the C&A mine. Greenway said he needed to consider the matter, and referred him to restaurant owner Bill Truax, who had long experienced problems with the miners due to his anti-union sentiments. Truax sent him to see R. A. Clampitt, assistant postmaster of Bisbee, as well as secretary of the Warren District Rifle Club. Clampitt was all in for the proposed roundup and said that the seventy-five to eighty members of his club were all that would be needed to carry it out.

Beeman informed Greenway of his meeting with Clampitt, and Greenway responded that he feared the plan wasn't immediately workable and might cause violence and loss of life. He went on to say that a movement was underway to form a Loyalty League and that Beeman should join in the process. In the meanwhile, he should "mark time" with his plan and wait to see how the Loyalty League panned out. By the time of the deportation, the League supposedly had two thousand members. Greenway strangely criticized Sheriff Wheeler for refusing to deputize additional men, though on June 29 hundreds of men had, in fact, been sworn in as deputies.

It is more a sign of the ambient anti-miner feelings than of reality that the bosses seem to have had doubts about Harry Wheeler's reliability. He is said to have required much convincing of the pro-German and anti-patriotic nature of the strike before going along with any extraordinary measures. He is even described as being "out of balance where patriotism was concerned." It should be noted that Wheeler had been a popular figure in Bisbee before the deportation, respected by workers and bosses alike.

Once Sheriff Wheeler decided to bring additional deputies on board, he worried about the additional expense, doubting the county board of supervisors would accept it. The chief watchman for the C&A Mining Company reassured him: "The expense would be taken care of by the companies." Wheeler, ever prudent, worried about "overt acts" carried out by the deputies and the expenses it would cost the bondsmen, but he was assured that John Greenway would see to it that no loss was incurred by the county. Greenway later assured him this was the case. With this, Beeman reported, the path was clear to the deputizing of three thousand men.

After the testy July Fourth celebrations, at which blows were exchanged between marchers and IWW members, Wheeler called a meeting of the "loyal citizens of the district to help him in his effort to maintain order and protect the lives and property of the citizens of the camp." All of the seventy to eighty attendees agreed to participate in the task, and Wheeler said he would choose ten men to set up the organization. All of those involved would supposedly be legally deputized. This was far from the case, as the testimony at the coroner's inquest on the deaths of Brew and McRae revealed, as we'll see in subsequent chapters, as only one man on the scene of the killings was officially deputized. One deputy marshal, at the invitation of the town's assistant postmaster, attended the inaugural meeting of the Loyalty League, and despite his position as a protector of law and order, he later said that he "looked over the men there [and] concluded I didn't want to work with them." The attendees were "bosses, generally, from the companies. I didn't see any of the rank and file of citizens about town."[111]

A week before the deportation, then, the organization that would carry it out was set. The town was divided into ten districts, each with one leader, and those ten leaders met at least once each day. Mining company involvement was ensured by John Greenway, a veteran of the Spanish-American War, who suggested that the men be organized military style, with each leader having four captains, who would each be responsible for bringing seventy-five men on board. The goal was to have all ten sections prepared to enter into action on an hour's notice.

On July 9, these ten leaders informed Sherriff Wheeler that everything was ready: three thousand men were deputized and ready to restore order.

There is no solid proof that Phelps Dodge president Walter Douglas was in Bisbee, but his support for the imminent roundup and deportation are not in doubt. Even the official history of Phelps Dodge is clear on this subject: "The orders for the actual deportation by the railroad were issued by Walter Douglas, president of Phelps Dodge."[112]

Anti-Wob rumors were spread, and "word was being passed out by the strikers that they were getting ready to stage a repetition of what was staged in Morenci in 1914, when all men who would not join the union were lined up and marched out of town."

The situation in the minds of the vigilantes was such that, on the afternoon of July 11, Wheeler informed the ten leaders that a meeting had been called for 8:00 that night and would be attended by "a number of representative citizens of the district."

Though Beeman reported that around thirty men attended the meeting, "mine managers, doctors, bankers, merchants, machinists, miners and muckers," another attendee put the number at a hundred—"fifty businessmen and fifty captains of the Loyalty league," who were all company employees.[113] It was suggested that a drive be carried out the next morning, with Mexico the goal. This mutated into the call for a massive deportation, which was voted on and carried unanimously. Beeman claims that few knew of the existence of the armed units, and "they were all amazed when they learned that such an organization had been perfected."

John Greenway suggested shipping the men to Columbus, New Mexico, where they could be "detained as enemies of the government." Though some feared bloodshed, Wheeler reassured them. "I know the class of men you are dealing with; they are all yellow, and if you meet them in equal numbers, you can handle them like sheep." Wheeler is also alleged to have said that the strikers were preparing to exceed the bounds of the law, and that he'd heard there were three hundred rifles in the hands of the strikers, though he didn't know how true that was. Dowell, general manager of the Copper Queen, said there was a "cancerous growth" in the town and that he recommended an operation, at which point Bledsoe, chief surgeon of the C&A, continued the medical metaphor, saying that the men there that night were the surgeons who could perform the operation.[114]

Before the meeting was adjourned Wheeler was told that former governor Hunt, still hoping to be given back his office as governor, would be in Bisbee that night or the next morning. John Greenway, demonstrating the contempt common among the vigilantes for a government too friendly to the workers, stated, "Should the old Governor be in Bisbee after all his friends had been taken out he would be lonesome, and it will only be a kindness to send him along with his friends, so that is what we will do."

Before adjourning, two committees were formed: a transportation committee, headed by the manager of the Cooper Queen mines, who would arrange for the train; and a food and water committee. Beeman made the patently false claim that two cars of provisions were attached to the train that took the men from town.[115]

The plans were carried out to the letter on July 12.

CHAPTER FOUR

THE ROUNDUP

Armed mob of imitation men

Normally, newspapers report the previous day's occurrences. The *Bisbee Daily Review*, which appeared at 6:00 a.m. every day except Mondays, certainly held to this standard. Except on Thursday, July 12, 1917. On that day, a screaming headline issued a warning: "All Women and Children Keep Off Streets Today." Below the headline was a notice from Harry C. Wheeler, the sheriff of Cochise County:

> I have formed a Sheriff's Posse of 1,200 men in Bisbee and 1,000 in Douglas, all loyal Americans, for the purpose of arresting, on charges of vagrancy, treason, and of being disturbers of the peace of Cochise County, all those strange men who have congregated here from other parts and sections for the purpose of harassing and intimidating all men who desire to pursue their daily toil. I am continually told of threats and insults heaped upon the working men of this district by so-called strikers, who are strange to these parts, yet who presume to dictate the manner of life of the people of this district.
>
> Appeals to patriotism do not move them, nor do appeals to reason. At a time when our country needs her every resource, these strangers persist in keeping from her the precious metal production of this entire district.
>
> Today I heard threats to the effect that homes would be destroyed because the heads of families insisted upon their rights as Americans to work for themselves, their families and their country.
>
> Other threats have and are being daily made. Men have been assaulted and brutally beaten, and only today I heard the Mayor of Bisbee threatened

and his requests ignored. We cannot longer stand or tolerate such conditions! This is no labor trouble—we are sure of that—but a direct attempt to embarrass and injure the government of the United States.

I therefore call upon all loyal Americans to aid me in peaceably arresting these disturbers of our national and local peace. Let no shot be fired throughout this day unless in necessary self defense, and I hereby give warning that each and every leader of the so-called strikers will be held personally responsible for any injury inflicted upon any of my deputies while in the performance of their duties as deputies of my posse, for whose acts I, in turn, assume full responsibility as Sheriff of this County. All arrested persons will be treated humanely and their cases examined with justice and care. I hope no resistance will be made, for I desire no bloodshed. However, I am determined if resistance is made, it shall be quickly and effectively overcome.

HARRY C. WHEELER,
Sheriff Cochise County, Ariz.

What followed over the next six hours was the execution of the greatest mass kidnapping in American history, as almost twelve hundred men were picked up in their homes and on the streets, penned in the town's ballpark, loaded on boxcars, and shipped to the desert of a neighboring state, in contravention of all laws, local, state, and national.

By the time it was all over, about two thousand deputies were involved in the roundup, some wearing badges, all wearing white armbands to distinguish them from others in the town, particularly those being rounded up. Wheeler had commissioned hundreds of additional deputies when the strike broke out, and when the Presidential Mediation Commission met in Bisbee in November, commission secretary Felix Frankfurter asked police court judge Frank Martin if all of the men doing the rounding up on July 12 were officially commissioned. "That I do not know," he answered, "but they were all carrying guns." Frankfurter continued that it was possible for men to be deputized orally, without an official commission, and that, Martin said, was indeed the case.[1] We can thus estimate that fourteen hundred deputies had not been deputized according to procedures, and joined the events on an ad hoc basis. A resident of Bisbee wrote to Governor Hunt shortly after the roundup that the "armed mob of imitation men" who carried it out were "led by a number of mining company petty officials such as company doctors, shift-bosses, [and] so-called businessmen who fooled some of their dupes by giving them to understand that the US government had ordered the roundup of the IWW. Others tell me they had either to help or lose their jobs."[2]

* * *

It was essential that the world be kept unaware of the events in Bisbee. When the roundup was set in motion, telegraph lines were shut down, and the Associated Press was informed by Western Union that "military authorities" in Bisbee had placed censorship on "all dispatches from there relating to the IWW disturbances." Even more, military authorities were also said to have taken over the telegraph offices in town.[3] As the phone company manager reported, when the AP reporter in Douglas was blocked from filing a story on the deportation, he asked Kellogg if censorship had been imposed on the coverage of the events. Kellogg told him no but offered the reporter a "tip": "I advise you to get hold of some official of the Copper Queen and find out whether they want it to go out or not." Telegraphic censorship had indeed been instituted, and telegraph lines had been shut down, but none of this had to do with military authorities, who had no role in any of the events in Bisbee: it was the organizers of the vigilante raids who had cut Bisbee off from the outside world. Phone lines remained open, as Kellogg refused the demand of the supervisor of the Phelps Dodge smelter in Douglas to shut them down. Western Union complied.[4] The Associated Press had been blocked from sending reports as the deportations occurred due to the closing down of the telegraph lines, and in the days that followed they were unable to find out who had given the order. Those officials they demanded answers from were unable (more likely, unwilling) to provide any names.[5]

The decision to shut down contact with the outside world was, as we've seen, taken at the planning session the night before. The organizers would initially claim that this was done at the behest of army officers, but by the next day it was revealed that the army had nothing to do with it. It was two Phelps Dodge officials—Robert Rea of the Copper Queen mine and H. H. Stout of the Copper Queen smelter in Douglas—who had organized it.[6]

None of this was done with legal advice. A Copper Queen manager would later admit, "We absolutely avoided all lawyers."[7]

The *Daily Review*, which had done much to foment hysteria over the previous months and had depicted the strike of the miners, not only in Bisbee, but also all over Arizona, as a treasonous plot and a "reign of terror," waxed purple over the success of the roundup and forced termination of the strike.

The date was termed "a golden date on the calendar," a day likened to the lancing of a boil, as serving as a "house cleaning, mak[ing] for better conditions in the home," ridding the town of "the scourge of the age; the pestilence extraordinary; the menace of the day.... The 'Wobbly is no more.'"[8]

* * *

Despite the pleas for people to stay off the streets, the parading of the strikers and their sympathizers to the ballpark and their being loaded on the trains was witnessed by thousands, as photos of the day attest. There is also no shortage of firsthand accounts, both by eyewitnesses and victims.

For Marion Stodgehill, who was nine years old at the time, it was truly a golden day. She remembered it well; the schools were closed.[9]

As planned, starting at 2:00 a.m., calls went out to 250 men who were deputized or would be. Phone company manager Kellogg and his switchboard operators worked at this until 4:30. Kellogg had been asked to have "'girls ready to take care of a big load.'" "Sleepy voices cursed and swore" upon receiving the early-morning call but awakened to their duty: "I'll be there was the answer." While this was occurring, the Wobblies "slept comfortably in fancied seclusion." The watchword was spread: "Until the last IWW is run out."

The strikers "sensed nothing of the impending disaster to their cause: as they went to their picket lines at dawn, and "at 6:30 o'clock the streets and alleys burst and poured forth their torrents of heavily armed citizens of the Warren district." The roundup had begun.[10]

R. E. Thompson, a businessman who visited Bisbee regularly, had been in town from the night of July 11 to observe the state of affairs during the strike. He was staying at the Philadelphia Hotel, his room facing the street, and wrote Governor Hunt that, shortly after daylight on July 12, he heard "noise take place in the alley." He got out of bed and went to the window to see what the source was, and "to my surprise, this alley street was filled with men, each having a handkerchief or rag tied around one arm. Each man having a gun or revolver of some description." As he surveyed the scene from his window, wondering what was going on, "a man pointed a rifle up at the building. Not thinking it was intended for me, even though he said 'Get your nut back there,' I still stood gazing. Then he took deliberate aim at me and said 'Get your God

Damn nut back there.'" Discretion being the better part of valor, Thompson "retired out of sight," dressed, and went into the hall of the hotel, which was being raided by the vigilantes.[11]

At the post office, "the favorite gathering place for IWW pickets during the strike," there was a large crowd of strikers. A whistle sounded and vigilantes emerged from the building, "as if by magic," while others came from an alley behind it, and still others came from nearby Subway Street. The strikers were surrounded, lined up, and searched for arms. Despite the threat the strikers were supposed to have posed, not a man had a weapon on his person.

The vigilantes chose the Bisbee post office as the place where they would gather their captives, which took them until around 7:30. Those taken into custody were described as "known advocates of IWWism and those who were out in sympathy and others who could not give a good account of themselves, were literally herded into droves and brought to the gathering center."

Striker Fred Watson's future father-in-law, who worked as a clerk at the Phelps Dodge mine, had been ordered by deputies who came to his house during the roundup not to go to work and to keep off the street. Enraged by the vigilantes' conduct, he told them, "There's nobody going to tell me when I can go to work and when I can't go to work." The deputies grabbed him and put him in the line of men gathered to go to Lowell. He was seen there by the boss of the company store, who asked him what he was doing among the men who'd been rounded up. "'I don't know,' he says, 'I don't know a thing. They just put me here and told me to stay.'" The boss pulled him out of line and said, "'Come on, get out of there,' and he put a white rag around his arm. That was a token of surrender, you know.'"[12]

Mine managers also participated in the roundup. Mr. Gehringer, in charge of operations at the C&A mines in Bisbee, did not attend the July 11 meeting, but he did admit to carrying a rifle on the twelfth and explained that "I am an official of this company, but I am also a citizen and I told several people around in town that—the feelings I had—feeling as I did that the action of these Huns and invaders was outrageous [and] that I would feel sore if anything was started around here and if they didn't let me know about it. That was all I had to do, until the word was sent out along in the middle of the night on the 11th to report for duty and I reported for duty as a private citizen." Like everyone else, he couldn't report any specific seditious utterances or acts of violence. He was told of it by "a hundred of my friends in this town."[13]

The vigilantes went through the rooming houses, private homes, and the union hall on O.K. Street, adding to the number of captives. In one rooming house, "they took 12 men out of 13 [who lived there]. Another place just across the street the woman dared them to come in, and said there was 4 in her house they could get if they ventured in, and was afraid with guns in hand, one guard stood at each corner and the others went and got officers on horse back and searched the place. Did they get the clap [i.e., applause]? I guess they did, every woman and child around the place cheered."[14]

The deputies burst in on A. R. Crawford while he was shaving, and he was warned of his ultimate fate, claiming he was told right then, "We are going to take you to Columbus and there try you for treason."[15]

Fred Brown was by no stretch of the imagination a Wobbly, being a local AF of L organizer, but he was told by two deputies—one of them the future defendant in the sole case to go to trial for the kidnapping of 1186 men, Harry Wooton—that he was "too active in union affairs and had to get in line."[16]

Thomas English, a miner, later described how he was taken by the vigilantes. "Well, on the morning of the 12th, about 7:00 in the morning somebody knocked on the door, and I told them to come in, and they asked me if I was working, and I said, 'no sir,' and they said 'well, come out of there right away and dress, we want you.' And I said 'What is this for,' and they said, 'get in line with the rest of them.' That was all of the information I could get."[17] English also saw Bisbee Wobbly leader A. S. Embree jabbed in the ribs by a vigilante, "apparently hurting him severely."[18]

Some people disguised themselves to avoid arrest. Violet White spoke of how her father put on a white armband that morning just so he wouldn't be picked up, while two of her neighbors were taken away by armed men. She was convinced that the wife and kids of one of her neighbors, a Mexican, had no idea where he was the whole time of the deportation.[19]

* * *

How did the vigilantes know exactly where to go at that early hour? Months later, State Representative Rosa McKay would tell the Presidential Mediation Commission how on July 9 she saw men going around Brewery Gulch pointing at "this house and that house," and she assumed that "they must be going to survey for something or other." She wasn't certain they were looking for the houses that would be subject to invasion the day of the roundup, but she was certain that of "the houses they pointed out[,] they went to each and every one of those houses that morning [of the roundup] with the exception of mine." Sheriff Wheeler was not a fan of Rosa McKay or her husband, who shared her politics. He would tell the Mediation Commission that he was "only sorry that Mr. McKay was not there to be deported with the rest of them ... and it would not have done much harm if she had gone along with him."[20]

McKay's description of events is backed Herman Adams, a vigilante who, when interviewed about the deportation in 1981, said he knew about the deportation a couple of days before, since he was being trained for it.[21] Bassett Watkins, another man who wore the white kerchief around his arm, told the federal commissioners in November that the method for choosing who was to be rounded up was a direct one: picked up were "only those we knew and could see on the picket line."[22]

Some people were picked up with relative ease. Fred Watson, for example, was arrested at gunpoint by Charley Allen, his own brother-in-law. As he described it, after his roommate left for the picket line at 6:00 he slept in a bit, and "the next thing I knew I was looking down the barrels of a double barreled shotgun and was prodded with the butt of another gun, and told to get out of bed."[23] In extenuation of his relative's conduct, Watson said that Allen, who owned a successful furniture store that had catered to the miners for thirty years, held out against participating in the roundup, but the deputies warned him that he either went along with them or with the miners and their allies. "You either put a white rag around your arm or you left town," as he summed it up.[24]

Abbie Bigelow, whose father was a close friend of Harry Wheeler and who lived on a ranch outside of town, spoke three-quarters of a century later of three men hiding out from the deportation, her father having told the deputies they weren't to step foot on his land to seize them. He never spoke to Wheeler again. Though she wasn't involved with the deportation in any way, Bigelow spoke of how "terrifying" it was.[25] Bernice Barth, who witnessed the roundup, described the vigilantes as "goon squads."[26]

If it was a goon squad, it was one made up of the seemingly respectable members of the community. Mrs. H. B. McClellan, who lived on Chihuahua Hill looking out on Naco Road, had a clear view of all that transpired, and wrote to Governor Hunt that she "found all business houses closed, the proprietors evidently all out with guns, the town deserted except for the gun men. I was grossly insulted twice."[27]

* * *

State Representative Rosa McKay gave a vivid, if second-hand, description of the two killings that day to the Presidential Mediation Commission. Recounting what an eyewitness to the killings had told her, she said that James Brew, who worked at the mines but was not on strike and was simply home sick, told a friend that morning that "I have not done anything against the law and I have always been a law-abiding citizen and," he continued, "if they come here after me, they cannot take me from my home without a warrant." The deputies knocked on his door and, as McKay reported, Brew asked, "'Who is there.' They said 'Officers.' And he said 'What do you want.' They knew who he was and who they were after, and he said 'You can't have me unless you have a warrant;' they said 'we are officers, and we don't need a warrant.' He said. 'Then you can't come in here.' They said 'We will drag you out,' [and he said to a neighbor] 'I am not an IWW... I have taken no part in this strike and they can't take me out of my own home.' ... And they rapped on the door, and with that Mr. Brew shot, and the neighbors said that one of the men in the other yard, a gunman, shot Mr. Brew."

McKay confronted Merrill, the president of the Loyalty League, and told him in no uncertain terms that everyone involved on the vigilante side of the Brew killing was a murderer. As if it would be a valid reason for killing Brew, Merrill responded that Brew was a member of the IWW, and that he had the card to prove it. McKay was having none of it: "Mr. Merrill, if you have an IWW card of Mr. Brew I believe that you made it out after he died, for you didn't want to kill a man who wasn't an IWW."[28]

Fred Watson spoke of James Brew's killing as well. Watson was passing the boardinghouse after being rousted out of bed, and he heard deputy Orson McRae telling someone to come out of the house. "The man, Brew, came out of the house and said, 'McRae, if you come through that gate, I'm going to blast you.' He said, 'I'm coming through.' He come through the gate and he blasted him. Killed him right there. I was standing there watching them. He went back in, put the gun down and come back out with his hands up, and they shot him like a dog."[29]

Brew's political beliefs are unclear. He has been taken up as a Wobbly martyr since his death, and Dan Kitchell, an engineer in the mines at the time of the strike, roundup, and deportation, said that: "Jim Brew was a machinist, not on strike at all, a member of the Elks. He was Austrian, a communist."[30] He was indeed an Elk, but census and voter registration records show that Brew was a Scotsman.[31] Fred Watson claimed there was bad blood between Brew and McRae, who, he said, had known each other during the labor battles in Cripple Creek, Colorado, in 1903 and 1904, from which Brew had been driven for his union activities.[32] Though Brew's whereabouts in 1903 to 1904 are not known for certain, McRae, according to voter registration records, census data, and his marriage license, seems to have lived his entire thirty-one years or so in Arizona, much of it in Cochise County.

At the coroner's inquest, held just four days after the shootings, details of the deaths were difficult to ascertain. The number of men who had gone knocking on doors to take men along to the assembly point was variously reported to be somewhere between nine and fourteen men, or ten to twelve, and those questioned at the hearing claimed not to know those they were with. Charles Pound, who was on the scene at the two killings, told the coroner's panel that only Orson McRae had a commission as a deputy.

What was agreed was that, when they arrived at Brew's boardinghouse, they had already canvassed four of five houses and the leader of the group initially said there was no reason to search the boardinghouse where Brew resided. H. T. Weaver, a deputy on the scene, reported they were told, "I know the woman that lives here and she wouldn't have anyone here that was not all right." But he then changed his mind and said they should "investigate on general principles," and "three or four fellows, maybe four or five, went in the gate." Weaver went in another direction to make sure no one fled the house from the rear entrance, so he did not witness what followed.

J. A. Williams, who was with McRae, said, "We both walked up to the porch together and he walked up on the porch ahead of me and just as he got to the top of the porch there was three shots fired and killed him, and that kind of startled me and I ran back away from there; just as I ran back there was two more shots fired and the fellow that done the shooting he opened the door and ran out before these two shots were fired, and he fell over dead." Williams was certain that McRae didn't knock on the door, though Harry Walters was equally certain that McRae, who was unarmed, "tapped" on the door with a club he was carrying. Charles Pound, owner of the White House Café, who said he was with McRae, was certain that three shots were fired from within, the first two missing both of them, the third hitting McRae. Then what he described as "a quarter of a minute elapsed," and he heard four shots fired on the porch. He continued, "It must have been Brew come from the room; I should judge about seven or eight feet, come out of the hall onto the porch; when I come to myself there were three shots fired in back of me, seven altogether, four from the house, two from the window, and two from the porch and three shots from at my back; I don't know where they come from. One of the three shots gets Brew on the porch and he drops dead." When it was all done Pound was given Brew's gun, which had four empty shells in it.

According to H. T. Weaver, who only heard the gunshots and saw smoke from the gunfire, the door was kicked open and the man who'd been inside came out "and he taken a fair, square shot at some fellow, I don't know who he was." It's unclear if the shots referred to were being fired at McRae or at Brew.

Williams's testimony was the most controversial; he had previously said during the inquest that the shots that killed Brew were fired by Chick Walters, but he now backed off his statement rather belligerently. "I didn't say that. I must have been excited if I did, because I never seen Chick Walters shoot him at all. You must have got mixed up yourselves."

Walters saw McRae go down, shot once in the mouth, once in the stomach, and he attempted to fire back, but his safety was on.

The inquest was something less than thorough. No one examined the bullet holes inside Brew's flat, and the coroner was puzzled by the size of the bullet holes in the screen to Brew's room, wondering if Brew had two guns, or if anyone else was in the room, or if the bullet holes had come from both directions. There is no evidence that these questions were examined more closely.

None of the vigilantes say that Brew said anything before firing. And perhaps he didn't say any of the things he's credited as saying, or perhaps they didn't think it important. Geanie Stagdill, who owned the boardinghouse, gave her version of what led Brew to act as he did. "I feel Jim went insane, because he was of a quiet disposition; I say the man went insane because he had been acting strange; he had been sick; he didn't sleep I know for three nights; he was in a very rundown condition."

The coroner reported that James Brew died at 8:30 a.m. on July 12, "cause of death by a gun shot fired from an unnone [sic] person." Orson McRae died at the same time "by a gun shot fired by Jim Brew."[33]

* * *

Rosa McKay wrote about "deplorable incident[s]" during the roundup, when a group of deputies "broke down the door of a man's house, walked in and pulled him out of bed." When his wife protested that he be allowed to dress and have his breakfast, "she was slapped and pushed out of the way, and the man was dragged out of the house in the sleeping garment." His wife tossed his pants to him through the window and he dressed on the street.

The question most frequently asked of those stopped was "Are you working?" To not be working meant you were a striker or a sympathizer of the strikers, and so subject to deportation. T. H. Loftus was asked, "You're a Wobbly, ain't you?" He didn't deny it and was told to get in the line of men headed for Warren.[34]

Bonnie Petsche—a married woman whose husband wasn't rounded up— said she heard the shot when Brew was killed, and spoke of seeing the men who went to arrest him. She described how the armed deputies rousted sleeping men out from her boardinghouse: "Some of them were even barefooted ... and they dragged them out of there." She said "People thought it was a terrible thing to do," and described it as "surprising" that only one man was killed. She spoke of how well-organized Wheeler was, and how women lined the route to try to liberate their husbands: "It was a pitiful thing." "It was upsetting for everybody," and people "didn't know what was going to happen next." She had no idea how the deputies knew who was a Wobbly, though she credited Wheeler's intelligence and thought he might have known exactly who was and who wasn't.[35]

The vigilantes had no respect for age, as Rosa McKay described how an "aged, gray-haired man past the three score mark, was taken from his home," and when he stumbled the deputy jabbed him in the ribs and told him, "Step up there, we have no time to wait for you."[36] Florence Noulin, a child at the time of the deportation, said that the vigilantes respected age so little that "my baby brother was just ten days old and we were scared to death they were going to get him and take him on the train."[37]

They were also no respecters of property. Along with the reports of doors kicked in and windows smashed, miner Blagoje Gjurovich reported that the deputies, after firing a shot through his door to get him to open it up, searched his apartment and made off with a watch and nugget chain worth $175. Renio Merilo claimed two men broke the glass of his door, came into his apartment, and while one man searched, he relieved Merilo of $150 and a gold watch and chain worth $110. Carl Turner's tale was even worse: Walking down Brewery Gulch early in the morning of July 12, two men approached him, and while one pointed a rifle at him the other went through his pockets, taking $75 in cash and a watch worth $90. He was then walked to the ballpark, prevented from making a complaint about the theft, and made to get into a freight car, where there was water but no food, and its floor, he said, was covered in dung.[38]

More troubling was the search of the IWW offices in Bisbee (the exact date of which is unclear), which the Loyalty League carried out based on a search warrant, rather than a subpoena. They removed Wobbly records and took them to the offices of the Loyalty League, which happened to be located in the Copper Queen dispensary. The records were later turned over to Deputy Marshal McDonald by John Forster, a detective in the pay of the banks and mining companies, who had played an active role in the run-up to the deportation. Months later, these records were still in McDonald's possession.[39]

Despite the vigilantes' claims that they were rounding up dangerous strikers—members of the IWW—what Fred Watson witnessed raised some questions: "They took men out of the barbershops. Why is it they went into barber shops and trampled them under foot on the streets that morning? Why did they go into restaurants where we had cooks and waiters with their white jackets and big hats [and put them] in line? Why did they get those? They didn't work in the mines? There was a fellow in a white coat that worked in there and they wanted to know, 'Are you with these guys or against them?' He said, 'I've made my living off those fellows for ten years. Why wouldn't I be with them?' His pool hall was wrecked because he was in line with us. It was union busting and a good opportunity."[40] And what kind of threat was Amado Villalovas, who was grocery shopping when he was grabbed and made to join the line, his purchases left scattered on the shop floor?[41]

Loyalty League president Merrill denied there was ever any violence used during the roundup. In fact, he insisted, it was all carried out with the best motives. Asked a few months later about the violence of the day, he replied, "I heard that and gave very little credit to it, for this reason, that practically at 6:30 in the morning when the deputy sheriffs got to the picket line most of the men were there. As I said, I never saw anybody go into anybody's house.... It was conducted with the spirit of patriotism; no harshness; no knocking anybody over the head with guns. There was one or two who resisted...."[42]

Many statements later provided to former governor Hunt put the lie to this. John Lehtinen was kicked and clubbed and told by a vigilante, "You God dammed Bohunk, get in line there the same as the rest of these men are doing." Deportee Louis Asic reported that at various points in the process— when he was at Bisbee Junction and while he was still in his apartment with his family—he was hit on the head with a hammer handle, hit and poked with guns, thrown over a fence, hit over the head with a club. His wife, in attempting to defend her husband, was thrown down a flight of stairs and held at gunpoint. Mrs. Asic was not alone in this experience, as deportee Vuko Dalja said his wife had been kicked and dragged by a deputy.[43] Another deportee also spoke of a woman, who was trying to give the men water, being chased away by a deputy.[44]

Governor Hunt was informed of the vigilantes' violence shortly after the roundup and deportation; one man was struck in the head with a revolver by "a very brave doctor" and was supposedly hospitalized in the military hospital in Columbus.[45] Isaac Conky reported that he was smashed in the ribs with a gun and required medical treatment for his injuries when they arrived in Columbus. Frank Wheeler told of violence at the ballpark: a Mexican man, who was trying to cross from one side of the field to the other, had "a gunman [step] in front of him and hit him across the mouth with a single jack handle, breaking one of his teeth and cutting his lip badly."[46]

William Jones, a miner at the C&A mines, was rounded up but saved from deportation. Oklahoma born with a third-grade education, he came to Bisbee in May 1916 specifically to get a job in the mines. He was honoring the strike, and on the morning of July 12 he and his two brothers-in-law "were trying to stay out of the drive." Gunmen came to his home in Bakerville and Jones and his kin hid. The vigilantes asked his wife where he was and she told them he wasn't there. "But we were there. After they left I went out in the yard and one spied on me and they came back and got us all."

Three men came for Jones and his brothers-in-law, one with a gun, two with axe handles they used as clubs. They didn't have a chance to call the police, but told the deputies that "we were working and wasn't bothering anyone who was working. They said we were a bunch of 'wables' [sic]."

Jones recounted the violence exercised against the men being rounded up, of how when he called the deputies "gunmen," "this fellow gives me a kick. He kicked my legs out from under me. He said if I popped off any more I would get more than that."

From his home, Jones was taken to the Warren ballpark, where he said there were "a few thousand men." A train with what he thought were twenty-six boxcars pulled in and "they made a line of gun men from the ball park to the RR tracks with men on each side. They marched the strikers up through the line into the boxcars."

It was at this point that good luck—of a limited kind—intervened. As he was being loaded onto the train, two acquaintances had him pulled out of the line. He explained, "Any business man or farmers who knew you could get you out, and Jack Fischer knew me and said 'Bill, you don't want to go out in the box cars. You don't have to go. You go home and get your belongings and leave town. You can't stay here.'" Jones left Bisbee for Tucson and didn't come back until 1920.[47]

* * *

Calls were coming in from all over Cochise County, but also from Globe and Tucson, and people as far away as Phoenix knew about things by 8:00 a.m. Three hundred men were said to be coming from Douglas to help out, and Captain Stout, superintendent of the Copper Queen smelter, said the lines connecting Bisbee to the outside world should be censored. George Kellogg of the phone company wouldn't do this, but Western Union did after Stout called. He said to the manager in Douglas that "while this deportation is on in Bisbee I want you to withhold any messages out of Bisbee until that train rolls out of here."[48]

* * *

When the full number of victims was gathered, Sheriff Wheeler gave orders to set the men off for Lowell, down Subway Street to the depot plaza, over the streetcar tracks and those of the El Paso & Southwestern Railroad, owned by Phelps Dodge, which had cars waiting to be loaded in Warren.

Armed vigilantes marched at the sides of the procession and at its head and rear. When they reached Lowell, the pickets grabbed in the lower end of the district were added to those already in line and they all began the march over the country road to Lowell.

The deputies added men to the crowd soon to be deported as the procession advanced, "in some places ten abreast." The group was so large that "it blocked the road to all auto traffic and to pedestrians going in the direction of Lowell."

It wasn't just the number of captives that swelled: deputies from Douglas, some twenty miles east, arrived in their cars, parked them at this point in the march, and joined in. Among those rounded up and subsequently loaded on the train was local labor lawyer William Cleary. He had been headed to Douglas for an inquest that morning but, as a telegram to Governor Hunt explained, "he was overtaken by special deputy sheriffs in three automobiles brought to Lowell and under express authority of Sheriff Wheeler," placed in line, and then joined the march to Warren.[49] At some point during the roundup, Cleary had been able to send a telegram to Governor Hunt: "Two thousand miners being deported this morning by corporation gunmen from Warren district; stop that train!"[50]

Some women and children accompanied the procession, and the former would attempt to negotiate the release of their spouses when they arrived at their destination.

Some of the captives were offered the chance to escape their fate and become deputies even while in the line. Fred Brown, the AF of L organizer, said he was offered a choice by one of the men guarding him: "Americanism or Prussianism." Though he rejected those definitions, he chose not to join the deputies. Sheriff Wheeler used Brown—whom he called "Frank Brown"—as an example of those who went voluntarily to be deported. Brown wasn't "forced to go and there were men in town begged him not to go, and he went."[51]

Walter Douglas, son of *the* Walter Douglas, head of Phelps Dodge, was just a child at the time, but he witnessed the roundup. His governess, he later said, took the children to the second story window to watch the Wobblies being driven to the ballpark. "It reminded him of a cattle drive," since there were armed cowboys on both sides of them.[52]

The men left the paved road at this point and entered the "bithulitic pavement," heading south to the Lowell ballpark. Once there, the northwest gate was opened and the captives entered. There were too many men for the grandstand (the ballpark has since been renovated, but everything is still situated as it was on 1917), and the men spilled out onto the field, "using the cushion [bases] for playthings and listening to the harangues of several 'Wobbly' speakers."

The vigilantes formed a cordon around the park, and as more men arrived from other parts of the district they were ushered onto the field. According to one deportee, the temperature was 112 degrees. No one tried to escape once they were inside the stadium.[53]

John Glen Wilson was an independent contractor and a former carpenter who had been swept up in the roundup, though soon released. He spoke of the mood of the men: "I may say in the deportation I never saw a bunch of men that was more peaceful and quiet; in fact, they took the matter as a joke. They were all laughing, although there was some men badly bruised with cut heads and broken arms and so forth."[54]

Anita Ribic's grandfather was an English merchant, and she explained that though the papers said that all the merchants in Bisbee supported the deportation, he was a supporter of the IWW and refused to wear the white armband. When he went down to the loading place, he was pushed into the line of people to be shipped out, but was taken off the line by Harry Wheeler, who recognized him as not being one of the strikers. Her father-in-law, though, who was deported, later spoke of the violence of the day.[55]

At 11:00 a.m. a freight engine with twenty-three boxcars pulled up on the tracks beyond left field and, according to the *Review*, "the 'Wobblies' gave the train a rousing cheer. They knew the edict. All seemed resigned to the trip and only desired to hasten the time of departure."

Mike Pintek, a jitney cab owner well-known in Bisbee, was able to take advantage of the delays in the deportation process to avoid getting on the train, but he also bore witness to the callousness of the deputies and the confusion of ideologies among the deportees. At a deposition in the case of *Arizona v. N.C. Bledsoe* (Bledsoe was a company doctor and armed deputy on July 12), Pintek was asked if he was a member of the IWW, to which he answered "I don't know....If I was I don't know." He finally stated he never joined asking "for what purpose? I didn't have a reason to join." From his house in Bakerville, along the route to the ballpark, he spoke of seeing and hearing men being rounded up, of the screaming and cries of women and children. Then, looking out his window, he saw "ten or fifteen [men] sitting there and I got so excited I pretty near fainted and I went into the room and laid down in bed, and my wife milked the cow and she was just getting me a glass of milk when the deputy came to take him away," "without rapping or anything, just pushed [the door] in and said come along."[56]

Dr. N. C. Bledsoe was at the ballpark with the other deputies, waving his gun, and ignored Pintek's pleas to help in staunching the blood he was spitting. Bledsoe simply pointed his gun at him and told him to get in line. While in the ballpark, Pintek saw a deputy sheriff he knew who asked him, "What the dickens are you doing here?" He walked around the fence, and took Pintek away before he could meet the fate of the other men.

Even as the train was waiting for them, as the ballpark was beginning to empty out, Mrs. H. B. McClellan reported seeing from her vantage point that, at 1:00, men were still "going down the road."[57]

The deputies formed a line from the ballpark to the train, and between forty and fifty men at a time exited the park and climbed into the boxcars. Milos Vukotich, who was in one of the cars, said "the car was dirty and there was no place to sit except upon the floor. I ruined a new suit of clothes as the car was very dirty. The clothes were worth $40. There was water but no food."[58]

Fred Watson spoke later of the conditions in the boxcars. His, he said, held "nothing but sheep dung." Bread and water might have been in other cars, he said, though he was certain there wasn't, since "the boxcar I was in had nothing and I never saw any sandwiches." Any assertion to the contrary, Watson said, "was a big farce." Later, he had "a piece of hardtack and a drink of water, and I vomited it right back."[59] Mary Harper said she was told that there had been food in the boxcars for the deportees but they threw the food and drink out.[60]

Dan Kitchell, an engineer in the mines, remembered being threatened that if he didn't put a white armband on he'd be put in the train, to which he replied, "You son of a bitch, you put me on it I'll kill you if it's the last thing I do." Kitchell, like a few other witnesses, also remembered there were machine guns trained on the men, saying there was a company of troops with a dozen of them.[61] Katie Pintek, wife of Mike, also said she saw machine guns trained on the men from the nearby offices of the C&A mines. She said years later that "that day they had their machines gun on the roof. They were bragging how they were going to shoot if anybody tried to stop them" from taking the men to the ballpark and then out of town.[62] Frank Vaughan of Bisbee wrote to Governor Hunt about a machine gun mounted on a car in Lowell, and of "2 rapid fire guns trained on" the ballpark, one from a hill and the other from the building of the C&A Mining Company.[63] In the days immediately following the roundup, lawyer W. B. Cleary said there was a car that herded the men to the ballpark that was armed with a machine gun.[64] A close examination of photos of the roundup does indeed seem to show a man and sandbags on the roof of that building; the presence of machine guns there cannot be proved definitively.

It took something over an hour for the men to be entrained, and the *Review* smirked that "in some of the larger cars ... greater numbers of men could be placed with excellent ventilation and a fine opportunity for the tourists to see the country, through which they passed."

Oddly, the characterization of the day's events by the mine owners' organ was largely true (if we except the two deaths): "The deportation of the vagrants was consummated with little or no friction, without a hitch in the plans and with a minimum of trouble."

* * *

In a news-filled letter to an old friend back in New Berlin, Ohio, amid reports on the daily storms (the letter was written July 21, 1917, in the heart of the rainy season), the cost of groceries, and her children's' feelings about school, Mrs. O. Snyder described the events of July 12.

The day, she said, was "worse than war, it was h—l with it." The perpetrators, she was clear, were "the capitalists of our town [who] with their scabs formed a parade, white handkerchief tied around his right arm and a gun in hand."

The armed force went from house to house, seeking men who weren't working: "First report was IWWs but [they] took every man not at work, some places upset mattresses to get them out of bed, took watches from some, some money, and worst of all, took husbands and fathers away from their families and marched them through the hot burning sun for 3 miles then loaded them on cattle cars with manure 3 in. thick where they just unloaded cattle and some box cars 23 in all with 1200 men inside and about 200 guards on top and sent them to a desert to starve with out [sic] food and water. Some did not have hats, some with-out shirts and others without breakfast."

Mrs. Snyder wrote of the heroism of the wives of the miners, some of whom "took guns and dared [the deputies] to cross the door sills and others took rock to defend their husbands." Though her account is well-informed, it does include exaggerations, as she wrote of "several" men being killed, when only two were, as well as of "some skulls crushed and some broken limbs." But she did not stray from the truth when she said, "It was one of the saddest and most out-rageous sights ever happened in the state or union."

It was an event that had to be seen to be understood, for the "papers publish it [it] is all for the companies side, and all our Bisbee papers are owned by the company."

Those in the right were obvious: "The miners did not strike for any thing unreasonable, and the working man must have his rights some time."[65]

Mrs. H. B. McClellan wrote to Governor Hunt describing how deserted the town was, ending her letter by expressing what many people felt: "I feel like hollering or getting a gun myself."[66]

Despite these events, the strike movement throughout Arizona was a source of great pride within the IWW. The Metal Mine Workers Industrial Union bulletin dated July 13 boasted of that Local 800 "has engaged in the greatest strike in the history of American mining." Bisbee, Globe, Miami, Jerome, Swansea, all in Arizona, and Butte had all gone out on strike, despite opposition from "companies[,] soldiers, [and] W.F.M thugs." The deportations from Jerome and Bisbee, they were confident, would be "of no avail as they must deport all miners if they wish to deport all IWW's." The Wobblies were confident of their ultimate victory, for "deportation will not help because it is we who are the ones who mine the metals and they cannot do without us."

The enmity between the IWW and the IUMMSW was reported to be "in the open," and the latter union was accused of having participated in the roundup in Jerome and then, after having deported the IWWs, "gone back to lick the boots of their masters in the mines." They showed their true colors by expelling the Bisbee local of their own union, "who were red blooded men who believed in fighting the boss." Resorting to the worst of insults, Moyer's union was said to be a replacement for the scab outfits of Pinkerton and Farley, and Moyer himself "must want to work for the government as he did back in 86."[67]

The Wobbly paper, *Solidarity*, published a full report on the deportation, and detailed that two thousand people were rounded up, including three women, which was not the case. The *New York Times* also reported the presence of three women, who were described as being deported because of their "sympathy for the IWW" and their "outspoken expression of it." For *Solidarity* this was "the Iron Heel at work," carried out by the "lickspittles of the copper lords, cockroach business men who grovel in the dust at the feet of corporate greed, scabs who know no manhood, living offal that stinks to the high heavens and are rotten with cowardice." The paper also asserted that among the deportees were many businessmen, who were included with the strikers as a way of "eliminating some of the competing business men from the town."

The final question, all but impossible to answer, is how many of the deportees were actual Wobs. One opinion, which seems entirely reasonable, is that of J. L. Donnelly, president of the Arizona AF of L, who said at a statewide gathering in October 1917, "of the 1200 men rounded up by 300 armed men ... 35 per cent were IWW's and the rest were peaceful citizens and professional men who had antagonized the copper barons."

"The so-called Loyalty League of Arizona," he declared, "was formed by the mine owners to stamp out unionism and would not stop at murder to accomplish its purpose."[68]

The deportees were not only miners, though here again there were cases of dual membership. They deported thirty of thirty-nine members of the Painters' Union. Three of the carpenters claimed they themselves were IWWs ... out of 139 members.[69]

The (unproved) presence of machine guns among the armaments of the vigilantes particularly enraged the Wobbly organ, and led them to easily answered questions: "Since when has it become possible for private citizens... to obtain possession of machine guns belonging to the state? Can it be that the copper barons are really the state of Arizona, and that the people of that state are only their industrial serfs? Is it possible that the copper barons of Arizona, like the coal kings of Colorado, maintain their own private army? Is this the state within the state? The answer to all three questions is, 'Yes.'"[70]

The day after the deportation, Phelps Dodge, through a spokesman in New York, tried to distance itself from the events. Company president James Douglas's assistant asserted that if the deportation had really taken place as described, Phelps Dodge officials on site had not acted in their capacity as Phelps Dodge managers, but rather as members of the Citizens' Protective League. This professional schizophrenia was a fairly transparent ruse.[71]

CHAPTER FIVE

THE DEPORTEES IN NEW MEXICO

Striking miners would be more welcome than would be
1200 Cochise County corporation deputies

The train with the deportees left Bisbee headed east at around 1:00 p.m. At least some of the cars had sixty-gallon barrels of water, and one had ice. When the train changed engines along the way, the men were offered bread crackers, which had been stored in the car attached to the wagons. The food, such as it was, was tossed to the men when they got off the train to stretch their legs during a halt, and there was a mild melee as the men tried to get some food.[1]

AF of L organizer Fred Brown confronted a brakeman on the train, asking if he was a member of the Brotherhood. When the man said he was, Brown asked if he wasn't "a little ashamed of the extent he was playing, and he said, 'No, we are doing this for Uncle Sam.'"[2]

The train reached Columbus, New Mexico, at about 10:00 p.m., after making stops in Douglas, Arizona, and Rodeo and Hachita, New Mexico.[3] Harassment of the men continued, and a deportee later recounted that when the train briefly halted, a man who had jumped off to answer a call of nature, was fired at by one of the five hundred armed men he estimated were accompanying them, barely missing him.[4]

In Columbus, there was further trouble. Deportee Brown told the Presidential Mediation Commission: "They tried to turn us over to the Army officials, but they refused to take us, and there was quite a squabble there between the constable, who wanted to arrest all the gunmen, but it seems that the prosecuting attorney gave his permission, or something to that effect, and anyway the outcome was they turned the engine around and went to the other end of the train and pulled us back to Hermanas," about seventeen miles away. The men were deposited in Hermanas, and attempted to sleep inside the cars.

In fact, it was reported that Walter Douglas, vice president of the rail line, which he also ran as president of its builder, Phelps Dodge, ordered its superintendent, F. B. King, to take the men to Columbus. King said that "the idea in taking them to that point was to force their care on to the military authorities stationed there."[5]

During the night, they heard the sound of men running overhead, and, when they went outside, they realized the running men were the gunmen, abandoning them and taking the early-morning train back to Bisbee, while the locomotive headed for El Paso. While they were there, one deportee reported that the gunmen fired two hundred shots around the boxcars.

Word spread of their abandonment at around 3:00 a.m., and the men got up and built fires. Still on their own, and in an early indication of how well organized the men would be, at 2:00 that first afternoon they passed the hat to collect money for tobacco—for which $72 was collected—and "to bring back grub."[6]

Hermanas had a telegraph office, and it was besieged by those men who had money to pay for the service, who sent protests to politicians and messages home asking for aid and informing their loved ones of their status. The small Western Union office was so overloaded that some of the messages had to be forwarded to Columbus to be sent out.[7]

As for the deportees in Hermanas, the rumor mill had them throwing rocks and threatening to halt the next Bisbee-bound train "to wreak vengeance" for their deportation. "Battle [was] feared." As with every other allegation of threatened violence, this one was groundless.[8]

Under orders from New Mexico governor Lindsey, on July 13 the district attorney of Luna County, New Mexico, along with the sheriff and fifty deputies, went to Hermanas to arrest the roughly twelve hundred men. But on that same day the district commander of US forces in Columbus, General George Bell, ordered that the men be brought from Hermanas, that—by order of the War Department—they be given rations and housed at Camp Furlong, a stockade that had been occupied by Mexican refugees who had traveled with General Pershing's forces when he had returned from Chihuahua and his raid against Villa. Though housed in a stockade, Bell made it clear that the men were not to be considered prisoners: the War Department had simply agreed to feed and shelter the men "until arrangements could be made for their disposition." Water was being supplied by a cavalry detachment, which transported it to the men.[9]

The day after the deportation, Bill Haywood issued a statement calling it an "outrage," continuing that "I wish to deny emphatically that German money, German influence or wartime motives are behind the western copper mine strikes. It is simply an effort to get living wages and just working conditions for our miners."[10]

He also sent a telegram to President Wilson, protesting the events: "More than two thousand men who were dragged from their homes and forcibly deported from Bisbee, Arizona are adrift in the desert at Hermanas, New Mexico. The men are miners, useful citizens, residents of Bisbee, Arizona. The United States can ill afford to permit these Prussian methods to go unchecked. We demand that these men be cared for and restored to their homes and families."

President Wilson issued a protest, writing Governor Campbell of "the greater danger of citizens taking the law into their own hands ... I look upon such actions with grave apprehension. A very serious responsibility is assumed when such precedents are set."[11]

Rumors that reflected and were intended to encourage fear of the deported men and the IWW continued to circulate. On July 13, the deportees were allegedly on the march, either to Bisbee or El Paso, and the cavalry was supposedly ready to seize the marchers. "Citizens" of the two cities 250 miles apart were getting ready to handle this unlikely situation, with El Paso supposedly preparing to feed the marchers when they arrived there and then expel them from the city. The dream of intervention by federal troops had still not died, and even after Wilson's telegram condemning the deportation it was thought the president would send federal troops to the mining camps.

General Bell sent the men supplies from El Paso, while others came directly from Columbus, which was not terrified by the presence of the deportees. Indeed, the New Mexicans' reaction to the men was overwhelmingly positive.

Unlike Cochise County's Sheriff Wheeler, Sheriff Simpson of Luna County promised the "exiles" fair treatment and protection from violence. He told them, "Not knowing the pros and cons of either side or the differences," he would have to take them in charge for the time being until instructions were given for the final disposition. He asked their cooperation in keeping down disorder.

Whether or not they were Wobs, the men set up their own systems to control the situation: their camp was, given the size of its population, a small town. And this town, there in the New Mexico desert, had its unofficial spokesman:

W. B. Cleary, the Bisbee lawyer who had always taken the side of the workers and who had been deported with them—though he was lodged at a Columbus hotel and not in the camp.

The day after the deportation, at 8:09 a.m., Cleary sent a telegram to Governor Hunt describing how dire the situation was, with "no food no shelter no money." He predicted a difficult stay, telling the governor there would be "much suffering if men kept here more than a day."[12]

Cleary issued a statement describing the roundup and deportation of, by his count, 1,286 men—almost all of whom, he averred, were "underground miners." This, we know, was not the case, since almost a third of those deported were Mexicans, none of whom were allowed to work at the prestigious post of miner and instead worked above ground. He laid out their strike demands, how they had wanted two men to work on a machine, how they had wanted an end to the physical examination every job applicant was forced to submit to and which served as a pretext to put the politically suspect on a blacklist.

The lawyer's statement also attempted to dispel any notion that the men now in New Mexico were in any way disreputable. "Among the men deported are property owners, Bisbee business men, Liberty Bond subscribers, men between the ages of 21 to 30 inclusive, who have registered under the selective draft law and others who are reservists."

Some of the "exiles" had gone even further, proposing to Cleary that they organize a regiment under his leadership to go immediately to the trenches in Europe in order to demonstrate that they "are not slackers or influenced by German propaganda or money, but men with a principle fighting for that principle and asking only for a square deal." Another report had it that Cleary had announced in Columbus that all deportees under forty would receive military training, an announcement that "was received with cheers."[13]

The men's conduct was by all accounts exemplary. There had been "no attempts to raid farm houses in this district, no alarm prevailed among the inhabitants, and considerable good feeling between residents and the exiles prevails."

The goodwill between the residents of Columbus and the men, and the outrage of the New Mexicans was amply demonstrated by an article in the local newspaper, the headline of which was indicative of the rest: "Striking Miners Would Be More Welcome Than Would Be 1200 Cochise County Corporation Deputies."

The Columbus paper, unlike all other newspapers of the time, wrote the facts as history has accepted them: that the "deported men were rounded up early Thursday morning in Bisbee by the sheriff and a large number of deputies, supposedly by orders of the Phelps-Dodge corporation. They were loaded into box cars and an order issued by Walter Douglas, vice president of the E.P & S.W. (and president of Phelps Dodge) that they be brought to Columbus and released." We learn from this paper that the news of the train—twenty-three cars reported—coming to New Mexico was sent by the owner of the Meadows drug stores of Columbus and Douglas.

When the train arrived, the mayor of Columbus and two trustees told the railroad supervisor that the deported men couldn't be let off the train, and one of the trustee's "first moves" was to place F. B. King of the railroad under arrest. The sight of the 250 armed men guarding the miners also found the Columbus officials, "very much in favor of arresting these guards and fined for carrying arms in this state."

The deportees were "all totally unarmed and Mr. Cleary kept them under his complete control. Of the twelve hundred and over men approximately 25 percent had their registration cards and one hundred forty-two were subscribers to the Liberty Loan. Many of them claimed they were not IWW."

> There is every reason to believe that in sending these men out of Arizona to New Mexico, a great outrage has been committed, not only against the deported men but the state of New Mexico and Luna County has been committed. The *Courier* is certainly not in sympathy with agitators and law-breakers, but in dealing with such people it is not necessary to commit an even greater crime than such agitators have been charged with.
>
> Among the people of Columbus the men interned are just as popular as the armed deputies ... and the Phelps-Dodge corporation and Arizona officials certainly are not held in very high esteem by the whole of southern New Mexico.[14]

Former and future governor George Hunt and Judge John McBride, both of them appointed as federal mediators by the Department of Labor, contacted the president immediately after receiving Cleary's statement.[15]

In the meanwhile, the men settled to work in their "small city of canvas"—the tents put up thanks to the soldiers garrisoned in Columbus.[16] On what was described as the hottest day of the year, under the desert sun, they dug pits for field kitchens, cut and hauled firewood, and dug latrines. The soldiers also provided the men with rations: canned beef, canned tomatoes, and bread, with coffee promised for the coming Sunday, "the first they have had since leaving Bisbee." The men were organized into a regiment of battalions and companies by the army's provost marshal.[17]

An unnamed IWW leader in the camp is quoted as saying that he believed the men would be in Columbus for two weeks "but gave no reason for his belief." Whoever he was, he was badly off the mark.

Lawyer Cleary, on the first full day at Columbus, counted the men and came up with 1,140, not 1,286 as had been originally claimed. Certain that none had left, he explained the discrepancy by the fact that the original figure was given during the heat and confusion of the loading of the cars. Subsequent, more detailed lists would also have different figures, as men did begin to filter out of the camp. After all, they were not prisoners.

The reporter credited the New Mexican and military authorities for the absence of "boot-leggers" and alcohol from the camp, but the record indicates they were not the principal impediment. As we have seen, the Wobs had consistently fought against the presence of alcohol and bootleggers among, first the strikers, and now the deportees.

There is no reason to doubt that the residents of Columbus were genuinely offended by the way the Bisbeeites had been treated, but it shouldn't be ignored that the men were allowed to go to town under military guard "to make necessary purchases." As a result, "the merchants in Columbus have been doing a thriving business supplying clothing and bedding to the exiles." Wives and children of the deportees were also arriving daily.[18] Columbus had become a kind of boomtown.

The men in their camp demonstrated great faith in the federal government. They discussed the possibility of wholesale suits for damages, though proposals that they demand release under habeas corpus were dismissed by the leaders for fear of "embarrassing" the federal government, which they felt was attempting to find a solution to the situation. In fact, the belief was widespread that the men would be returned to Bisbee under military guard and that their rights would be protected.[19]

* * *

Now that the deportees have been settled in Columbus, we can perhaps answer the question, who were the deportees?

According to a speech by Cochise County's state senator Fred Sutter in June 1918, which was almost certainly based on information provided by the mining companies, 4,718 men were employed in the mines of the Warren district, which had a population, all areas included, of approximately twenty thousand.[20]

Though the number of deportees is a solid 1,186, based on the count taken when the men were loaded onto the train cars, the numbers we have for analysis are smaller, since the men were not prisoners in Columbus and some left before the census could be carried out on August 5, 1917. We have fairly complete information on nine hundred deportees, and historian Katherine Benton-Cohen, whose book on Cochise County, *Borderline Americans* includes a thorough, fair, and thought-provoking account of the deportation, has added to this list the names of all those she came across not included in the Columbus census.

The first, perhaps most important, breakdown is that by nationality.

Americans 167	Bohemians 3
Croatians 35	Finns 76
Montenegrins 24	Serbians 82
Spanish 7	Swedish 18
Austrian 40	British 32
Canadians 6	Dalmatians 14
Greeks 1	Polish 2
Australians 5	Bosnians 1
Germans 20	Norwegians 4
Swiss 4	Irish 67
Danish 5	Lithuanians 3
Hungarians 4	Dutch 2
Scotch 3	Russians 7
Bulgarians 2	Italians 8
French 3	Ukrainians 1
Luxembourgian 1	Welshmen 7
Armenians 1	Slavonians 3
Mexicans 229	

Other categorizations are vital for us in understanding the deportation:

Married Men 230

Men with children 226

Men having taken out first citizenship papers 241

Men having taken out first and final citizenship papers 71

Men who purchased Liberty Bonds 169

Men registered for selective army draft 355

Men owning property 773

Men with bank accounts 281[21]

Fred Brown provided the union membership figures, saying there were 426 "acknowledged" IWW members, 381 AF of L members, and 361 who were members of no labor union.[22]

Senator Sutter's speech included breakdowns of the deportees by mining company, which showed a wide discrepancy. The Copper Queen mine, the largest of the three companies, and which employed 2,201 men, suffered 168 deportations, or 7.6 percent of the total mining staff. The Calumet and Arizona Mining Company, with a slightly smaller contingent of mining staff (2201 at Copper Queen, 1926 at C&A) had 163 men deported, or 8.4 percent of the miners. The Shattuck mine, with only 591 miners, had a shocking 153 men, or 25.8 percent of its miners, shipped to Columbus.

Governor Hunt, in a message to the legislature a year later, reported that the full number of men registered for the draft, drawn from the full 1,186 deportees, was 472. Given the high percentage of foreigners deported—355 of 900 men in the above table, or 39 percent, or 472 of the 1,186 total deportees, or 39.7 percent—this seems to be an extremely high percentage of men registered, one that, from the point of view of the government in any case, would be considered admirable. It would thus seem that everyone liable to register for the draft had done so. That Sutter went on to say that only thirty-three men had been called under the colors and that "the remainder were either alien enemies, aliens, or men not subject to the draft" is of little consequence and doesn't prove that the men were in any way "shirkers," as the authorities loved to depict them. If few men were called, that was a decision of the draft board, not the men who'd registered.[23]

* * *

Bisbee-based historian Mike Anderson, in his investigations into the later fate of deportees, has tracked down at least twenty-eight inducted into the US Army after the deportation, as well as four who served in the Canadian Army and one in the British.[24]

Among them were John B. Taylor, who returned to Arizona after the deportation and reported for induction days after being called a slacker in the *Bisbee Daily Review*. After serving in France, he returned to Bisbee and worked in the mines until he retired. The Finn Eric Isaacson was inducted after leaving Camp Furlong, and after the war worked in various western mines. Of the four Croatian Segulja brothers, John and Felix were shipped to France after induction, where John was buried alive when a trench collapsed. He was pulled out but spent much of his later life in veteran's hospitals due to the shock he received. Brooklyn-born Joseph Patrick Reddy enlisted in the Canadian Army and later worked in the Old Dominion mine in Globe, Arizona. Italian immigrant John Clerico left Camp Furlong for the mines of Morenci, Arizona, until drafted in June 1918. Fred Watson, who left such a vivid account of the events of 1917, also enlisted in the Canadian Army.[25] If there were any men who engaged in draft resistance, we don't know of them.

* * *

Liberty Bonds figure in the census taken in Columbus, and they were considered a vital measure of patriotism. Subscription rates and the relative success or failure of bond drives were a regular feature of American newspapers during the war, particularly in the early days of the war, when patriotic frenzy was at its height. According to the Columbus census figures, 18.7 percent of the deportees had purchased Liberty Bonds, and because this was considered a way to judge Americanness, mine owners would twist and turn this figure in every possible direction, as long as it was to their benefit. In contrast, one in six American households, or 16.6 percent, purchased Liberty Bonds in the first drive, begun April 28, 1917—a figure lower than the rate at which bonds had been purchased by deportees.[26] Certainly, the number as stated in the Columbus census did not back the mine owners' claim that the deportees were not contributing financially to the war effort.

The mining companies provided figures vastly different from those of the Columbus census, claiming 111 bond subscribers from among their deported miners. The discrepancy can certainly be explained, at least in part, by the fact that not all the deportees were mine employees.

The mine owners used this lower number, as well as the number of bonds redeemed early or bond purchases that were canceled, as proof that the miners were unpatriotic. For example, of the forty Copper Queen miners who purchased bonds, only one had made a full payment of $250—the rest either making only partial payments or withdrawing payments and canceling purchases. Of the seven C&A miners who subscribed, only one had made full payment, and none of the sixty-four Shattuck miners had made full payment. Adding five who became bondholders through banks, Sutter claims that only seven deportees were bondholders (presumably omitting the nine who purchased theirs as part of the Serbian or Croatian societies' $100,000 purchase).

All those who purchased bonds and canceled or asked for refunds did so before July 12, which, according to Senator Sutter "leav[es] but one conclusion; which is, that after joining the IWW they were compelled to cancel their subscription for bonds."[27]

Though it is impossible at this distance to verify the figures provided by either the deportees or the mine owners, it requires little imagination to cast doubt on this typically anti-Wobbly conclusion.

All of the refunds and cancellations occurred *after* the strike declaration. As this was not an era of unions with strike funds, there is nothing surprising in the men asking for refunds or being unable to continue payments for the bonds. They didn't need to be ordered or compelled to do so by the IWW (and there is no evidence they were). Survival dictated it.

* * *

A week after their arrival in Columbus, Mayor Erickson of Bisbee received a telegram from the officer in charge of the encampment about the plight of the Mexican families left behind when the men were deported. The families were "destitute [and] further no aid is being given them by the Aid association or Copper Queen store, being laughed at when they ask for aid." Erickson responded that the "Citizens' Relief association [is] caring for every person asking aid. Mexicans not barred."

That the situation in Columbus was not going to be short-lived was also made clear a week into the arrival of the "exiles." The men voted unanimously that they would remain in the Columbus camp "pending further action by the federal government"—this after the officer in charge of the camp had informed them they were free to go whenever they chose. Though the headline of the article on their decision to stay in the camp said that they "prefer government grub to steady labor," the resolutions passed tell a far different story:

> Whereas most of us have our homes and families in the Warren District of Cochise county, Arizona, and
>
> Whereas, we were forcibly deported without proper sanction of law from our homes on the 12th day of July; and
>
> Whereas, the federal government has today given us our choice whether we stay in this camp or return to the Warren District, where we would be at the mercy of company thugs and gun men, or wander to other parts of the country; therefore, be it Resolved, That we, as striking miners, stay in the camp as a solid body until the federal government sees fit to return us to our homes with adequate protection against lawless acts; and further be it Resolved, That we form our own police force guarding the camp and carrying on the necessary work systematically.
>
> Resolutions of thanks and appreciation were extended to the regular army officers who have looked after the men and to the white and negro soldiers stationed here for their kind treatment.

The release of the men who, again, were never prisoners, caused no disquiet in Columbus. Mayor R. W. Elliott issued a statement praising those in the camp as "law-abiding citizens and working-men." The mayor went on to say how "no attempt has been made by them to come to town or to cause any disturbance." Their self-organization of a police force was also praised, a force that has "curb[ed] any attempt on the part of their members to start individually or collectively into town or for other places." The mayor was confident that as long as the men were supplied with the food and housing the government had promised, "there is no cause to apprehend these men will become a burden on the settlements of this country."[28]

The deportees self-organized, and one of them recounted that while they were encamped in Columbus they were broken down into companies of seventy-five, each given specific chores, and, oddly for these antimilitarists, "treated as if they were in the army." They also fraternized with the soldiers in Columbus, most of them Black. When the latter showed sympathy for the Bisbeeites, they were replaced with white soldiers.[29]

John MacDonald, a Wobbly organizer among the deportees in Columbus, wrote to Grover Perry in Salt Lake City on July 23 to update him on the situation there. He confirmed that, on July 21, the War Department had told the men they were free to leave, though the government would continue to feed all those who remained. The men in the camp held a mass meeting and "all agree unanimously to stick together and stay here until the government send us back to Bisbee." Mail from Bisbee was arriving only sporadically, and the men were convinced that some of it was being opened and then resealed after having been read. MacDonald was convinced that the intention was for the men "to drift away one by one and scatter out, but the spirit shown so far is fine, and but a few are restless." The Wobs were sure that the men would hold out: "All of the Old Rebels here are contented to stay here, so long as the grub continues."[30] The grub would continue, and the Old Rebels stood their ground.

One July 24, the leadership sent a telegram to Governor Hunt, thanking him for his assistance and support, and telling him that "we will remain in one solid body until returned to Bisbee."[31]

Even so, there were reports on July 26—by which time the men were free to move about the area as they wished—of men from the camp making their way to small towns in New Mexico like Rodeo and Lordsburg, mainly searching for other men who had been victims of the roundup. In Rodeo, though, a mile from the Arizona border, it was alleged that "IWWs" had gotten into fights with Cochise County deputies.[32]

Also on July 26, two weeks after the roundup, IWW leader A. S. Embree wrote to both Bill Haywood and Grover Perry about the situation in the camp, and though Embree was able to tell the leaders that "the spirit among us is undaunted," the strike considered won, and a return to Bisbee a certainty in the "near future," the letter reveals interesting insights into the political and emotional state of the deportees.

If the IWW saw the strike as hinging on the six-hour day, Embree felt obliged to tell Perry and Haywood that the rank and file considered this demand "a chimera." This situation was not about to change, for he felt "it will require the lesson of this strike and months of educational work afterwards to get them ready for the six hour struggle." The men in Columbus simply did not see the "object and necessity for it as part of the whole revolutionary program." But even more, Embree felt that "the majority of us do not yet regard this strike as part of a revolutionary movement," though they did indeed "grasp the idea of industrial solidarity as they never could have done had it not been for this strike."

Wobbly ideology, such as it was, had only permeated the working class to a certain extent. The overthrow of the system remained foreign to them.

A certain pique with the leadership is also revealed in this letter. The camp at Columbus had sent a telegram collect to the IWW office in Salt Lake the previous day, and it had been refused. Embree expressed his puzzlement at this, since Perry knew full well that the men "have no money individually or collectively, so their only option when informing the central office of anything was to send the message collect. At this time all our boys are naturally suspicious and quick to resent anything that savors of procrastination."[33] The time in the desert was beginning to wear on the men.

* * *

The men in Columbus continued to come up with ways to leave their camp behind and make themselves useful, though only on terms they considered dignified. On August 3, representatives chosen by the miners sent a telegram to President Wilson making a bold offer: they would return to Bisbee and dig copper, but only on the condition that the mines were nationalized: "Miners deported from Bisbee voted unanimously that they were willing to dig Copper for the United States government provided that the government will take over and operate all copper mines and smelters in the country." If they received a response, none is recorded, though the flow of copper was essential to the war effort.

An angry restlessness began to make itself felt among the exiles, at least if we are to believe the Phelps Dodge organ. A candy store owner complained that men from the camp got soft drinks at his establishment and "refused to pay, saying they would pay when Columbus gave them work." It was also alleged that a bread wagon was raided and its contents expropriated. The men were also beginning to drift away from the camp, some of them making their way to El Paso to the east or back into Arizona.[34]

Jack Norman, a Wob leader among the deportees in New Mexico, wrote to Grover Perry on July 30 that he had "just received word from Bisbee that they are shipping scabs in from Salt Lake." And telling Perry that if his investigation proved the truth of this that fellow workers still in Bisbee would carry out "sabotage and other last resorts."[35]

In an undated letter to Grover Perry from fellow-Wobbly M. C. Sullivan in Columbus from around this period (the letter can be approximately dated from its reference to the killing of Frank Little, which occurred on August 1, 1917), the spirits of the men are described: "Just a few lines to let you [*sic*] that we are still in the land of the living and every thing fine and dandy we have a good bunch here...every one standing solid for a victory we have a bulletin board here send us all the news you can... I think it was to [*sic*] bad about Little I suppose you and your family got tunder [*sic*] struck when you heard it."[36]

Fred Watson left an account of the conditions and spirit in Columbus, having spent six weeks there, staying until the camp broke up. A tribute to the workers' spirit was his statement that, "you never saw a bunch of men in your life stay together like we did." He also fills out the picture of who was among the strikers: the deportees included cooks from a notoriously anti-union restaurant in Bisbee, the English Kitchen. They'd gone on strike in Bisbee and been sent to New Mexico, where they went on strike in the camp as well.[37]

* * *

Deported Wob Jack Norman wrote to union leader V. V. O'Hair from the Columbus camp on August 18, and his concerns were not only for the men in the camp. He had received a letter a few days earlier that strikes were spreading and were breaking out in the Masabi Range, and complained that they were "damn slow" about it. Passivity was not an option for Norman, who said that "action is what is needed all over the god damn country." And not only strike action. The situation in Arizona, with strikes and deportations all over the state's map, led him to wonder "if it will not wake up the cats I don't know what will." The "cats" in question referred to the Wobbly symbol for sabotage: the black cat, the Sab Cat.

Norman was frustrated at the paucity of relief being sent to the deportees, saying he had written to all the locals he could think of and that a few had sent funds, and that it was "time that some ore was jarred loose from their spare change."

Finances were ever more an issue in the camp. Money was tight and there were ten or fifteen men a day in need of shoes and shirts and overalls, along with tobacco and stamps. Like most of the correspondents from Columbus, Norman spoke of the high spirits of the men, "all cheerful as long as they get good news," though he admitted to having "a hell of a time with some of them."

Norman had some doubts about the goal of holding out in New Mexico and an eventual return to Bisbee. He expressed a wish to stay put, asking,

"What the hell would we do without a relief fund [if we are to be returned to Bisbee]?"—however unlikely that might have been, given the guards at the border of the town. He added with more than a touch of irony that being stuck in New Mexico was "the finest thing that could of [*sic*] happened to us, if we had been in Bisbee until now I think the strike would have been broken." His vision of events was not without humor: "Pretty soft for us the company feeding the family in Bisbee and the government feeding us here, pretty soft."[38]

This softness of their situation led a Wob leader, likely Grover Perry, to explain to Norman the reason the men in New Mexico were not receiving much in the way of funds. However tough it might be for them "to stick in that detention camp with no shade but your sombrero," they at least had the satisfaction of knowing that nothing could be mined without them. As for funds, the "couple of dozen" men the IWW had doing collections were sending the bulk of their gleanings to Miami, Globe, and Butte, whose men "really need support worse than you fellows, as they do not even have a 20 cents a day ration served to them."[39]

Even with this, the camp was a political focus. Governor Hunt, representing President Wilson in the striking areas of Arizona, arrived in Columbus on the afternoon of August 20 to meet with the attorneys for the exiles and was expected to speak to the assembled men on August 22. But again, as proof of the orderly nature of the encampment, when city officials requested that the men stay off the streets of Columbus after 6:00 p.m., "the executive committee of the deported men addressed their followers at the camp to comply with this request."[40]

* * *

Fraternal organizations were a key element of life in Bisbee, and politics and class seemed to matter little there before the deportation. Bosses and workers were Elks or Masons in the same lodge, and it is a particular oddity of the deportation (and unusual in the history of working-class dissent) that the alleged Wobbly James Brew, the only person killed on the miners' side, was a member of the Elks and was buried in the Elks' section of Evergreen, the town cemetery. This fraternal sentiment carried over to the Columbus camp.

Governor Hunt wrote a letter on August 21, during a visit to the deportees' camp in Columbus, to the "Worshipful Master" of the White Mountain

Lodge in Globe informing him of a serious violation of Masonic principles. Four Masons in Columbus had made themselves known to Hunt. What made their presence in the camp especially disturbing was the fact that one of the leading forces among the vigilantes was Dr. Bledsoe, Worshipful Master of the Bisbee Lodge. Bledsoe could not claim ignorance that fellow Masons were among those loaded on the train, since it was Bledsoe who officiated at the entry of one of them to Freemasonry.

Whatever the law might do to those responsible for kidnapping the miners, Hunt wanted the Sovereign Lodge of Arizona to be notified of the situation and for it "to call to task a Brother Mason who so shamelessly assaulted one of the members of his own Order." He felt it was incumbent upon the Order, of which he had been a member for many years, "to see that some action be taken by the Order to see that so disgusting and so inhuman proceedings should never be allowed to be tolerated in the Jurisdiction of Arizona."[41]

* * *

For a certain class of capitalist, the men in the desert and all their kind were just so many unused hands that could be put to profitable use. I. W. Wallace, a real estate man in Bisbee, received an "inspiration" while returning by train from the coast. Seeing the need for a military road from the desert around Yuma, Arizona, and across the railroad bridge over the Colorado River, he determined that "the thing to do is to arrest all Wobblies in the towns, cities, and camps of Arizona on vagrancy charges and put them to work building a fine road across the desert. The state needs the road and the Wobblie [sic] needs to be put to work. Cochise County is using her bootlegger prisoners on a fine county road with good results. Why not a great state road, built by men who are thrice the menace to the community at large than the boot leggers ever were?"[42] Wallace was perhaps unaware—or perhaps not—that this county road was suffering occasional delays due to fluctuations in the labor supply, as was the case a week before the strike in Bisbee began: "The force of men was reduced ... on account of the sentence of several having expired."[43] Wallace was confident enough in his proposal to suggest that California also use Wob labor to continue the road across the state: "She has plenty for this work, and from what I heard on the coast she considers them as much of a menace to her progress and prosperity as we do here in Arizona."[44]

After Governor Hunt's August visit to the camp in Columbus to investigate the condition of the nine hundred to a thousand men who were still encamped, he sent a telegram to President Wilson on September 1, telling him in no uncertain terms that he felt "repugnance for an act so unamerican, so autocratic, as that which forced them from their homes." He implored the president to grant the deportees "an early recognition of their constitutional rights and a resumption of American justice in this State."[45]

* * *

On September 3, Hunt followed this up with an ardent plea to the president on the workers' behalf. He told the president that he hadn't been able to fulfill his role as mediator and conciliator in the labor dispute in Bisbee, since before he was even able to reach the Warren District there was "no one [there] to whom I could appeal for a settlement of existing differences. The workingmen were gone, and it is not to be presumed that the operators, successful and defiant in their stupendous act of usurpation of the functions of the law, or of lawlessness, were in a frame of mind to listen to appeals to their fairness."

Foiled in his role as mediator, Hunt had gone to Columbus to talk to the strikers and learn their mindset, their psychology, their attitude toward the war, and their attitude toward their employers, all of which Hunt hoped "would likely shed a little light upon the causes of labor's unrest."

After speaking to a third of the men in Columbus, he told the president that despite all claims of German influence, "there was not to be found the slightest evidence of German money, now or heretofore." This charge he had no hesitation in calling "a hoax pue [sic] and simple."

Hunt stated that half the men in Columbus were Wobblies, which was "*more than there were at the time the deportation occurred*" (emphasis added). He considered this the logical outcome of the owners' methods. The rest of the men were members of other unions and men unaffiliated with any labor organization. Hunt had been informed by a friend in Bisbee that "not even ⅓ of the men deported were members of the IWW."[46] AF of L organizer Fred Brown gave the Mediation Commission precise statistics on the union membership of the deportees—416 were acknowledged IWWs, 381 were members of the AF of L, and 361 were members of no union—36 percent, 33 percent, and 31 percent: near enough to Hunt's estimate.[47]

Far from the demons spoken of in the press, the men he met were "just ordinary human beings, struggling in their own ways and according to their own lights for a betterment of the conditions which they expect will be their lot through life."

The men couldn't understand "why the war should be so one-sided in its effect upon capital and labor, as to justify extraordinary gain to the former while denying to the [latter] the right to organized action to secure a living wage." However, they were not interested in readjudicating these issues; rather, they wanted their constitutional rights restored, and though aware that should they be allowed back to Bisbee, their conditions there would be untenable and life would be made "unendurable" for them. But even if it was certain that they would ultimately have to leave Bisbee, they insisted they be allowed go back, and this was why they remained in Columbus. Their demand, their sole demand, was "THEY WANT THEIR LIBERTY, AND THE RIGHT TO SUPPORT THEMSELVES AND THEIR FAMILIES, BUT THEY WANT THAT LIBERTY TO BE RESTORED TO THEM WHERE IT WAS TAKEN FROM THEM" (emphasis in original).

The poison of the Bisbee Deportation was a powerful one, Hunt told the president, and "it would be destructive of the patriotic ardor which burns in every true American breast" if it were to serve to prove that "there exists a class of men in this country so powerful, so influential, that they can disregard the laws of society, take the administration of justice into their own hands and within the borders of a state. If this Union set up an autocracy, defying both state and Federal authority," all by using the "camouflage" of patriotism while "they are in reality using the nation's extremity to serve their selfish ends."[48]

The deportees remained firm and organized in their desert camp, but after two months both sides were beginning to suffer from frayed nerves. On September 8, the military authorities posted a notice in the camp that the rations distributed to the men would be cut in half. Telegrams of protest were sent to the president and the secretary of labor, but to no avail, and on September 11 the reduction was implemented. Feeling that even the previous amounts were insufficient, another protest, again to Secretary of Labor Wilson and the president's secretary, J. P. Tumulty, was issued over the signature of Wobbly organizer A. S. Embree.

The telegram to secretary Wilson read: "Does federal government want us to leave this camp? If so please tell us plainly to go. Do not be school boys and cut down our rations as was done this morning. We are willing to leave if you will tell us plainly that the federal government wants to get rid of us and does not consider we were wronged when we were forcibly deported from our homes. Men here are loath to believe the government approves the government of Sheriff Wheeler in deporting us from Bisbee. An immediate reply is demanded."[49]

Meanwhile, the IWW was doing fundraising for the various strikes under way from Arizona to Montana. A letter from V. V. O'Hair, seized in a raid later in the year in the union's Salt Lake City office, told the Wob deportee Jack Norman that two dozen IWW organizers were raising money for strikers in Globe, Miami, and Butte in special need. Because these strikers' situation was worse even than that of the deportees, no funds could be sent to them, though it was hoped that "funds will come in sufficient quantities so that I may be able to send money down for your urgent needs also." Even if no funds were being received by the men in New Mexico, they were told they had "the satisfaction of knowing that no copper can be dug as long as you boys stay out of the mines."[50]

Which is not to say that the national office had abandoned the Bisbeeites. Jack Shean, the financial secretary of the Pittsburgh recruiting union, wrote to Bill Haywood, on August 28, that a large fundraising meeting had been set up for September 16 in the steel town, and that half the collections would go to the Bisbee strikers, the other half staying in Pittsburgh for organizing purposes.

There was a significant note struck in this letter, one that is indicative of the Wob attitude toward sabotage. Shean told Haywood that "we shall absolutely ignore the term sabotage in all our educational activities in this district, and do not wish to distribute any literature treating on this subject."[51]

Though the men reportedly declared they were not going to leave the camp until replies to their telegrams were received, the executive committee of the deportees also wrote to Governor Campbell and President Wilson that they intended to return to Bisbee. The telegram to Campbell informed him that, "unless the federal government restores rations we will leave Columbus. Six hundred men have belongings in Bisbee and will go there to settle their affairs and get their belongings." We can read this to mean that half the men were still in New Mexico two months after being forcibly removed from their homes, and the military declared that, after the reduction in rations, "a few men were missing from the camp," though whether they had departed for Bisbee or elsewhere was unknown. A count would be done to determine how many were left, but the army was certain that "no considerable number have yet left the camp." Other reports from Columbus, though, stated that "ten men from the IWW camp boarded the westbound train here at midnight with the avowed intention of returning to Bisbee. Twenty more are reported at Hermanas, sixteen miles west, having made the trip from Columbus during the day. These men were also expected to take the night train to Bisbee."[52]

Among those who left the camp were A. S. Embree, who returned to Bisbee for his wife and son. Embree explained to a journalist that despite the receipt of assistance from Wobbly offices in Chicago and Salt Lake City, "the army cut our rations from 23 cents worth of food a day at Columbus to less than eight cents worth, and we could not live on that. In fact, one major gave us to understand that we were not wanted there longer."[53]

* * *

The newspapers reported the camp's demise on September 17:

> Columbus officially ceased to be a rendezvous for the men deported from Bisbee, Ariz., July 12, when the tents in the detention camp were torn down today and the army commissariat ceased issuing rations to the few men remaining here. Only a small group of the men deported from Bisbee remained here today. One was an organizer for the American Federation of Labor and had the fact blazoned on his sombrero. Another was a Finn, another a Mexican and the remaining three Americans. They said they expected to leave soon for the west.[54]

CHAPTER SIX

BISBEE AFTER THE DEPORTATION

A new and better community

The day after the deportation, the *Daily Review* described Bisbee as "a new and better community." Life had returned to normal now that what the paper described as "a sordid, unlikely job had been accomplished." The *Review* admitted that "though there was regret felt that such stringent proceedings were necessary, the feeling of relief that pervaded the entire community was open and undisguised."[1]

However, the deportation of 1,186 men didn't satisfy the authorities and mine owners that the town was safe from dissent. Despite the forcible ending of the strike and the demolition of the unions, Governor Campbell "wished" for army troops to be stationed in Bisbee, Kingman, Jerome, Clifton, Morenci, Ajo, and Ray: every town where there was an active strike, or where one had been crushed, or where one was feared. Campbell's wish did not give birth to a formal request at the time, as he wanted to carry out a more complete investigation of the situation.

For the moment, order was maintained by several hundred men—deputized and mostly armed—who covered the entire Warren District. They had set up six permanent camps where all arrivals to the district were made to explain their business in Bisbee, and all those suspected of sympathy or participation in the strike turned away. Or, as the authorities' organ explained, would be "induced to [explain their business] in another direction."

How were these kangaroo courts organized? Workmen's Loyalty League head, M. W. Merrill, said they grew spontaneously in the immediate aftermath of the deportation. The morning after the deportation, a "telegram came that they were all coming back in, and I did not know but what maybe they were or weren't, and it was up to someone to investigate, and who was going to do the work?" Everything that followed happened without being willed, Merrill insisted. "A rustling card system was established. It automatically took place." Though he correctly said that "the committee" never promised anyone a job, he was far from truthful when he said they "never told anybody that I know of that he had to get out of town." When asked if the men blocking the roads didn't serve as a warning for those deported not to come home, Sheriff Wheeler disingenuously answered, "No, I don't think so."[2]

The casualness of the violence that followed the deportations was exemplified in the instance of a Mexican man who got off a train coming into town but lagged in getting back on it when ordered to do so. "A good shot unlimbered his rifle and kicked up the ground behind him. Another shot followed and the would-be 'deserter' lost no time in getting back into his car."

Whether true or not, it was reported that the majority of those deported from town were "foreigners," and a few apparently were Americans.[3]

Two days after the deportation, it was reported that "deputy sheriffs are still busy working on many cases of agitation and sedition." Though some were found to be innocent of the allegation—the word "charge" can't fairly be used since it is not a crime to agitate, and sedition was far from proved—some were found to be members of the IWW or simply sympathizers. "Such men were informed that their presence in the camp was not needed."

The owners' newspaper also reported that "outgoing trains were again crowded," while incoming trains were also packed. This, readers were told, was owed to the fact that the news was spreading that Bisbee "is a camp without 'Wobbly' influences at work and a good place in which to reside."[4] Though not for unionists: Frank Vaughan, head of the Painters' Union, escaped the deportation, but two days later was "ordered" out of town. His union, which had thirty-nine members before July 12, was down to nine.[5]

It wasn't paranoia when S. W. White, a lawyer in Douglas, wrote to Governor Hunt that he had been told in confidence that a roundup like Bisbee's was being planned in Douglas. He'd heard that he was to be caught up in it on account of his "Hunt and labor sympathies." Though White wasn't sure if another roundup was really being planned, he doubted anything could be done to "forestall such action, if it is contemplated." To prove the possibility that a roundup was planned, White told the governor that the number of special deputies in town had been increased to 4,500, and that "it is announced five hundred more will be added." White told Hunt that the workers in Douglas were not IWW sympathizers, but were men convinced that what had happened in Bisbee was a step too far, and in order to quiet their "rumblings," which reached the bosses through their "big flock of detectives," they might convince the mine owners "to conclude that another 'drive' would be expedient." None occurred.[6]

The death of vigilante Orson McRae, killed by the alleged Wobbly James Brew, was seen as part of the fight for democracy going on in Europe. It was announced that "the Warren District recognizes that the faithful employee of the C. and A. Company died no less in the nation's cause than will those who perish on the battlefield of France or on the great white ways between this country and the scenes of carnage abroad."[7] McRae was put to ideological use in service to the cause of anti-unionism.

Dan Kitchell, a mine engineer at the time of the deportation, considered the event "the most deplorable thing that ever happened in the United States," and spoke highly of deputy McRae, saying that "Orson McRae was a wonderful fellow…. It seems like every man, woman, and child walked down to the cemetery for the funeral … Jim Brew was an Elk and they couldn't get enough Elks to serve as pall bearers, that was the difference. People were scared to death."[8]

Fred Watson later recounted how McRae was buried with honors, "with a flag draped on the casket in the rotunda of the P[helps] D[odge] store, and the Elks buried him with a big fanfare." Brew, on the other hand, was buried in the dark of night in the Elks section of Evergreen Cemetery. The poor attendance, according to Watson, was an enforced act, for he said that "Jimmy McDonald [a deputy sheriff] was an Elk, and he was going to the funeral. And they told him nobody could go to this funeral. Jimmy pulled his gun and says, 'Hell there ain't!' He said, 'I'm going,' and *he* went to the funeral. That's why I tell you, it don't make any difference what you belong to or who you are, in a day like that you're on the picket line, you're just riffraff."[9]

Perhaps that's why a movement was started in the district on July 16 "for the erection of a monument in the square in front of the post office to the memory of Orson P. McRae." All of the organizations behind the roundup and deportation backed the collection drive: the Citizens' Protective League, the Commercial Club, the city government, and Sheriff Wheeler, but "the Workmen's Loyalty League will take a particularly strong part."

The subscription was set at a trifling amount, "not less than ten cents nor more than twenty-five cents," with the name of every contributor to be engraved on the monument. "By placing the subscription at the nominal sum which had been fixed, every man, woman, and child in the district can have the honor of taking part in the erection of the monument."

The monument would not be a simple reminder of a passing event; rather its backers intended it to be "a reminder during all the remainder of the history of the district of the patriotism of which its people are capable as Americans."

McRae had fallen, according to the organizers, not trying to arrest a workman who refused to have his home violated but on a battlefield equal to those to which the Doughboys were being sent. "The monument will stand as marking the first life to have been given from among American manhood in the present war—given in conflict with enemies of the country and wholly in the spirit of service to the flag."[10]

* * *

The *Daily Review* reported during the strike that most workers were disobeying the strike order, and yet, almost a week after the deportation it said that though 70 percent of the workers at the Copper Queen and Calumet and Arizona mines had returned to work, only 34 percent at the Shattuck mine had done so.[11] Something was still wrong in Bisbee.

Workers entering the district were being thoroughly vetted. Every man on the incoming trains "brought a letter from some prominent resident of their home or from the town in which they formerly resided, attesting to their citizenship and character." These men were welcome.

But a new system was put in place; it no longer sufficed to go to a mining company's hiring office to get a job. The system of "rustling cards," was established. In fact, entering Bisbee was now regulated by the Citizens' Protective League. No one could set foot in town without a card issued by the vigilantes, and the card would only be granted "after a thorough investigation." Only once this card was issued could the prospective employee go to the hiring offices. As the *Daily Review* laconically put it, "Several IWW's were investigated yesterday by the Citizens' Protective League and the Workmen's Loyalty League. Several left the city last night for other points." In short, the leadership of the town, still in the hands of the vigilantes, had established a border around Bisbee and had arrogated to itself the right to decide who could live within it.[12]

Fred Watson, who spent six weeks in Columbus, insisted that they didn't suffer; the ones who really did were those left in Bisbee when the kangaroo courts functioned. "Anyone who came back from Columbus was thrown in the hoosegow and treated the same—brought before the kangaroo court. Men with money in the bank and everything. They were given a certain time to sell their property at what the company wanted to give them and a certain length of time to leave time." According to Watson, once the arrangement was settled on—at gunpoint—those forced to leave went to the bank with gunmen in front of and behind them.[13]

The town leaders could not have been more open about how Bisbee functioned. A pamphlet issued in August 1917, informed prospective newcomers that Bisbee "has all the conveniences to be found in any city of its size in the United States." But they also warned them that "it is the determination of the residents and mining companies in the district to maintain a community of American citizens. No members of or sympathizers with the I.W.W. can secure employment in the Warren District." This official pamphlet, which included wage levels and the prices of goods found in the stores of Bisbee, was signed by the sheriff, the mayor, and the heads of all the mining companies, but at the top of the list of signatories were M. W. Merrill, president of the Loyalty League of America, and M. J. Cunningham, temporary chairman of the Citizens' Protective League. The vigilantes ruled the roost.[14]

Frank Thomas, the Bisbee police court judge, could certainly not be accused of having a predilection for the miners' cause, but he was disgusted with what he saw at the kangaroo courts, which he considered "detestable and unAmerican." The members of these unofficial courts, as far as Thomas was concerned, were completing the work of the roundup and deportation. For him the men who were being turned away were not just IWWs, "they were union men.... They were making a clean-up and included them in the clean-up." And whatever the supposed purity of the motives of the vigilante judges, Thomas was not fooled. Asked by Felix Frankfurter of the Mediation Commission if the members of the kangaroo courts were company employees, Thomas didn't hesitate: "I think invariably they were, every one of them was."[15]

Sheriff Wheeler issued a statement via the Associated Press that "if the IWW's who were deported from this district should come back of their own initiative we would meet them and put them in a bullpen we have arranged for just such a purpose." He admitted to having no solution to the "problem" presented by the deportation and detention in New Mexico, but he refused to believe that "the United States will force these men upon us after we took the action we did through pure Americanism."

And not just "Americanism." Shoring up the case for the deportation by appealing to xenophobia and a fear of radicals, Wheeler now claimed that "*American* women were told their houses would be blown up" (emphasis added). Alleging that almost no crime, however petty, was beyond the strikers, Wheeler justified the deportation because "dinner pails were stolen from the miners," a common complaint during the strike and a constant refrain after the deportation. Finns were a small but united element among the strikers and their supporters, and their wives, according to Wheeler, were no better than the men, since "Finnish women sympathizers with the strikers attacked the miners going to work."

Wheeler also told a rather unlikely story about the union hall calling him three hours before the "first move was made" to tell him that the union men had heard that gunmen were going to be sent for them and that if they were, they would meet "serious resistance." Wheeler boasted that "we had a machine gun and we met with no resistance." Since the roundup began at around 6:00 this would have meant he was called at 3:00 a.m., and as we have seen, the roundup took the strikers completely by surprise. Wheeler did not reprise this story in later justifications of the deportation.

Finally, Wheeler claimed that there were 4,500 men organized in the two citizens' leagues and that he expected to increase the number to 5,000. The goal of all this was tantamount to ethnic cleansing: "We are pledged ... to make this an American camp where American working men may enjoy life, liberty, and the pursuit of happiness unmolested by any alien enemies of whatever breed."[16]

Despite the abuse of the word "American," many of the deportees were attempting to return to Bisbee to answer draft calls, one deportee going so far as to say it was the majority of men, and that they all would have gone back had they the means. Fred Brown apparently tried to return twice, at least once to meet his selective service obligations. He attempted to return in time to answer the draft board's call but the kangaroo court pulled him from the train and held him overnight. He asked if he was under arrest and was told, "If you want to take it that way, all right." He refused to go to police court and insisted on seeing Sheriff Wheeler, who lectured him on patriotism and anti-patriotism. He then went to Tombstone, where he was offered clearance by the kangaroo court, which he refused, and returned to Columbus. He came back to Bisbee on August 19, and was able to get into town. But two or three days after arriving he was arrested and held incommunicado for nineteen hours. He was able to sneak a note out to a friend, who sent bail for him. He asked that his trial be delayed so he could prepare his defense. It was postponed several more times, and after two weeks the case was dropped.[17]

* * *

Sustaining the fear of Wobs was clearly a part of ruling-class strategy in Arizona. If we can't go so far as to say that to the authorities and the mine owners "the only good Wob was a dead Wob," it's certainly the case that everything possible was done to show that as long as there was an IWW in the state there was a danger of death, ruin, and sabotage.

On July 18, a letter was sent from California by a certain "Rowan," who was apparently running a group of informants in Bisbee. Rowan was far from confident the job was finished and thought there was still work to be done "in ferreting out those who may have escaped the dragnet and of whom we understand there are quite a number." The dangers of undercover work due to the widespread nature of the continued roundup were underlined by Rowan, who advised that agents "exercise due precaution in getting a line in these, as you are apt to be taken up and turned in by one of the Loyalty League plain clothes men." Sowing dissent among the miners was also a part of the strategy of their opponents, and the addressee was encouraged to get in touch with an AF of L leader to see if they had plans to reestablish the closed-down local in Bisbee now that the Wobblies were gone. "Such a correspondence might develop something worth while."

Despite the deportation, despite the kangaroo courts investigating those entering town, despite the absence of any violent acts by strikers still in Bisbee, Rowan continued that "there are still Wobblies in the district and what is more, others are coming in from all parts of the country with the announced purpose of bringing sabotage onto play."[18]

And so it was reported that there was fear in Mesa of a Wobbly plot that, "if carried out would result in an attempt to destroy the crops on the Salt River Valley." Having learned from Jerome and Bisbee, it was considered necessary to appoint "a sufficient number of deputies whose principal duty would be to keep a close watch on all incoming 'tourists' and inquire into their antecedents. *If there is suspicion that the arrivals are in any way affiliated with the IWW*

or other disloyal organizations they should be compelled to move on or placed in
confinement" (emphasis added).

In Kingman, Arizona, the sheriff planned to lock up any IWW strike agitators for the duration of the war. Having heard that Wobblies from Globe and Bisbee were heading his way, he defiantly said, "Let them come. We'll round them up and put them in an internment camp and ask the government to send a military guard to take charge of the prisoners."

But it wasn't only Arizona that was at risk. The Bisbee paper also reported the "discovery" of a plot to burn down the entire town of Mojave, California, and though the person who had set the fire—he claimed accidentally—was in jail, troops were sent to the town and reports had been received that a large number of Wobs had arrived "bent on stirring up trouble among fruit canners, pickers, and dryers." The local marshal postured as a West Coast Harry Wheeler and said "he is planning to drive the IWW's out at once. He estimates the unwelcome arrivals number about 100, and of the number about 25 active agitators."[19]

* * *

The anti-union tactics employed in Bisbee received praise from press around the country, and the *Los Angeles Times* was especially strong in its support of the deportation. After talking about how Americans have been sent overseas "to crush and overwhelm Germany," the *Times* warned of the danger within, of how "on our own soil is an enemy, swearing by oft-repeated oaths to perpetrate all the destruction that violence can wreak, preaching revolution and invoking anarchy; yet our government has taken on official recognition of these villains, the I.W.W.'s."

Across the country, from north to south, from east to west, "that international organization, filled with foreigners, officered by convicts, and attempting vaguely to guise its sabotage behind the specious title of 'Industrial Workers of the World,' is in open warfare against our government; and as yet no stern measures have betokened that our American leaders realize the danger or even the significance of this whirlwind of threats and strikes in those mining districts from which America and her Allies are drawing the war's supply of copper."

This group, whose "agitators are for the most part foreigners," were hypocrites, according to the *Times*, for though "they talk of freedom and equality for the workingman, of higher wages, and all that; yet in this crucial hour they bend all their efforts to aid the monarchy where workingmen are disenfranchised, where wages are small and eaten by taxation that goes to a hereditary aristocracy."

Among the deportees there "was no one man who wanted work." All "twelve hundred [of the deported] refused to labor and were run out of the country—driven out in an orderly and peaceable manner by citizens who knew that ruin and disaster awaited their community if these ruffians and agitators were not suppressed and deported."

The events in Bisbee were applicable elsewhere, and "the citizens of Cochise County, Arizona, have written a lesson that the whole of America would do well to copy. In these days America cannot afford to trifle with rioters." Vigilantism has moments when it is justified, and "if there ever was a case where the doubtful expedient of taking the law into the hands of those not lawfully authorized to execute it, this is one."[20]

The *Nation*, the venerable voice of abolitionism at its founding, and of liberalism—or of enlightened conservatism[21]—at the time of the deportation, did not justify the deportation, but the point of view of its editor, Oswald Garrison Villard, nevertheless betrayed a certain ambiguity, showing that if liberal opinion did not countenance what was done in Bisbee, it held both sides guilty. A week after the deportation, the weekly roundup of news and opinion in the magazine spoke of how the IWW's "awakening" in the West was as "ominous" as the methods employed to suppress it. Evidence of this was the union's attempt to "bankrupt" Spokane with its free-speech campaign, which overloaded the city's jails, and referred to "revolutionary industrialists" as "ugly customers" to whom unionized workers are "as antagonistic as anyone." Even so, Villard insisted that "the whole country has an interest in seeing that local and state authorities in the west do not let panicky mob violence develop around those accused of IWW leanings."[22]

A month later, with deportees still camped in the New Mexico desert, Villard was even harder on the Wobs, saying that the recorded speeches of Wobbly leaders "are such that it seems likely that leaders can here and there be arrested on substantiated grounds of sedition or disorderly intent." These arrested "would give a salutary lesson to prospective lawbreakers," though Villard was clear that any salutary lessons should be "left to the sense and energy of the Department of Justice and the States."[23]

Men continued to seek employment in Bisbee, those passing the kangaroo courts all having references from respectable citizens, and "in this way the working forces of the mines are being built up with the best of men, all Americans." One "bad case" presented himself to the kangaroo court, "a Mexican by the name of Rodriguez." He said he was the secretary of the Mexican branch of the IWW and "maintained that he would always strike when he got an opportunity."

Unions not otherwise involved in the strike or deportation went into action against the kangaroo courts, which they correctly viewed as aimed at all unions. A flyer was distributed, headed "Stay Away Notice," and signed by W. H. Hayden, organizer of the United Brotherhood of Carpenters and Joiners, informing carpenters that "the Kangaroo Court of the self-appointed Law and Order League of Bisbee, Arizona has declared Bisbee an open shop in all building crafts, with the determination to disrupt every Union in the city and make collective bargaining an impossibility."[24]

On July 21 an order was issued to arrest for vagrancy all unemployed men in Bisbee who had failed to apply to the so-called Investigation Committee for "clearance cards." Sheriff Wheeler began a roundup of the unemployed that morning.[25]

* * *

Keeping with a tradition of vigilante justice, which in its shamelessness included the selling of postcards depicting lynchings, the first advertisement for postcards of the deportation appeared on July 19, a set of them available at Sasse's Candy Store.[26] Days later, the set taken by local photographer Dix was available, twenty-four photos for $2.00, available either as postcards or "paper prints for albums." Potential purchasers were warned that "orders [would be] filled in rotation." The ad was accompanied by two photos of deportees being led from town, headed "IWW agitators get a free ride out of Bisbee."[27]

The purge of the working population continued unabated. Two weeks after the deportation, "vagrants by the tens and twenties are being rounded up by the county and city authorities." The local paper of record minced no words: the arrest for "vagrancy" of men with no visible means of support was part of a "general 'clean up' of the city [which] has been and will continue systematically."[28]

The measures taken after the deportation was suspected to even include the opening of the mails. Frank Vaughan, in concluding a letter on the situation in the town, wrote to Governor Hunt that "I have every reason to think that your letters to me was [*sic*] opened here so am going to post this in some other town."[29]

* * *

Cleansing Bisbee was absolutely central to the life of the city, and despite the driving out of strikers and their supporters, despite the destruction of unions, despite kangaroo courts that blocked entrance to the city to anyone with a past tainted by union activity or dissent of any kind, Bisbeeites were warned more than two weeks after the deportation that "the time of greatest peril to the Warren District is right now." The front-page article on July 28 is worth quoting in extenso:

> Just because Bisbee arose in her might and drove some twelve hundred red flaggers out of the district is no sign that her work is done. Our real task is yet to do. WE MUST KEEP THEM OUT! Many of the small fry escaped the meshes of the net.... They must be gathered up one at a time, and ousted from the community....
>
> The IWW and its sympathizers do not work. They have only one object, one ambition, and that is to hinder those who do work...The only thought behind their unwashed, hairy faces is to tear down, cripple and destroy....
>
> Any citizen of the Warren district who allows himself to be lulled to sleep in the thought that his work was finished on the morning of July 12, is sure to have a most unpleasant awakening....
>
> Every citizen must do his part. Keep a look out for the vag and the loafer and the agitator. When you see one or hear one, spot him and tell the authorities....
>
> The deputies who were at the city's borders were greeted as heroes, each "with a rifle in the hollow of his arm.... Their alertness and tireless vigilance and stern determination should be an inspiration to every one of us here in this sheltered valley." They were a model for the shopkeeper, the clerk, merchant, miner, worker, lawyer and office man, all of who were abjured to "DO YOUR PART."[30]

Despite the climate of fear that had been installed, not everyone in Bisbee was in favor of what had occurred, and if active resistance wasn't possible, more passive forms occurred. Mary Bugen, who was a young girl at the time of the roundup and deportation, remembered that her father wore a white armband and that afterwards she and her brother were ostracized: people said about her and her family, "Forget them, they're scabs, their father's a scab."[31]

* * *

Weeks had passed and still the vigilantes were at work—now against lawyers for the deportees. Fred Moore, a lawyer from Los Angeles and best known as primary counsel for the IWW, was fresh from his defense of the IWWs in Everett and, more recently, a visit to the deportees in Columbus, where he'd promised to visit the men's families in Bisbee. Moore came to Bisbee on July 30, bearing a letter of introduction from Arizona governor Campbell to Mayor Erickson and Sheriff Wheeler requesting that Moore be allowed to undertake his business unhindered. Upon arrival in town, Moore was told Wheeler was in his office in Tombstone, and Erickson was tied up and wouldn't be free till late afternoon. He met with the kangaroo court that was then deciding the fate of a returned deportee. He was then ushered into a room where some twenty-five to fifty men were gathered, who told him that Wheeler was out of state and that he would not in fact be meeting with the mayor. The vigilante group, which never left Moore's side except when he was in his hotel room—and even then kept an eye on him from inside and outside the hotel—informed Moore that his visit was "highly undesirable" and that his "presence would give moral support to the men and women who sympathized with the deported men."[32] The *Daily Review* reported that when the conference was over, Moore "was advised to go to Columbus or some other point on his itinerary." Phrased less delicately, after spending six hours in Bisbee, informing the governor of his treatment, and meeting with Rosa McKay for only two or three minutes, he was ordered by the Loyalty League to leave, dragged from the Copper Queen Hotel, telling the clerk that "a guest was being forcibly ejected without reason," and "forcibly placed in an automobile." He was taken to Osborn Junction south of Bisbee and placed on a train to Douglas and points east.[33]

Despite all the hardship, the solidarity between Bisbee and Butte had not been forgotten. Congresswoman Jeannette Rankin, on August 7, 1917, in her first speech on the floor of Congress, called for the nationalization of all "metalliferous mines" in order to better serve national needs. She also spoke of the telegrams she'd received from Butte miners requesting protection after the Bisbee Deportation.[34] She was applauded loudly when she attacked the "copper trust," whose actions and attitudes she said were the source of the problems in the mines of the West.[35]

The strike in Butte had led to one of the great tragedies of Wobbly history, the lynching of Wob militant Frank Little. Little had broken his leg in Oklahoma while driving to Butte, where he was headed to take charge of the strike. He gave a speech at the Butte ballpark and then returned to his hotel room. Six armed men broke into his room, beat him, carried him from his room, and attached him with a rope to the back of a car. They dragged him behind the car to a railroad trestle outside Butte, pulled him up by the neck, and left his dead body hanging.[36] The note pinned to Frank Little's body read, "First and last warning! 3-7-77 D-C-S-S-W-T," and the *Butte Daily Post* explained that "the six letters total the number of men supposed to have taken part in the hanging."[37] Another theory is that, despite the hatred between the IWW and the IUMMSW, they were both targets of vigilante violence. An alternative theory is that these were the initials of the men the vigilantes were aiming for next: six members of the IUMMSW.[38]

* * *

Investigation of the roundup by state authorities was going on at the highest levels, with both Governor Campbell and state attorney general Wiley E. Jones spending part of a week in Bisbee, gathering information, though they refused to discuss any of their findings when they left town on August 13.[39] It would take almost two weeks for their findings to be made public.

Despite the investigation, with the deportees still in Columbus, though now free to roam freely, the anti-Wob, anti-union frenzy in Bisbee continued well into August. Sheriff Wheeler had warrants prepared on charges of vagrancy and inciting riot that would be used to arrest anyone on the list of deportees who tried to return. The list was in the hands of the city officials, and whenever a man appeared in Bisbee whose name was among the deportees "he is immediately arrested. He is then brought before one of the several courts of the Warren District and the case disposed of." The idea was to "rid and keep rid the city and District of those who were eliminated from Bisbee on July 12." All of this expressed "the determination of the people of the city ... to continue without IWWism or its kindred evils."[40]

Governor Campbell insisted that he would stay in Cochise County "until the officers of Cochise County promise to keep within the law, or the situation is otherwise cleaned up in its entirety." His investigation was aimed at determining whether residents' constitutional rights were being respected, and he warned, "Only the armed force of a State or a federal force will overcome these unlawful deportations as well as denials of entrance into Bisbee as now conducted."[41]

After this, Wheeler, Mayor Erickson, and their aides could only feel relief at the findings of Governor Campbell's investigation, in which IWWism "is flayed ... and acknowledgement made that complaints, alleging that relief was not being extended to many needy families, were erroneous."[42]

The word "flayed" is hardly strong enough for the way the IWW was treated by the governor. The principles of the IWW are described as "a stench in the nostrils of decent Americans" and "a menace to civic well-being and industrial progress in time of peace." This was not enough for the governor, for he went on to claim that "such doctrines, during a state of war, is treason."

The governor's report was a point-by-point attack on everything done by the strikers: the presentation of the demands to the companies and the calling of the strike without a vote are described as "unfair"; their tactics, particularly the "preaching of impossible doctrines and ridiculing [of] national war policies" resulted in "a reign of lawlessness, invading the constitutional rights of the whole body politic of the district." Wheeler is approvingly quoted as providing an explanation that was seldom used by supporters and participants in the roundup: federal military authorities failing to provide relief during the strike—because they felt the situation did not require it,—and the "legal machinery" unable to cope with a situation where the number of prisoners was beyond the capability of local jails to hold the men, and "desiring to effect the removal of a menace," Wheeler decided to deport the twelve hundred men to New Mexico. It apparently never occurred to the governor and the attorney general to ask why the men were sent across state lines and forced to travel 180 miles. Were there no jails in Arizona? Campbell maintained that $1,200 worth of subsistence goods were distributed to the men on the trains, "but much of this was destroyed in anger." As for family members left behind, they were all taken care of, except in cases of "concealment or stubbornness." The governor made the unsubstantiated claim that the actions of the mine operators, the Citizens' Protective League, and the Workmen's Loyalty League were aimed strictly and solely at the IWW and not against "regularly organized unions," except in isolated cases. That there were nowhere near twelve hundred Wobblies in Bisbee is carefully elided.

Nevertheless, in his conclusions, Campbell describes the deportation as "illegal." Everything done was justified and should have been done, but none of it was legal. Contradicting all known facts, the governor claimed that "lawlessness" prevailed in the Warren District, but instead of sending out deputies in the morning hours, "arrests should have been made and trial given under proper jurisdiction." He was clear: "The deportations of July 12 and those subsequent thereto were illegal." Campbell, in this, quoted the response of President Wilson on the deportation: "May I not respectfully urge the great danger of citizens taking the law into their own hands." Not only the deportation, for the president averred that the kangaroo courts determining who can and can't enter Bisbee were "without legal status and unjustified" and insisted they immediately cease.

Campbell ordered that anyone arrested for infringing the law "must be accorded a thorough investigation before a legally constituted tribunal ... [and] the rights of Sheriffs and deputies to search and detain must be exercised with caution and judgment."

The governor, after excoriating the IWW, ended by calling for labor and capital to work in harmony; for both sides, in this age of "federation and combination," to refrain from dictatorial actions. "Organized capital and organized labor must know that in the end they must be brought into harmony with one another in the interest of the general public."[43]

* * *

It was possible to fight the decisions of the kangaroo courts, but few availed themselves of the opportunity. Judge Frank Thomas of the police court asserted that only six or seven men contested its decision.[44]

Keeping people in line, getting them to continue to support the authorities both in their past actions and going forward, whatever critics might say, was a priority, and on August 23 activities aimed at ensuring support from women and Serbians were held. At the YMCA, in the heart of Bisbee, the Women's Loyalty League was founded and decreed that, despite the governor's chastisement of the sheriff, "we most heartily commend the action of our fearless sheriff for his loyal and patriotic stand in the deportation of the undesirable element on July 12, 1917."

Serbs, who were a significant portion of the mining population of the Warren District, whose homeland was part of the Austro-Hungarian Empire, and who were, as a result, suspected of enemy loyalty, needed to prove their bona fides as Americans in the eyes of many. Indeed, on the day of the roundup, the *Review* published on its front page a telegram sent to two members of the Serbian community of Bisbee written by the inventor W. I. Pupin, warning his compatriots to have nothing to do with the strike, telling them that he had "reliable information that strike called by Industrial Workers of the World is directed against allies by German interests. Please get Serbians in Arizona to do everything they can to defeat this German move."[45] John J. Grgurevich, the secretary of the South Slavic National Council, headquartered in Washington, then came to Bisbee to "encourage his countrymen to loyalty to the United States." Grgurevich, a veteran and special agent of the United States Department of Justice who had left the latter position to "help his people," came to Bisbee to discover "if my people were not misled by false stamen [*sic*] of labor leaders who are really foes of labor." He felt that anyone who did follow the IWW did so in error: "I am sure my people did not realize what their action meant when they followed the IWW agitators in that strike to close the copper mines and thereby cripple and hamper our government." The government, he claimed, was an ally of Serbia.

Grgurevich believed a hundred of his countrymen (the list that's come down to us shows eighty-two Serbs, thirty-five Croats, one Bosnian, fourteen from Dalmatia, and three Slavonians, for a minimum of 135—which puts southern Slavs third behind Mexicans and Americans) were being held in Bisbee and Columbus, and he intended to "impress upon all the Slavic workers the necessity of not going on strike during the war. It is disloyal to do so." That they did do so meant they were "misguided," and again, despite their presence among the strikers, the patriotic Serb was "already convinced that my countrymen were satisfied with their wages. Something else was behind their action. Intimidation for one thing."[46]

The meeting for which Grgurevich came to Bisbee was held on August 26, and at it were passed a series of resolutions aimed at affirming the patriotism of the Serbian and Croatian communities and their opposition to anything IWW. Coming on the heels of the deportation, and at a time when their countrymen were fighting the US in Europe, the nearly hysterical tone of patriotism of the resolutions can cause little surprise. The first resolution affirmed that the South Slavs "have always been, are now, and desire to remain unequivocally and absolutely loyal to the United States." All of the resolutions that followed flowed from this: that a "patriotic and loyal workingman must not undertake any steps which brings the interests of this country and its industrial and military preparedness into jeopardy"; it spoke of how the conditions in the mines were so good that "we had no reason, nor have any to complain, and still less to go on strike or sympathize with it." The assembled Slavs "positively assert[ed] that we have not, nor intend to adhere nor to sympathize with the principles of an organization known under the name of Industrial Workers of the World." They of course "emphatically condemned" the strike and considered the deportation— called here "the measures adopted" to be a "war measure," which the citizens, according to their belief, thought they were obliged to adopt.

The committee expressed their regret that "a considerable number of our countrymen" were victims of the roundup, convinced as the assembled were that they were simply "misled," and hoped that no one from among them "is under suspicion of having committed anything for which the citizens should or could regard him as an undesirable resident." Knowing that the large number of South Slavs rounded up placed them in an uncomfortable position, they expressed pride in their group's having maintained the confidence and respect of "this community."

Who "this community" was was made clear, as the resolutions were to be submitted to the Citizens' Protective League, the authorities, and the mining companies. This new committee of Slavs had but thirty-seven members.[47]

The great fear that had seized the mine owners across the West and their allies in government continued apace, and if the Wobs continued to be the main target, other unions too were in the gunsights. Despite the distance between them, what happened in Montana was intimately tied to Arizona mines; the Anaconda smelters in Washoe were shut down after a strike call of the IUMMSW, defined as a "radical threat," putting fifteen thousand men out of work.

The *Review* continued to make war on the IWW on its front page, showing that the courts around the country continued to work on behalf of the mining companies, making use of the now-standard canards against the IWW. A judge in Spokane refused a writ of habeas corpus for the district secretary of the IWW and seventeen of his fellow workers, based on "evidence that many Industrial Workers of the World accused of fomenting strikes in the northwest are German citizens and draft evaders." Even more damning, the prosecuting attorney testified that "many of them were disbelievers in religion, marriage or organized government." Wobs in the northwest were alleged to have sabotaged fruit trees and to have beaten and thrown men off trains.[48]

When accusations against IWWs for their politics weren't enough, accusations of personal turpitude were often attributed to them. Repeating a report from the *Los Angeles Times*, Bisbeeites learned that IWW attorney Fred Moore, "who is contemplating a visit to the Warren district in the interests of the deported men [in Columbus]," was being sued by his wife for divorce on the basis of desertion. Saying his whereabouts were currently unknown, though he was thought to be in Phoenix, his estranged spouse complained that "what money he has sent during the past year has not gone far toward supporting her and their three-year-old child."

Moore, the complaint continued, "has been giving a great deal of his time to the defense of IWW's." He had allegedly been paid $4,000 for his defense of them in Seattle but had only sent Mrs. Moore $100 of that sum.[49]

Though the local press had long reported that the mines were back to normal, as late as September 1, *Solidarity*, the IWW paper, was reporting that "the Bisbee parasites [are] desperate." While the workers in Columbus were "sitting tight," back in Bisbee "the mines ... are in bad shape and the bosses are more than worried, they are desperate." Scabs were certainly working the mines, but "it takes miners to produce ore," so the companies were placing ads in Texas papers to encourage "farmer boys" to come work in Bisbee. According to the Wobs, the production in the mines was reduced from the usual 185–190 cars daily before to the strike to "not even fifty." For the IWW, "this certainly refutes the mine managers' statement that the strike is broken and that the mines are working almost normally."[50]

The bad blood generated in July continued, not sparing even those who held guns on the strikers and pushed them into the boxcars. Sol Morgenstern was a merchant in Lowell who had served as a deputy on July 12, and whose name appears on the regularly published lists in the *Daily Review* of business and professional members of the Citizens' Protective League. These ads, which also listed those who were not members of the League, were aimed at encouraging residents to do business with the former and shun the latter. Morgenstern—a Jew from the East Coast—had been the subject of rumors in town that he was an enemy alien. So serious was the situation that he felt obliged to send an open letter to be published in the newspaper, insisting that reports that he had gone to New York so he could claim exemption from the draft because he was an enemy alien were false. He wrote that "I wish the public to know I claimed no exemption. I have my first papers and have applied for my second, so that I could serve my country, and I wish the public to know I am willing to serve in any capacity that I can be of use."[51]

The impunity with which the vigilantes continued to act was demonstrated in the fall when a delegation from the AF of L appointed a committee of five to go to Bisbee to report on conditions there. Carrying credentials from the governor, the committee was greeted in Bisbee by armed vigilantes "who stopped the unionists in full view of a regiment of federal troops and commanded them to 'get out of Bisbee.'" The union said that "every Arizona official, from the Governor down, has acknowledged that the stand of the unionists is correct, but refuses to do anything."[52]

That the situation in Arizona had barely improved after the departure of the Mediation Commission in November, indeed, even after its scathing report was issued that same month, can be seen from a letter sent by the adjutant general of Arizona to the Chief Military Bureau in Washington, DC.[53]

Like the Mediation Commission, the army described the "military" activities going on in Arizona as carried out by "illegal organizations that have been organized from a supposedly patriotic motive, and that are known as loyalty leagues." Acting governor Campbell was directly involved in these activities, since it was he who had procured a large cache of weapons and ammunition that he then had sent to a minister in Globe whom he addressed as Major F. M. Johnson, Jr., the adjutant general, specifying that "this man has no commission as major and is known as the head of the Loyalty League at Globe, Arizona."

Virtually everything about these leagues and their being armed was illegal. Arizona law forbade any body of men from military-style drills except at educational institutions where military science is taught, and though the governor had been advised of the violation of this law by the "home guards … he either neglects or is disinclined to take any action for the enforcement of this law."

The governor's active support of the arming and exercising of the leagues had dire effects and had culminated in the Bisbee Deportation. "I feel confident," he wrote, "that had this law been enforced from the commencement of this year, many other violations of law, covered by the report of the Secretary of Labor, would not have occurred." Governor Campbell's responsibility was abundantly clear, since he hadn't taken any action against the violation of state law.

The adjutant general recommended that sufficient troops be maintained in Arizona "to promptly suppress any insurrection which might arise, and TO ENFORCE THE ORDERS OF THE COMMISSION, OF WHICH SECRETARY WILSON IS A MEMBER, ISSUED UNDER AUTHORITY OF THE PRESDIENT OF THE UNITED STATES, FOR THE CONTINUATION OF THE PRODUCTION OF COPPER IN THE MINES OF ARIZONA."

That it is the employers who are the insurrectionists decried above is made clearer later in this letter, when the adjutant general outlines that trouble was feared in Bisbee, Globe, or Clifton-Morenci. He goes on to say that "it is the absolute intention of the *employees* to carry out the agreement, but if the same willingness is not shown by the *employers* it is possible there might be further trouble" (emphasis added). The adjutant general even named the culprits: "The districts that I have mentioned where further trouble might possibly occur are those controlled or dominated by the Phelps Dodge corporation."

Four and a half months after the deportation, the employers were still acting with impunity. As well as being a threat to liberties, this constituted a threat to the country's ability to meet its war needs. The adjutant general wrote that federal forces needed to protect the industries key to "purposes of the war." The mine owners, who had claimed strikers and Wobblies were a threat to the war effort were revealed as the actual threat.

Months after the deportation, men were still being "vagged," charged with vagrancy, and sentenced to ninety days in jail or given two days to leave town. One deportee, who returned to town at the beginning of November in order to testify before the Presidential Mediation Commission, was "vagged" anyway and, instead of testifying, worked that day as prison labor on the county road.[54]

* * *

The hatred between the IUMMSW and the IWW was no secret, and the former's disavowal of its Bisbee members who participated in the strike was a shameful episode. But this union, too, wrote a letter about the situation in Arizona, addressed to, among others, Labor Secretary Wilson, in which, echoing the adjutant general, they said that the Mediation Commission made a serious mistake "in allowing the Loyalty League or any similar organization to remain in existence." In doing so, they left in force an organization that had established itself as a law-breaking body ... a body that was organized for the distinct purpose of oppressing the workers." In contrast, the IWW defined the Loyalty League as "merely a blacklisting system, unheard of, yes, undreamed of by even the most stringent provisions required by any of the companies under their system of employing men before the war."[55]

If the President's Mediation Commission would soon come to Arizona to fairly investigate all that had occurred there, other arms of the federal government acted in a more expected fashion. As the sweep of IWW offices across the country was going on, the headline of the *Bisbee Daily Review* on September 6, 1917, screamed, "Government takes step to kill treason of IWW." Arizona IWW offices in Globe were raided, and "among many articles seized by the authorities in the raid on IWW headquarters were a number of copies of a German paper published in New York."

Despite the headline, and the allegation in the wire service story that "many Austrians" were in the ranks of the IWW "who have been active in stirring up strife intended to hamper American industries, doing work handled by Germans before the United States declared a state of war with Germany," the paper had to admit that, "continued investigation has failed, it is understood, to connect these activities with German money."[56]

* * *

Bisbee had been tamed. In December 1919 a special agent at the Bureau of Investigation (predecessor to the FBI), reported that the Communist Party, the new bugaboo of the authorities, had no presence in the Bisbee-Douglas area.[57] A few months later, in March 1920, IWW organizer John Graham was arrested in Bisbee while "soliciting" individuals to join the organization. The pretext for his arrest was his distribution of a handbill, headed "The Crime of Centralia," about the railroading of IWW members in Centralia, Washington, for murder. The authorities in Bisbee had promulgated a law that banned the distribution of flyers without a city council permit. Perhaps in another period this would have led to a free-speech fight in Bisbee, but the IWW had been crushed nationally, and unionism had been squelched in the town.[58]

CHAPTER SEVEN

THE PRESIDENTIAL MEDIATION COMMISSION

We are not a democratic government,
that in fact we are a plutocratic government

On September 19, 1917, President Wilson, following a recommendation made by Secretary of Labor William B. Wilson, issued an order establishing a commission to investigate the events in Bisbee and labor conditions in the Pacific Northwest.

The president's order attempted to be evenhanded, speaking of "charges of misconduct and injustice that representatives of employers and of employees have made against each other." The commission was not to be focused on the past, but rather the president wanted to see "some kind of working arrangement arrived at for the future, particularly during the period of war, on a basis that will be fair to all parties concerned."

The commission's members were Secretary Wilson, Colonel J. L. Spangler of Pennsylvania, Verner Z. Reed of Colorado, John H. Walker of Illinois, E. P. Marsh of Washington, and—most importantly, as it would turn out—Felix Frankfurter of New York as secretary.

The commission's remit called for it to visit each of the western state governors to inform them that the group was there to lend "sympathetic counsel and aid to the state government in the development of better understanding between laborers and employers, and also to deal with employers and employees in a conciliatory spirit." In order to do so it was authorized to call conferences between the two parties whenever it deemed them advisable, but it should "also endeavor to learn the real causes for any discontent which may exist on either side, not by the formal process of public hearings but by getting into touch with workmen and employers by the more informal process of personal conversation."[1]

Ten days later, the commissioners left for Arizona, the first state to be visited by the group, which also planned to stop in California, Utah, Nevada, Oregon, Washington, Idaho, Montana, Wyoming, Colorado, and possibly New Mexico. Among the issues it was expected to address was the allegation made by the AF of L that the IWW in the West was being financed by corporations in order to "discredit" the rest of the labor movement.[2]

During the hearings, Secretary of Labor William B. Wilson, a former union organizer himself, spelled out the function of his commission:

> This commission is here because of the great need of the government for copper. The government is vitally interested in the production of copper; the government is vitally interested in the production of ships; and the government is vitally interested in the production of lumber. The labor troubles in this western country naturally made the President uneasy, because this western country is the greatest producer of copper, and it is the producer of ships, and it is the producer of the great bulk of the spruce lumber necessary for the manufacture of airplanes. Anything that interrupts the continued production of these things is of vital importance to the government.[3]

The commission made its way to Bisbee on November 1, arriving there from Clifton in two special cars. The train was described by the *Review* as the "Mecca" for the many who wanted to speak to the commissioners, and though the names of some of those who were called to see Secretary Wilson and his fellow commissioners *was* known, what they were asked was not.

The commission was already able to boast of success in mediation of active strikes, informing the president on October 31 that they had effected a settlement in the strike that had started in July in Clifton-Morenci. Boasting that the settlement would result in the production of ten million pounds of copper per month and the employment of over five thousand men, Secretary Wilson credited the settlement to "the spirit of cooperation with which the commission was met both by the managers, the national as well as the local leaders of the strikers, and the patriotic service rendered by Judge Ernest W. Lewis of Arizona."[4] Wilson and his fellow commissioners thus entered Bisbee full of confidence.

Organized labor, in the form of the Warren District Trades Assembly, an AF of L group, had already written the commission with its testimony, signed by a minister and leaders of the painters', electricians', butchers', and carpenters' unions.

The Trades Assembly testified that the peace and quiet that currently reigned in Bisbee was not that "of a free community, but the quiet of a group of men and women intimidated to silence by an autocratic power." Since the day of the roundup, "the powers in control of this district have trampled at will upon the legal safeguards of our citizens." The deportation was "a clear example of the triumph of the most atrocious misuses of power of the capitalists in defiance of the democratic rights of American Citizens."

In keeping with AF of L policy, they stressed they were "not in sympathy with IWW methods and tactics. We have fought them at every turn." They went further, though, claiming that "we feel positive that the mining companies have encouraged the IWW men to come into this camp in order to disrupt the local miner's organization affiliating with the AF of L." Even so, the accusations that the IWW workers were planning on wrecking the town, and themselves deporting its prominent citizens, were "of a piece with the method of the Teutonic autocracy which, when it wishes to perpetrate a crime in defiance of all the rules of warfare it first accuses its enemies of having done that which it intends to do."

The union men engaged in understatement when they wrote, "We cannot feel that Mr. Wheeler was uninfluenced by officials of the mining corporations," and were more than suspicious of the source of the money used to pay the deputies, and requested that the commission investigate the source of the funding.

It is to the AF of L organization's credit that they directly pointed their finger at Phelps Dodge and cast doubts on the spontaneity of the roundup on July 12. They wrote that they wanted to call attention "to the fact that the El Paso and Southwestern train was ready for the men whom the 'Loyalty' League had at the tips of their rifles on July 12th." They reminded the commission that the president of Phelps Dodge was at the same time the vice president of the railroad that carried the deportees into the desert.

But that wasn't all. They didn't hesitate to assert that "the mining companies, through the Phelps Dodge store, furnished rifles to many of those who acted as gun men," guns they were all but certain were the ones distributed to deputies at the post office, giving the entire roundup the air of a government-endorsed action.

They called on the commissioners to find out who was blacklisting men involved in the strike or deportation, but they ended by warning the commissioners that "many who could give you convincing testimony would not dare to do so for fear of consequences." In fact, the writers of the memorandum insisted that "those appointed to compose it do so at the risk of being impoverished or driven from the district."[5]

This statement from the labor council contained much that the Mediation Commission would address in the coming days.

* * *

It was thought that there would be a predictable order in which the men were being called before the commission: labor sympathizers, followed by "unattached miners," then businessmen, and finally the mine operators. At no point would any Mexicans be interviewed. This, indeed, turned out to be more or less the case. The visit to Bisbee was the first regional deportation to be dealt with, Jerome being the next city scheduled on their list.[6]

By November 3, the commission had already spoken to Sheriff Wheeler, local businessmen, deportees, and various workers, but still offered no comment on their work as they prepared to speak to the mine operators that day.

In California, a strike was feared by the workers of the Pacific Telephone and Telegraph Company, and the Mediation Commission was contemplating leaving Arizona for California to settle the dispute preemptively.[7] The work in Arizona being so complex, this counterplan quickly fell by the wayside, as Secretary Wilson telegraphed the mediator on the spot in San Francisco to tell him they wouldn't be able to reach the coast for two weeks, and the commission settled in to meet with the mine operators.

The commission made clear its sentiments on the deportation on many occasions during the hearings. If the mine owners were concerned that the IWW were German agents, the commissioners were concerned that the mine owners were acting like Prussians. Commission head Wilson expressed shock early in its sessions that "following the hue and cry that had gone up all over this country against the deportation of the Belgians by the Germans, and right in the face of that expression of horror on the part of our people, that people in responsible positions, intelligent men, should be parties to the wholesale deportation of that time. It is one of the strange things of it to my mind."[8]

The commissioners homed in on a key question posed by the deportation: By what authority was it carried out? Sheriff Wheeler showed little concern for expressing his justification in legal terms, responding "in case of great disorder ... I am empowered to use all necessary force." He was open about the absence of a basis in law for his actions: "Perhaps everything I did wasn't legal. I tried to make it legal as far as I could." Having already admitted that there had been little violence, merely threats during the strike, he made the roundup a result of thought crime. The conflict in Bisbee was "between the man who loved his country and the man who didn't. It became a question of, 'Are you an American or are you not?'" How was this determined? "Well, we asked and stationed men at the gates."[9]

On the matter of legality and jurisdiction, Secretary of Labor Wilson, whose exchanges with Wheeler were sometimes heated, said that he was personally willing to admit that everything that had happened in Bisbee was within Wheeler's jurisdiction (though he makes no mention of it being legal), but that shipping the men out of town, out of state, meant exceeding his authority, as did the cutting off of communication with the town. Though it's difficult to understand the distinctions drawn by Secretary Wilson, it is nevertheless clear that the commission had already decided at the hearings that the sheriff and other authorities had crossed lines in Bisbee that were unacceptable.[10]

If loyalty was the issue, as Wheeler said, the commissioners were puzzled by the deportation of so many men who were registered for the draft, and who had then and since been blocked from reporting to the local draft board.

Sheriff Wheeler disputed the numbers of men who had registered for the draft in the army's official count—namely, 472. In any event, Wheeler doubted the draft issue was a real one since there were so many foreigners among the strikers. "I counted one hundred and ten one morning on the streets of Lowell on the picket line ... and I believe there were three Americans among the bunch." He was certain there couldn't even have been twenty men among the deportees who reported for registration.[11]

The commissioners were not convinced by testimony given by a committee of members of the Warren District Commercial Club and the Citizens' Protective League. Claims of IWW control of the strikers and of the presence of professional pickets were made, and the county engineer, J. C. Ryan, head of this committee of business and vigilante interests, read a statement from Sheriff Wheeler that he "had reasons to believe that many Mexicans had Villa rifles cached away and still believe so." As would be expected, Ryan also made claims of threats of violence, alleging that lunch pails were being taken away from men who broke the strike![12]

Ryan and his companions attempted to appeal to any possible xenophobia lurking in the members of the Mediation Commission, telling them that workers' wives "were being visited by delegations of Austrians and sometimes Mexicans while husbands were at work. These delegations never failed to tell the women they visited that unless their husbands ceased work their homes would be blown up."[13] Ryan later spoke of women reporting that strikers "would blow up certain buildings," though under questioning he had to admit he didn't know who precisely was making these threats.[14]

The commission session with a committee of managers was a testy one. Secretary Wilson asked on what legal grounds the deputies, both those officially sworn in and those serving unofficially—supposedly four thousand men—acted. "What legal grounds did the sheriff or any of you people act upon in deporting people from this community into another state?" Ryan punted, saying, "That is a question that should be asked of the sheriff himself as the chief peace officer of the County." An important question that Ryan also couldn't answer was how the deputies, deputized in Cochise County, Arizona, maintained their status when crossing into another state. Secretary Wilson grew frustrated, both with Ryan and with the general situation, returning to the Belgian example: "I wonder whether or not those who had counselled with the sheriff, who had advised with the sheriff along the lines of this question of policy had stopped to consider the similarity of this and the practice of the Germans in deporting the Belgians, which had horrified the entire world." Ryan fought back, saying it was different, because "the Germans invaded Belgium and the IWWs invaded Bisbee."[15]

The commissioners had already pointed out that the deportation was being used to give the US a black eye on another front: in revolutionary Russia. There, "a certain element that have gone across from this country ... for the purpose of promoting the interests of Germany ... [is using it] against us with the Russian workmen and peasants, trying to make them think we are not a democratic government, that in fact we are a plutocratic government."[16]

Nothing Ryan said was making the events of July 12 and the months after more acceptable. He went on to assert that 59 percent of those deported didn't work in the mines, to which Wilson asked about the other 41 percent. "Consequently, that would mean in the neighborhood of five hundred of these people, at least five hundred of those people who were picked up bodily and deported from their own homes, from places where they were earning their livelihood were sent into a strange land, and not only sent into a strange land, but sent into a desert land."[17] Ryan's response was that the deportees could have remained in Bisbee, "if they remained as loyal Americans."[18]

The Mediation Commission had been made aware of the blocking of an August visit to Bisbee from the Arizona Federation of Labor, and commission secretary Frankfurter wanted to know if that visit would have been illegal. Ryan appealed to a different set of standards: was it unlawful for them to come to Bisbee? Ryan said there was nothing unlawful about it, but everyone in the community who had gone through all the "strife and grief. Every man who owns property and was a property-owner and taxpayer in Bisbee was certainly interested as to who came in to stir up more strife and trouble."

To Ryan, anyone who made threats was necessarily a Wob, but Wilson wanted a more precise definition. How, he asked, "do you know any of those twelve hundred people deported were any more guilty of those threats than (roundup organizer) Dr. Bledsoe? How do you know that they were guilty?" Ryan's reasoning was circular: "Because they were affiliated and associated with the IWWs. They were in control of this whole situation, and naturally they must have belonged to it."[19]

As he ended his testimony, Ryan told his listeners that "all of us here were connected with the deportation under the direction of the sheriff, and if we have done wrong so has the sheriff, and if there is any recourse by the civil courts or otherwise we are all subjects to that recourse." Wilson reminded Ryan the commission wasn't there to prosecute, but admonished him that all those who rounded up the men should have considered whether their acts were not "a conspiracy to deprive those people of their rights under the constitution."[20]

By the time these hearings took place the government of which Secretary Wilson was a member had made a radical step in the war against the IWW, raiding offices all over the country. E. E. Ellinwood of Phelps Dodge turned the tables on the commission, which had accused the companies and deputies of imitating the Prussians the US was fighting in Europe. Felix Frankfurter spoke of the "ferment" left behind by the deportation, to which Ellinwood said, "You might as well say that the raids that the government has made in Denver and Chicago have had the same effect." Frankfurter was unshaken, explaining that the difference was that the raids were carried out by the government, and that the Copper Queen was not the government. Ellinwood was undeterred. "It was done by the sheriff and legally appointed deputies; he simply anticipated the Department of Justice; he did exactly what the Department of Justice has done since, except as to the deportation."[21]

It was an odd tactic on the part of the mine owners' representatives to focus on the nefarious role of foreigners in the strike and of their presence and actions as necessitating the deportation. After all, the commission's head was born in Scotland, and its secretary and most forceful member was a foreign-born Jew, Felix Frankfurter of Vienna. But so ingrained was their suspicion of anyone not native-born that Arthur Houle felt at liberty to testify that "the trouble makers at the time of the strike were mostly foreigners." Frankfurter demurred, saying their names "sound to me very much like American names," to which Houle replied, "The leaders are American, but the men who were the forces or the biggest part of the forces that remained out on strike, were all aliens."[22]

Continuing along that track, Houle said that all but eighteen of the fifty-three aliens he had succeeded in selling Liberty Bonds to had cashed them in before July 18, and "I think that situation goes to prove that inasmuch as these fellows withdrew their money before the 18th of July, they were not good citizens." Secretary Wilson pointed out that had they been bad citizens they'd never have purchased them at all, a point that held no water for Houle.[23]

If Frankfurter and Wilson both spoke warmly of America as a land welcoming of immigrants, fellow commissioner John H. Walker joined the mine owners in pointing out that labor had vehemently supported the 80 percent law, which required 80 percent of all those hired in companies with more than five employees, to be American. He added "they tried to get that law through at that time for the very same reason that the employers in Bisbee are now insisting that Bisbee be made an American camp and that only American citizens be employed. At that time the Mexican alien, as they saw it, was being used to reduce their standard of wages and to prevent them from making progress ... and the companies at that time bitterly opposed it, and there is no use to try to be camouflaging about it."[24]

* * *

The same day that the report was issued, the Mediation Commission sent a letter to representatives of the mining companies as well as IUMMSW head Charles Moyer, laying out an agreement as to how disputes at the mines were to be handled in the future. The letter contained five points:

1. —No man shall be refused employment or be discharged or discriminated against in his work because he does or does not belong to a union.

2. —Grievance committees representing the employees and made up of active workers were to be recognized by management when grievances arose and were presented to them.

3. —Should the grievance committee not be able to settle the dispute, a US Administrator was to be called in, whose decision was to be final.

4. —Workers whose case was presented to the administrator were to have representative of their choice.

5. —This machinery was to take the place of strikes and lockouts.

As one would expect, the companies were not enthusiastic. G. H. Dowell, manager of Phelps Dodge, replied that "it is our conviction that the adoption of any such plan in this district is unnecessary in view of existing conditions and this action is contrary to our best judgment."

Harry Clark and W. B. Gohring of C&A "protest[ed] that conditions here did not necessitate the appointment of a federal administrator and maintain that the most harmonious relations exist between ourselves and our employés." Even so, they accepted the missive and continued that "the government assumes responsibility for the successful continuation of our operations during the life of this agreement—we promise our utmost cooperation."

Arthur Houle of Shattuck also accepted the agreement while washing his hands of it: "The Shattuck-Arizona Copper Company does not assume responsibility for the successful outcome of the plan of the President's mediation commission, except as concerns its own part to this agreement."[25]

The ill grace of the mining companies, who had already swept the city clean of opposition to their unimpeded rule, is shocking even today.

* * *

The discontent of the Mediation Commission and its head, Secretary Wilson, was clear from a letter the secretary sent Governor Campbell on November 6, just days after leaving Bisbee and after seeing and hearing about the practices that were continuing in the district months after the deportation and the ending of the strike. Wilson was dismayed that during their visit they "found practices which you have heretofore declared illegal still existing."

The governor wrote that "I am sure that Sheriff Wheeler will fully live up to the assurances he has given and that strict observance of the requirements of the law will be adhered to by him and other officials of Cochise County."[26]

* * *

Only days after completing their work in Bisbee, on November 6, 1917, the Mediation Commission issued a "Report on the Bisbee Deportations," a scathing account of the events in the Warren District. The report reiterates that the work of the commission was aimed at "securing peaceful industrial relations for the future," rather than judging the past, "but it is impossible to make for peace in the future unless the recurrences of such instances as the Bisbee deportation are avoided."[27]

The commissioners, in their exposition, denied there was any need for a strike, the "grievances" not being "of such a nature as to have justified the strike." If so many men went out on strike, it was not because they believed in the demands, but "as is common among workingmen," it was out of loyalty to "the cause represented by the strikers," as well as their desire to avoid being considered and called "scabs." Whatever the grievances, justified or not, the strike was unavoidable in the eyes of the commissioner since there was no neutral mechanism in place "for the adjustment of difficulties between the companies and men." Optimistically, and despite the hostility still demonstrated by the operators just days before during their testimony, the report avers that "a plan has been worked out establishing such machinery" in any future disputes.[28]

A century later there is nothing in their review of events that causes one to dispute their account or its conclusions:

That army officers came to Bisbee at the request of Governor Campbell on June 30 and July 2 and saw no reason for military assistance in the town, and that in fact Bisbee was "peaceful and free from any manifestations of disorder." That the deportation of 1,186 men was carried out by about 2,000 deputies under the command of the sheriff and that the decision was taken the night of July 11 at a meeting at which the managers of the mining companies were in attendance and that "those who planned and directed the deportation purposely abstained from consulting about their plans either with the United States attorney in Arizona, or the law officers of the State or county, or their own legal advisers." The commission dismissed the belief held by those behind it that the strikers and their sympathizers were contemplating violence: "The belief has no justification in the evidence in support of it presented by the parties who harbored it." Even more, the commissioners found that this ungrounded fear was never communicated to the governor so that he could call for further review of the situation by federal troops.

The conclusion of the Mediation Commission's findings about the roundup and deportation are the most damning. It called the deportation, in no uncertain terms, "wholly illegal and without authority in law, either State or Federal." It quoted Governor Campbell concerning the kangaroo courts set up to screen people entering Bisbee as saying that "the constitutional rights of citizens and others have been ignored by processes not provided by law," and that well into August "the function of the local judiciary was usurped by a body which to all intents and purposes was a vigilance committee, having no authority whatever in law."

Since the deportees included men who had registered for the draft, the commissioners also determined that the deportation interfered with the carrying out of the selective service law.

Its recommendations were not such as to strike fear in the hearts of those responsible for the illegal acts, as they called for the ceasing of "all illegal practices" and the right to free movement into and around the Warren District, that appropriate remedies be taken "for the vindication of [Arizona] laws," that the attorney general of the US be informed of the obstacles placed to the implementation of the draft for appropriate action, as should the Interstate Commerce Commission be informed of the blocking of phone and telegraph lines. But it ended by admitting its impotence in an important regard, for "deportation such as we have set forth have not yet been made a Federal offense," it advised the president that he should recommend to Congress that such acts be made criminal.[29]

In carrying out the deportation, the commissioners felt it proved that the "leaders of the enterprise" made use of the local offices of Bell Telephone and exercised censorship over the telephone and telegraph lines in order to prevent news of the roundup and deportation from being spread.

* * *

In January 1918, in the secretary of labor's annual report, his judgment of the mine owners remained harsh. The strikes in the copper areas had resulted in a loss of one hundred million pounds, and the fault in the three months of slowdown was largely down to the owners. Wilson found that the "solidarity of interest among the various owners checks the views of any one liberal owner from prevailing against the autocratic policy of the majority."

The purpose of the commissioners, we will recall, was mediation, the bringing together of the two sides to reach a compromise. But Wilson found that "the managers fail to understand and reach the heart of labor because they have not the aptitude or the training or the time for wise dealing with the problems of industrial relationship." Foreshadowing the field we would come to know as labor relations, he bemoaned the fact that the managers, who are "technical men," lacked the knowledge base to deal with a diverse workforce, and that no one was assigned the task of dealing with labor problems. "In fact it has hardly begun to be realized that labor questions call for the same systematic attention and understanding and skill as do engineering problems."

Adding to this indifference is the complication of the "polyglot character of the workers." Wilson pithily put it that "the industry contains within itself the Balkan problem on a small scale," with unspecified camps, ones much like Bisbee if not Bisbee itself, having twenty-six and thirty-two nationalities among its employees. In camps with fewer nationalities, language and ethnic divisions nevertheless remained, given the presence of non-English speaking Mexican workers. "The seeds of dissension among the workers render difficult their cohesion, and the presence of non-English-speaking labor tends even to greater misunderstanding between men than is normal in American industry." Wilson nowhere here acknowledges the Wobbly demands in support of Mexican workers, who they treated as equals in the struggle, and despairingly notes that "the movement toward Americanization, so fruitful in its results in different parts of the country, has hardly penetrated into these outposts of industry." In those (and these) days of anti-labor frenzy, it was odd to read under the pen of the secretary of labor that the "trade-union movement is the most unifying spirit among the workers." He then went on to give his reading of the etiology of the troubles in Arizona: "The progress of the movement, however, is impeded by the traditional opposition of the companies, by difficulties due to racial diversities, and by internal dissensions in the miners' International. The resulting weakness of the organization deprived the industry of the discipline over workers exercised by stronger unions and gave the less responsible leaders a freer field for activity. Thus a numerically small minority could compel a strike because of the solidarity of workmen in time of strike."[30]

More expected is a furious and wide-ranging letter to Felix Frankfurter from former president Theodore Roosevelt, written after the issuing of the Mediation Commission's report. Though he went through phases where he would pass himself off as a progressive of sorts, Roosevelt's hatred of radicals and affection for a white man's America were among the sentiments that dominated his activities.

Frankfurter had written to Roosevelt about the trial of Tom Mooney, the labor activist sentenced for the bombing of the Preparedness Day parade in San Francisco in 1916, which he had gone to San Francisco to investigate. Roosevelt, never one to show any hesitation in touting his own virtues and attacking others, accused Frankfurter of taking "an attitude which seems to me to be fundamentally that of Trotsky and the other Bolshevik leaders in Russia."

Roosevelt was hardly kinder in his reaction to the Mediation Commission report. After boasting of his friendship with John Greenway, one of the main forces behind the deportation, the former president went for the jugular. "Your report is as thoroughly misleading a document as could be written on the subject." The report was faulty at its heart because of the members' "failure to know, and clearly to set forth, that the IWW is a criminal organization." Its movement within Bisbee was formed with "criminal intent," and though there are no facts to back this up, Roosevelt felt safe saying that "no human being in his senses doubts that the men deported from Bisbee were bent on destruction and murder." Roosevelt asserted that the vigilantes were simply doing what needed to be done and, without evidence, that "no efficient means [were] employed to guard homes, upright and well-behaved citizens from the most brutal kind of lawlessness." Though Sheriff Wheeler had deputized hundreds of men in the days immediately after the strike was declared, Roosevelt claimed that no protection was provided against IWW violence.

Frankfurter, finally, was accused of "excusing men precisely like the Bolsheviki in Russia, who are murderers and encouragers of murder, who are traitors to their allies, to democracy, and to civilization, as well as to the United States."[31]

This letter, it should be remembered, was sent *after* the Everett massacre of 1916, *after* the lynching of Frank Little, *after* the tar and feathering of Wobblies in Oklahoma in 1917, and *after* the raids on the offices of the IWW just weeks earlier.

CHAPTER EIGHT

THE DEPORTATION ON TRIAL

It was a government of the rich and they thought it ought to be
put on the bum and by god they were going to put it on the bum

There would be several trials that followed the deportation, and all of them, whether they involved deportees or deporters, resulted in the perpetrators remaining unpenalized.

Even after the government's blazing criticism of the vigilantes in its reports, the first trial, held in November 1917—thus almost in the immediate aftermath of the work of the Mediation Commission—was of IWW organizer A. S. Embree. The trial was moved, not only from Bisbee but from Cochise County, 150 miles away to Tucson, in neighboring Pima County.

Cochise County attorney John F. Ross attempted to prove that Embree was guilty of destructive rioting based mainly on two incidents: Embree's alleged presence during an alleged beating of a Mexican workingman, as well as his participation in the seemingly eternal and ever-changing alleged threat to blow up a laundry in Bisbee during the strike. Embree's lawyer, A. A. Worsely, concentrated on demonstrating successfully that Embree had only ever advocated peaceful methods and had, moreover, taken no part in any of the alleged violent events.

The evidence against Embree was weak: Deputy Sheriff Tom Hargis testified that he'd seen Embree on the picket line during disturbances and that he had heard threats made by pickets against scabs. He admittedly did not hear Embree make any threats, and the best he could come up with as a damning remark by the Wobbly organizer was his saying that "the government is about to set the price of copper at $6 and we want to get our $5 day flat before they do. We've six of the biggest logging camps shut down and practically every copper mining camp in the west, and we are going to tie up every copper mining camp in the United States. You make your demands. We don't give a damn what they are. We'll stay with you if you stay with us." Not a word of violence or rioting.

Townswoman Helen Grass said she heard a miner speak of turning a machine gun on the Copper Queen dispensary, headquarters of the deputy sheriff, and of blowing up the mines while the scabs were in them. Not a word of Embree.

Embree, described as a "slight, wiry young man," testified that he had lived in Bisbee for a year, working as a mucker at the C&A mine, and was a member of the Executive Council of the metal miners' union.

The committee he was a member of in Bisbee held to a policy against violence, "repeatedly" warning the strikers not to threaten men breaking the strike or to call them scabs or "hurt their feelings," believing that acting kindly and conversing briefly but congenially with the scabs, telling them to "be a man and join us," would encourage them to honor the strike. He admitted to speaking several times in City Park and even meeting with Mayor Erickson.

The jury deliberated five minutes before finding him not guilty.[1]

* * *

Those responsible for the deportation would next be the target of the law. On May 15, 1918, twenty-one of the leaders of Bisbee's business community were arrested for "conspiracy to injure, oppress, threaten and intimidate citizens on the exercise of the right to peaceably reside in the state of Arizona." Those charged by the grand jury were among the highest placed citizens of the town: Walter Douglas, president of Phelps Dodge; Copper Queen General Manager Grant Dowell; Lemuel Shattuck, president of Shattuck-Dunn; and president of the Loyalty League, Miles Merrill. Indictments were prepared for others, including Sheriff Wheeler, John Greenway, James Douglas, and W. H. Brophy, manager of the Phelps Dodge company store, all of whom were in the US Army and serving in France.

Walter Douglas's lawyer in New York issued a statement in which, after blaming IWW "mischief makers" and "Austrian and Mexican miners" for the strike, he justified the deportation by asserting that federal authorities made no effort to return the men, "the general feeling being that there could be no temporizing with a movement that aimed to keep the government from getting the copper it needed."

The defendants were arraigned in Tucson at the US courthouse on the conspiracy charge, as well as that of kidnapping, and defense attorney E. E. Ellinwood immediately moved for dismissal on the grounds that no federal laws had been violated. The case was postponed by the judge so the motion could be reviewed, and on December 2, 1918, Judge William Morrow of San Francisco upheld the motion, determining that the indictments for conspiracy to deprive the deportees of their constitutional rights did not constitute a federal offense, since whatever laws might have been broken were state laws, and it was in state court that charges should be brought. Morrow considered that if any law was violated, it was that against kidnapping, but that even though they crossed state borders in the course of the event, making it an interstate matter, it still didn't constitute a federal offense. The judge, in issuing his decision, criticized the deportees for not submitting their "character and conduct to a tribunal in their community where they resided, rather than the federal courts." The situation was "lamentable," and even "deplorable," but that didn't place it within his constitutional authority. An appeal was filed with the US Supreme Court, which, in November 1920, sustained the dismissal of the federal case. Those responsible for the deportation had escaped the first attempt to hold them responsible for it.

As expressed in the *Nation*, liberal opinion in this case was most unhappy with Judge Morrow's decision. The hypocrisy of the dismissal of the charges was the heart of the matter for the *Nation*. "A gross and scandalous outrage was committed against the striking miners, and the public is by no means convinced that a serious effort has been made to fix the responsibility for it." But while the perpetrators of the kidnappings and the kangaroo courts were granted impunity, the IWW had just been found guilty in a massive trial in Chicago and the defendants sentenced to an aggregate of eight hundred years and $2.5 million in fines. "The brisk and energetic certitude of our legal processes when applied to the IWW, as compared with their reluctant and indolent methods with the anarchist mob of 'leading citizens,' is utterly offensive to a natural sense of justice."[2]

The victims of the mining companies and their allies next tried civil court—272 of them suing Phelps Dodge, Calumet and Arizona, and the El Paso and Southwestern Railroad, the transport arm of Phelps Dodge that had provided the trains that carried away the deportees. Civil suits totaling in excess of $6,150,000 were filed against Phelps Dodge Corporation, Phelps Dodge mercantile, the Calumet and Arizona Mining Company, and the El

Paso and Southwestern Railroad. Figures of $1,250 for men with children, $1,000 for married men with no children, and $500 for single men were discussed for "pain, inconvenience and loss of income suffered," though the amounts demanded were $20,000 per individual, except lawyer W. B. Clearly, who sued for $40,000. Though some payments were made by smaller defendants, the mining companies refused to make any payments until all payments could be made. Given the dispersal of many deportees to parts unknown, this made payouts impossible, so none were made by the major companies. The mining companies managed to turn the lawsuits to their benefit: a list of some five hundred plaintiffs was sent to mining companies around the state, which served as a blacklist.[3]

In preparation for the state criminal trial that would finally confront the Bisbee Deportation, on October 8, 1919, hundreds of documents were filed in Bisbee against deputies involved in the deportation "for the offense of kidnapping." Many familiar names can be found on it: Lemuel Shattuck, head of the Shattuck mining company; Jacob Erickson, mayor of Bisbee; company doctor Bledsoe.... Interestingly, Neither Harry Wheeler nor any Douglases appear on the list. The defendants were each released on $2,000 bail.[4]

Affidavits were filed in January 1920 stating that "because of the bias and prejudice of the Honorable A.C. Lockwood, Superior Judge of the County of Cochise, he cannot have a fair and impartial trial."[5] He would be replaced by Judge Samuel L. Pattee.

Finally, more than two and a half years after the deportation, the trial was set to begin in February 1920. The mining company representatives were in no way unhappy that the trial was taking place: they immediately cut off negotiations for out-of-court settlement on pending civil charges, knowing that if the criminal case resulted in a victory for the vigilantes it would be less than likely they'd have to pay any damages.[6]

Defense attorneys sent investigators to interview men who might be called as members of the jury, and their reports reveal the mindset of the mine owners and authorities. Reading through them, the phrase "fair minded and conservative and has no use for the IWW or the radical element" is the highest praise possible, along with "always fair to corporations." Support for the IWW was not the only black mark held against some potential jurymen: support for Governor Hunt was incriminating in the eyes of the defense attorneys. Membership in fraternal organizations or lack of same, like the Elks or the Odd Fellows, was considered a key piece of information, as was the newspaper read.

Bad men were those like the plumber A. Baxter, who was a "bootlegger, belongs to the radical element." Damningly, he was described not only as an IWW sympathizer, but as a "Hunt Democrat." He "did not approve of the deportation," and so he was "no good."

Henry Dunbar, an English-born miner, was "a drunk, very ignorant, unreliable proposition, NO GOOD."

Jesse Bean was doubly suspect: his father was "considered pro-German," and he "rather radical."

Louis Bauer was a butcher in Douglas but was "rather shiftless and does not have a job long." Perhaps more damningly, he was married to a Mexican woman and was "inclined to be radical and was a strong follower of Hunt; was against the deportation and is not to be trusted."

Sometimes a potential juror could straddle the two camps, someone like Frances Bowden, a pipefitter who was in Butte during the deportation and "believes it was German propaganda." Though he was pro-union, he was "sorry the unions allowed themselves to be led by the radicals." His "sincere loyal[ty] to the mining companies was supposedly owed to how kindly the Phelps Dodge mercantile store treated him when his wife died.

The defense attorneys were willing to overlook past peccadilloes. Though L. J. Dunagan had been arrested for bootlegging in Douglas and served time in the county jail in Tombstone, he was a defendant in the deportation case and "has no use for the IWW or the radical element."

Horace Beach was "Good." With a "quiet disposition," he was also "not inclined towards the IWW." Not only had he bought Liberty Bonds (not all that impressive, since many of the deportees had as well) but he was "Fair to corporations. A Republican in national politics."

Sherman Beale had good bloodlines, his brother being a member of the Los Angeles Police Department, while he read the reactionary *LA Times*. He was the very type of the ideal juror for the defense: "Is fair minded, conservative, and a good loyal American citizen and has no use for the IWW or radical element ... Approved of deportation."[7]

Along with these investigations, the seating of a panel sympathetic to the defendant and thus the deportation had been made simpler by the reality of the period following the deportation. Though the county attorney, Robert N. French, was elected on the promise that he would right the wrong of the deportation, the city and county had undergone a quiet terror after July 12, 1917. The greater part of the "radical element" had been driven from Bisbee and from Cochise County. Making someone pay for the kidnapping of almost twelve hundred residents of Bisbee was always going to be an uphill battle.

The trial of the first members of the vigilante gang that had carried out the deportation—Fred Sandtner, James Boyd, and Phil Tovrea—was set to begin on February 2, but the trial immediately hit a roadblock. Two key state witnesses were not in Cochise County, nor was their arrival thought to be imminent. The case against the three men was dismissed, and it was decided to move on to hardware store owner Harry Wooton as defendant.[8] Sheriff Wheeler, given his popularity, would have been the first choice of the defense, so County Attorney French requested that charges against him be dropped. Wooton would now be the stand in for the two thousand men who carried out the roundup.

The difficulty of impaneling a jury immediately made itself evident. Two hundred men were called for the voir dire, 122 of whom appeared. Eight of those who showed up at the courthouse in Tombstone, the county seat, were themselves defendants in one or another case related to the deportation.[9]

The charge against Wooton, as it was against all the deputies, was that they "did forcibly take, arrest, and convey into the state of New Mexico, without right under State or Federal laws, one Fred W. Brown, in violation of section 185 of the Penal Code of Arizona," which defined this act as "kidnapping."[10]

Judge Pattee ruled on February 3 that anyone employed by the mines or by any companies whose officers were potential defendants was ineligible to serve on the jury. In a county like Cochise, where the mining companies dominated two of the largest towns—Bisbee and Douglas—this severely limited the pool of eligible jurors.[11] Attorneys on both sides made free use of their right to reject jurors for cause. One local rancher was excused because he had been heard to say that "it was a shame the way they treated the men who were deported."[12]

County Attorney French dropped a bombshell on February 5 when, in conference with Judge Pattee and defense counsel, he declared that after the Wooton trial he would move to dismiss all the remaining individual cases, while pursuing a blanket case against 123 individuals and companies. French explained that he had made this determination because of the inordinate length of time it would take to choose a jury, as well as the likelihood of the cases against the other defendants being dismissed.[13]

As it had done at the time of the strike and deportation, indeed, as was its general wont, the *Bisbee Daily Review* worked assiduously at frightening right-thinking citizens with scare headlines about revolution and bloodshed planned to be shed by radicals in the US and Mexico. An IWW strike in Utah and a bloodcurdling account of the events in Centralia, Washington, were reported ("IWW owns to plot to murder ex-soldiers on Veterans Day"). Readers were also informed that Morris Hillquit, the mildest and most reformist of Socialist Party leaders, was threatening violence (though he had actually said that if the Socialists won the election and the capitalists stood in the way, violence might be resorted to in order to ensure that the results were respected). Even Samuel Gompers was reported to be calling for labor to take over the country.[14]

This anti-red frenzy led to an absurdist comedy event that speaks volumes about the mood in Tombstone. When dawn broke on February 7, a red flag was seen to be fluttering at half-mast over the Cochise County courthouse. It was taken down, but "for three or four hours Tombstone hummed with excitement while city, county and government officials conducted rigorous investigations in an attempt to learn the identity of the persons who had hoisted the emblem of anarchy and revolution." Two young men, one working in a garage and the other a student in Tucson, were identified as the culprits, and the perpetrator still in Tombstone was held on $300 bond for contempt of court. He was reported as being "disappointed at the serious angle which his joke had developed."[15]

As the jury selection dragged on into mid-February concern was expressed for the expense the county would be incurring for the trial. With seven more jurors still to be selected on February 14, the process had already cost the county $4,600, and the sheriff was obliged to find four hundred more men from whom the remaining jurors would be selected.[16] On February 26, the jury selection process looked to finally be completed, with a full panel chosen. An event on that day goes far in explaining why the process was such an arduous one. Talesman Charles Mannus was questioned by defense attorney Curley about his failure to purchase Liberty Bonds or to contribute to the Red Cross during the war, while subscribing to the *Free Press*, described as a "German newspaper." When Mannus denied ever having expressed an opinion against the deportation, subpoenas were issued for his wife and a neighbor, who had claimed he had done so.[17] Not for a defendant, but for a potential jury member!

This resulted in testimony regarding Mannus's beliefs and the actions of the family of another challenged potential juror, one of whose brothers was accused of having deserted from the US Army after induction. These exchanges also resulted in defense attorney Bruce Stevenson, who had falsely reported Mannus's supposed comments against the deportation, being charged with perjury. Side issue was generating side issue, all of this delaying justice for the deportees. Both sides were jockeying for a perfect jury from their point of view. The result was constant delays, mounting expense, and a poisoned atmosphere in the courtroom.[18]

The following week, on Monday, March 1, after yet more testimony on the beliefs and actions of the *jurors*, Mannus and another supposedly "disloyal" juror, C. Haynie, were dismissed by Judge Pattee, who announced that Haynie "might be a good citizen in time of peace, but was worthless in time of war."

By day's end, it seemed all twenty-four jurors—twelve members and twelve alternates—had been selected.[19] But on March 4, one of the twenty-four announced that the questioning of the jurors had revived his old opinions on the deportation, and he asked to be removed, resulting in the need to call a further panel of 250 men from which to choose only one![20]

More days passed, with new jurors selected while others fell by the wayside. Finally, on March 5, after five weeks of voir dire, costing $15,000, a full panel was ready, but a four-day adjournment was called because the courtroom was needed for other purposes, including—ironically—naturalization ceremonies.[21]

As the trial was getting ready to begin, Harry Wheeler got in a final shot in defense of the actions of himself and the deputies, alleging again that there were former Villista soldiers among the strikers, men "arrogant and boastful," who had a thousand Mausers stashed near the border. The roundup had prevented the activation of what he called the "San Diego Plan," an uprising of Mexicans in the area. Wheeler and his men had saved Bisbee and Arizona from revolution.[22]

On March 10, the trial finally began. The report the following day in the *Daily Review* announced that "Germany's victory and armed overthrow of US Government plotted by Bisbee IWW."[23]

* * *

The deportee Fred Brown was the first witness called, and his testimony was brief and to the point. He had known Wooton prior to the roundup, and recounted that on that day he was brought by an armed deputy to the defendant, who asked Wooton if this was the man he wanted. Wooton confirmed it, and Brown asked what he'd done. Wooton responded, "You came up to my place a week ago and declared it was unfair" to labor, which Brown denied ever having done. Brown was, however, the head of an AF of L grievance committee which had, indeed, found that Wooton was unfair to organized labor.[24]

Only two other men testified to the events of the day, but when one of them, Thomas Green, was asked if he was an IWW the state objected. The issue of whether or not to admit testimony concerning the IWW caused a delay in the trial as the judge required time to review precedents, followed by a lengthy explanation by Frank Curley, one of the defense attorneys, aimed at diminishing the reliability of anything said by any prosecution witnesses.

Curley first insisted the question was legitimate because if the witness was an IWW member it would reflect on his character and reliability, since, as laid out in the writings of the union's leaders, "one of the principles of this organization is that right and wrong does not concern them." Even more damningly, no doubt, was that "the Christian religion to them is but a joke," which he supported with a reading of an excerpt from an article condemning the hypocrisy of some religious figures. The state objected, and the judge sustained the objection. The prosecution reminded the court of the findings of the Presidential Mediation Commission, and the prosecution was done.[25]

Defense attorney Curley's opening statement was a lengthy rehashing of anti-union, anti-striker notions about the threats of violence surrounding the strikes that had been occurring across the country around the time of strike in Bisbee. He had little to say about his client Harry Wooton. His opening remarks were, rather, an expansion of the questioning of the prosecution witnesses, aimed at putting the IWW, already beaten in federal court and so an established enemy of society, on trial.

Curley announced that he intended to prove that "in or about the year 1908" (nine years before the deportation!) Bill Haywood, Vincent St. John, "and a great many others, running probably into the thousands," conspired to overthrow the government of the United States by violence, and ultimately to do away with private property. In order to do this, the conspirators "proceeded to apply the axe at the very roots of civilization in an effort to rob those who could not be reached by an insidious propaganda, of the benefits of religion, rendering them less immune to the virus of anti-patriotism and anti-government."[26]

Curley was followed by his colleague William Burges, who brought the IWW's alleged conspiracy to the local level, showing that the activities of the IWW up through July 12, 1917 fit their general schema. These activities constituted threats "that any reasonably prudent man or set of men was and were justified in believing and acting upon." On a practical level, the jail of Cochise County did not have sufficient room to hold all the local conspirators, which explained the need for the deportation. The deportation was a matter of necessity.[27]

It was the so-called law of necessity that could be invoked, and not self-defense, the judge then specified before the defense began calling witnesses. Mere threats, the judge informed the jury, do not allow for a defense based on a claim of self-defense. The law of necessity, though, "justifies by virtue of necessity the invasion of another's rights" and doesn't require an immediate act as a self-defense does. The presence of a threat suffices.[28]

In his charge to the jury, Judge Pattee explained the law of necessity at length.

"Necessity is a defense when it is shown that the act charged was done to avoid an evil both serious and irreparable, that there was no other adequate means of escape and that the action was not disproportionate to the evil." This admirable language, gentlemen, sums up in its briefest form the so-called rule of necessity. It is obviously a rule that can be rarely invoked and only successfully invoked under extreme circumstances but when the circumstances are such as to justify its application and the one charged with the crime has acted strictly within such rule it completely excuses an act which would otherwise constitute a criminal offense. The law of necessity simply excuses one when threatened with an overwhelming peril, a peril imminent and immediate and which ordinary means are insufficient to avoid, in taking it upon himself to take such steps as may be necessary to avert the threatened peril even though it involves the invasion of the rights of others. An individual, a number of persons, or a community which faces threatened destruction of life and property and the peril of such destruction is imminent and immediate and overwhelming may, if necessary to avert such peril, not await an attack or the actual consummation of the threatened destruction in whole or in part but may act affirmatively to avert the threatened peril and if in so doing the rights of others are invaded such invasion is excusable and the one committing the invasion is guilty of no crime. But, necessarily, the evidence claimed to present such a situation should be viewed by the jury with caution and only in the event that such immediate threatened peril is shown and no reasonable means of avoiding it except by commission of the act complained of is shown can the law of necessity be given effect. Before you can find that an otherwise unlawful act is excused by reason of the law of necessity you must find from the evidence that the impending danger feared by the defendant was actually present and in operation and the necessity must be based upon the reasonable belief that no other remedy was available under the circumstances.[29]

The judge did not exclude morality from his reading of the law, for it was clear from all precedents that "an officer has no right to command another to perform an unlawful act, and one summoned by an officer to assist him acts at his own peril." Whatever the individual's good faith, his conduct cannot be justified if the action of the officer summoning him was illegal. In short, if Wheeler acted illegally, so did Wooton and all his fellow deputies.[30]

The law of necessity was not a law vested in a public official, the judge continued, but only in individuals. Everything done on July 12 was thus done outside of any official duty, "and their right to claim to be excused on the ground of necessity depends upon the existence of a situation which would warrant individuals in acting under that rule."[31]

As for the charge of kidnapping, it can only be applied to a case if a person was forcibly taken. If Brown, then, was not taken forcibly, and his removal to New Mexico was "voluntary on his part," then Wooton and his fellows were not guilty of kidnapping.[32]

When testimony for the defense was finally given there was virtually nothing new in it, all of it a repetition of tales recounted in the newspapers of threats against scabs, of the blowing-up of the laundry, of lunch-pail stealing....[33] In all, the defense called ninety-two witnesses.[34] One miner, speaking as a defense witness, recounted an event that at least sounds true as an example of Wobbly language. He said he'd "heard the strikers say that they were going to win, that it was a government of the rich and they thought it ought to be put on the bum and by god they were going to put it on the bum."[35]

In his testimony, Harry Wheeler insisted on the practical problem that had already been brought up, that the local jail had room for only 150 men, so the men had to be moved out of town. As for the seriousness of the threat, new strike supporters were coming into town "all the time," while "loyal men" were departing daily. The town, Wheeler implied, was about to become Wob. "We were growing weaker; they were growing stronger." The *Daily Review* had, of course, been reporting the opposite during the strike.

Wheeler deported the men to New Mexico because his hand was forced: denied assistance by the president and the governor, he "wanted the troops to have them." Fearing there would be killed and wounded on both sides, "I was thinking of my county, too, as well as our district."[36]

On April 20, the judge made his most consequential statement, which all but determined the outcome of the case: "When a condition of violence and terrorism is charged to exist ... the character of those charged with causing that situation is a legitimate and proper thing to be shown in determining whether or not that situation actually existed."[37]

The defense was now given free rein to put the IWW on trial, and they did so with a vengeance. All that had worked so well in the federal trial of the IWW in 1918 was repeated, though on a smaller scale. The preamble to the constitution of the IWW was entered into the record, as were Vincent St. John's *The IWW: Its History, Structure and Methods*, the French syndicalist Gustave Hervé's *Patriotism and the Worker*, Bill Haywood's *The General Strike*, song lyrics from the *Little Red Songbook*, and pamphlets on sabotage.[38]

It already having been established at their 1918 trial that the Wobs were enemies of the good, the character was tarnished of all those in Bisbee accused of being either members or supporters—all 1,186 deportees, including the test case, Fred Brown, who was an AF of L member.

It was only on April 15, nearly two and a half months into the process, that defendant Wooton was called to the stand. Nothing in his testimony was particularly surprising, as he too told tales of name-calling and lunch-pail snatching and the alleged IWW threat of a cleanup of the city after victory.

Even so, one of his final answers stood out. Asked if on the morning of July 12 he thought the people of Bisbee were in danger of destruction, Wooton answered, "I did believe it. I had been told so often that I couldn't help but believe it." The constant beating of the drum of the danger of the IWW had borne fruit. And for Wooton, and doubtless for many of the deputies, this belief would suffice to justify all that ensued.[39]

When testimony ended, Judge Pattee told the jury that it was beyond doubt that Brown had been arrested in Bisbee and sent to New Mexico. This was established, but it was up to them to determine whether Wooton "forcibly took and carried Brown... into the state of New Mexico." It was their obligation to find that when Brown was taken "that he did not voluntarily go from one state to the other."

How could Brown possibly have been voluntarily kidnapped? The judge informed the jurors that if Brown had had "a reasonable opportunity" to separate himself from the rest of the men and failed to avail himself of it, then his deportation was to be deemed voluntary. As we have seen, several men rounded up had indeed been able to avoid deportation, and many were offered the opportunity to switch sides and put on the white bandana. Not to do so made the kidnapping voluntary. This being so, the doors were open wide for the jurors to exonerate Wooton.[40]

All the jury needed to do was to "believe at the time of the so-called deportation there actually existed in the Warren District a real, threatened and actual danger of destruction of life and property" for the law of necessity to be applicable.[41] This idea of *belief* in a threat was vital. The judge reiterated that the character of the IWW was allowed to be a factor in determining the nature of the danger.[42]

The looseness and danger of the law of necessity was analyzed by George Soule in the *Nation*. He laid out a counterfactual. He asked that readers imagine that the miners of Cochise County were able to gather enough strength to elect a sheriff sympathetic to their needs, and that in response the mine owners were to declare a lockout. By depriving the workers of their livelihoods, this would endanger their very existence, as well as that of their families. Soule then asked that we imagine that the workers formed a new union, and the employers bring in, "or *are reported to have brought in*, armed detectives and the workers *believe* that these gunmen are about to attack them" (emphasis in original). The logic of the defense and the judges makes it "difficult to see why the verdict of this jury would not justify the miners in thinking they would be within the law if, under the leadership of the sheriff, they could forcibly deport the detectives and the mine managers and seize and operate the mines." This so-called law led to the conclusion that "if two parties fear attacks from each other, the one who attacks first is protected by the state."[43] Logic, though, played little part in the trial or the jury's deliberations.

The defense, in its summation, returned to the matter that there was no alternative to deportation. Defense attorney W. G. Gilmore added that given how long this trial had taken, it would take between one hundred and three hundred years for trials of all those deported. The cost would bankrupt the city.[44]

As for the voluntary nature of Brown's deportation, Gilmore stressed that he was a liar and a Wobbly (the two being virtually synonymous) and that he had had many opportunities to avoid being put on the train and never took advantage of them.[45]

As the defense summations continued, they returned to the familiar themes, but Gilmore made the real issue clear to the jury: "There were two sets of people. There was a law abiding one and the lawless—the merchants and workers on one side, the working miners on one side, and the striking miners, including the IWW and their sympathizers and dupes on the other side."[46]

This led directly into the summation of defense attorney Burges, who also stressed that the deputies were not Bisbee's "lawless ones, not those that profit by disorder, but the men who came from their own homes, from their business houses, the men who make the town."[47]

Wooton and his fellow vigilantes were fully justified in doing what they did because he and they "knew the character of the people on the other side."[48] Wooton acted as he did on July 12 because he "believed" that his life and property and the lives of his wife and children were in danger, and "it was necessary for him and those similarly situated to band themselves together and protect themselves against imminent danger by the deportation," and so he and they were protected by the law of necessity.[49]

Burges appealed to the jurors' patriotic instincts by asking them to put themselves in Wooton's place and imagine what they'd have done. He asked if there was "a man on the jury who believes that when the call had come to him that night, he would have taken his place under the other flag," the red flag of revolution. Burges quoted the anthem written by James Connolly, asking if any member of the jury could adhere to its vow "To keep the scarlet standard flying high/Beneath its fold to live and die./Though cowards flinch and traitors sneer/To keep the red flag flying here."[50] In that time—of the Red Scare, of the Palmer Red Raids, of the IWW trials, of deportations of foreign-born radicals like Emma Goldman—the gauntlet thus thrown down could leave the jury little choice. Not that there was much of one, since the jury panel had been vetted to exclude anyone who might have gone along with the workers' anthem....

County Attorney French tried to ease the fears of the jurors, saying that many IWWs he'd spoken to had told him they'd joined "because they kept after me and I took a card to get rid of them." French accepted that there were dangerous men in the IWW, "but there are also good men who joined totally ignorant of its principles."[51]

It was essential that French establish that Brown was forcibly taken from town, and unjustly so, and that he went to New Mexico against his will. Due to the past dealings between Wooton and Brown, the former knew full well that Brown was not in the IWW, since he had headed an AF of L grievance committee. And given the condition of the day, with armed men rounding up the defenseless, as well as their ignorance of the fate awaiting them, Brown's deportation to New Mexico could only have been involuntary.[52]

If the defense attorneys had made the jurors the stand-ins for all patriotic, right-thinking citizens, the arbiters between the status quo and revolution, French appealed to their consciences. It was up to them to show that in America there wasn't "one law for the rich and one for the poor."[53]

On April 30, an hour after retiring for deliberations (which took only one ballot and twelve minutes) the jury returned a verdict of not guilty. One juror expressed disappointment that this one verdict couldn't settle all cases, but in fact, it did: no other deputies were pursued for their acts on July 12. The jury had saved America from revolution.

That America was saved can be seen from the front page of the *Bisbee Daily Review* on May 1, 1920, in which the announcement of the acquittal is flanked by two scare headlines. "Radicals Mark Congressmen and Unites States Judges for Assassination Today," and internationally, "Chihuahua City Is Taken by Revolutionists."[54] The vigilantes of Bisbee had done their part to forestall the onward march of the people. But the threat remained.

CHAPTER NINE

The Aftermath

I would like not to discuss anything about the deportation

Once the lawsuits were all settled or dismissed, the Deportation of 1917 became the great unspoken event in Bisbee's past. The mines closed in 1985 and the town suffered a massive exodus. Its beautiful setting, mild climate, and cheap housing served as a magnet and attracted young people, who have revived Bisbee. It's the county seat for Cochise County, so government employment plays a role there. Artists work in their studios, and older Bisbeeites, some natives, some recent arrivals, work happily as docents or research volunteers at the Mining Museum and participate in the local chorus. Even so, the characterization by a historian of the West is an accurate one: Bisbee "is a quintessential 'western' ghost town, where mostly white tourists from all across the United States come to play. Some will buy Native American or western paraphernalia in gift shops before driving north to watch Wyatt Earp fight 'cow-boys' in the streets of nearby Tombstone."[1] On the other hand, Cananea, the Mexican mining town invaded by Bisbee's American forces in 1916, remains a thriving and working metropolis.

Like so many cities whose glory has faded, talk of ghosts haunting buildings or specific spots circulate to add romance to the town's diminution. But whatever the talk about ghosts haunting the Copper Queen Hotel or the Queen Mine, open to tourists year-round, the specter that haunts Bisbee is the deportation. Finally, more than a century after the event, it is being confronted.

Lifetime residents speak of how, when they were growing up in the town in the '50s and '60s, no mention was ever made of it.[2] Fred Watson, when he told his story years later, reported that his wife didn't want him to do so, fearing "notoriety." Citing the sixty years that had passed since the strike and deportation, she asked why he didn't just forget it. "And I say, 'I'll forget it when I die!'"[3]

In a collection of oral histories stored at the Bisbee Mining Museum, former miner Ralph Hargis, when asked about the events of 1917, would only answer, "I would like not to discuss anything about the deportation."[4] (It's worth noting that in most of the interviews on file either the interviewer or interviewee gets the year of the deportation wrong.)

Robert Houston's novel *Bisbee '17* was published in 1979 and encouraged locals to look into their pasts. In 2018 a film titled *Bisbee '17* (no relation to the Houston novel), directed by Robert Greene, was released. It was a reenactment made in Bisbee during the centennial year, using Bisbeeites to play the role of the Bisbeeites of the era, while also allowing them to examine their own feelings about the occurrences of one hundred years before. The splits of 1917, it revealed, continue today.

Ruben Gomez comes from a family with a long history in Bisbee, the mining town becoming the endpoint of the travels of his Sephardic family after their expulsion from Spain in 1492. Part of his family arrived in Bisbee in 1880, shortly after the town's founding, leaving for a while and then coming back "the second time to stay" in about 1895. Ruben's paternal grandfather arrived in Bisbee sometime between 1900 and 1904 and worked as a carpenter. In 1917, he was a laborer at the Calumet and Arizona Mining Company, run by Lemuel Shattuck.

Like almost all of his peers, "as a child in the 1950s–1960s I was unaware of the deportation per se." Ruben's father worked for Phelps Dodge, and when he was "able to, my father joined the union, and actively participated in strikes whenever they took place. He was always suspicious and wary of 'the company.' Maybe the Deportation was a subtext in my dad's remarks about the company and the dominant population's attitude toward minorities."

Ruben recounts that shortly after Robert Houston's novel *Bisbee '17* came out, "out of curiosity, I asked my dad about the 1917 Bisbee Deportation. He responded that his father had been deported but returned 'soon' after." Though Ruben's father was only a baby at the time of the deportation, "he remembered there being lots of '*barullo*' (noise, confusion, yelling, and crying), however, my impression is that this was talked enough about in the ensuing months/years for him to remember it. My grandfather shows up in the 1916/1917 Bisbee directory and not again until 1924 at the location where my father grew up. My dad died at 93 years old in 2010."

When the film *Bisbee '17* came out, Ruben asked other family members about the family's connection to the event, and none had heard of any, nor does his grandfather appear on the existing list of deportees, which was compiled at the camp in Columbus about a week after their arrival and is short about 150 names.

Ruben is particularly proud of his Sephardic heritage, of how his father's mother's maternal grandfather was a Spinoza and perhaps related to the great philosopher. But in the end, he said, if the deportation "matters to me from a historical point of view.... It doesn't matter from a family story point of view. The fact that there is no documentation doesn't change what my dad told me."[5]

Perhaps no story is as heart-wrenching as that Steve Ray's family. Steve is a former law enforcement officer who now gives tours of his hometown. He told me that in the Arizona history he was taught in high school, "there was only one small paragraph in the history book about it. I asked my teacher if we could talk more about it because I had family on both sides and the teacher told me, Steve we can't talk about it we're not allowed to." Steve first heard of it when he was nine or ten years old and his older sister "was doing some research and writing a paper for 8th grade civics class."[6]

Steve is the great-grandson of E. L. Cooke, who acted as a deputy on July 12, 1917, but he is also the great-grandnephew of Archie Cooke, E. L's brother, who was deported that day. He told me, "I do remember vaguely my grandfather saying that he knew his dad had to do what he had to do because he had a family to support and my understanding is Uncle Archie really was not all that into the strike, he wanted better working conditions, better wages, however he was not as vocal about it as maybe some of the other strikers were. Initially he just went to go listen."

In fact, it was E. L. who rounded up his own brother and escorted him at gunpoint to the Warren ballpark and "personally put him into one of the cattle cars bound for Columbus." Allowed to return to Bisbee but unable to find work, Archie pressed charges for kidnapping against his brother, leading the latter to flee Arizona for Central and South America. He returned to Bisbee after the acquittal in the Wooton trial. The brothers finally reconciled in the 1930s.[7]

The reconciliation process was completed when Steve's mother had the idea of locating the graves of the brothers in Evergreen Cemetery in Bisbee—Archie's was unmarked—and giving them a common monument.

People from outside Bisbee but with roots in the town return there to research their family's connection to the events. Tom Carter of Nichols,

California, visited the Bisbee Mining Museum's library to see if his grandfather Ed Wilson was among the deported. He was able to verify that Ed lived in Bisbee in 1917 but didn't appear in subsequent city directories. He had been told by a great-aunt that Ed had likely fled Bisbee because he was an outlaw, but when Tom learned of the deportation he connected it to a story told by another family member that Ed had been visited by a group of men, after which he "packed up and moved to Bakersfield." Family lore has it that he had been warned of the imminent deportation.

Ed doesn't appear on the list of deportees, but as local historian Mike Anderson said, "There was no reason for anyone to make up having been a deportee, since there's nothing to be gained by it."

* * *

James Brew's death had gone virtually unmourned after he was killed on July 12, after firing through his door at the deputies come to arrest him, killing the deputy Orson McRae. Brew, possibly a member of the IWW, but definitely a member of the Elks, was buried in the Elks' section of Evergreen Cemetery, his stone simply bearing his name and date of death.

John Pintek is a lawyer in Tucson. His father was rounded up on July 12 but was saved by his mother Mary's pleas. He has spent years keeping the memory of the deportation alive when Bisbee wanted it kept buried. Back in 1984 he participated in a memorial service for James Brew, at which he gave an impassioned speech:

> Here in these barren hills sixty-seven years ago today isolated from America and the world by the de facto government of the copper companies which had taken all means of communication and ingress or egress, over twelve hundred free-thinking American citizens and residents of Bisbee learned before daybreak to their surprise and sorrow that eternal vigilance is the price of liberty. Had they been aware of the secret conspiracy which had been organized to drive them from their homes, they might have been prepared to defend their lives, their fortunes and sacred honor, as was declared by John Hancock and the founding Fathers in the Declaration of Independence on July 4, 1776 ... Let us hope that we will learn to treat each other with humanity [and] integrity and recognize the human rights of dignity and freedom.[8]

Pintek continued to work tirelessly on behalf of the forgotten deportees, and also collaborated with Todd Bogatay, a Bisbee architect, to erect a memorial for James Brew in the town. The hope was to place it in Vista Park, across the street from the ballpark where the deportees were held, but that was shot down at the last minute for fear it would be "an obstacle and subject to graffiti."

Finally, on May 30, 2005, Bogatay was able to inform Bisbee's mayor that an agreement had been reached with all parties concerned—including Phelps Dodge—about the erection of the monument, a simple "boulder, placed near but not on top of the grave." Phelps Dodge agreed to the move of the stone, and the dedication was to take place on July 4, 2005. The plan called for the plaque to read, "This boulder is dedicated by the citizens of Bisbee on July 4, 2005, in honor of the courage of James H. Brew, a Bisbee miner, killed at his home on July 12, 1917 in Bisbee, Arizona defending his rights as a free citizen to demand fair labor laws."[9]

In fact, the dedication was delayed a year, and the plaque on his grave, dedicated July 4, 2006, contains a longer, angrier message, which connects the fate of Brew and his fellow workers to the struggles that have gone on since: "Memorial to James H. Brew shot in his home in Bisbee July 12, 1917 after he shot one of the four men sent to get him. He refused to work under conditions of 'involuntary servitude' as defined in the 13th amendment of the Constitution of the United States of America. Brew's death and the 'deportation' on that day of 1185 persons are symbolic of our continuing struggle for freedom and equality."

* * *

For the centennial of the deportation in 2017 the IWW prepared a red pennant with a simple message: "We Never Forget."

CONCLUSION

Justifiable homicide at the hands of persons unknown

The Bisbee Deportation existed at the confluence of many currents of its time and of American history. Most obviously, it was an attack on a group of workers who refused to bend the knee, and their roundup was part of the fear and hatred of radicalism that was in the air and would lead, within just a couple of years, to the Palmer Red Raids and the deportation of American radicals. This time not just into the desert, but across the ocean to lands they had long since left behind.

The strikers in Bisbee and elsewhere in Arizona had to be painted in the most lurid light, the Wobbly presence exaggerated out of all measure, and the violence and supposed treason of the union made a focus. Control of the local press by the mining company made this all too easy, and fake news was circulated daily. Fictional threats of physical violence by the strikers, which those who lived there knew from experience were not really happening, became a fictive reality and a justification to do whatever was necessary to protect the lives and property of the residents of Bisbee.

On the local level, it was the crowning event in the righting of things from the corporate point of view. As James Byrkit, in writing about this time and place put it, "The Bisbee events reveal that a colonial relationship existed between the East and the West, the old and the new.... Evidence indicated that most Westerners felt relatively little fear specifically about war or the possibility of subversion.... By falsifying existing conditions [the Bisbee mine managers] persuaded many townspeople and much of the nation to share company antipathy toward labor."[1] Labor had been too assertive in demanding its rights; working people, organized and not, had voted for and approved politicians who limited the ability of mining companies a free hand in their fiefdoms and had passed laws that raised their tax bills. This could not be allowed to go on, and so labor had to be cowed and Arizona's natural rulers allowed a free hand. What better way to make real their rule than to organize the arrest and deportation of residents of the city?

The Bisbee Deportation was possible also because it occurred in an isolated town far from prying eyes—even more, an isolated town in the American West, which, Byrkit wrote, carried on "the reputed 'ethos' of the nineteenth century American West," an ethos that "should have been anachronistic." Bisbee was not a town of cattlemen, it was a mining town, with all the cares and issues that go with that. "Ethos" is only one possible word for the attitude of Bisbeeites: "mythos" is another one, the mythology of the American West, of the small individualistic landholder, of a man's right to do whatever he felt needed to be done to protect his life and livelihood. This in a setting that "seemed to more closely parallel Pittsburgh's than Tombstone's," and the citizens of Bisbee "were strongly possessed by the frontier mentality. This mentality enabled a twentieth century application of the old Western American legacy—vigilantism."[2]

In this mythologized Western city, taking the law into your own hands was perfectly legitimate: wrap a white handkerchief around your upper arm and you become the distributor of justice, bound by no laws written in the statute books. And in a case like Bisbee's, where the sheriff, the official representative of the law, is the man giving you the right to arrest men on no legitimate charge, deport them from their homes, and block their return, whatever little scruple a person might have against taking justice into their own hands would necessarily evaporate. Telling the bad man to "Get out of town before sundown," was the Western way. For the deputies involved in the Bisbee Deportation, all they were doing was helping the bad guys along their way.

Mike Anderson, a current red-card carrying member of the One Big Union and a long-time student of the deportation, describes it as largely "newcomers vs the established." This, he explained to me, was "something made all the easier since there was little personal contact between established residents and the newly arrived." It was "WASPS vs all the others," he said. And of course, it was a class conflict. But Mike makes clear that a little of everything could be found on both sides: one Japanese person was probably a vigilante, since he was a mining engineer working at Phelps Dodge headquarters, and according to Anderson only one Finn was among the vigilantes: in fact, Finns were so prominent among the deported that they all but disappear from the Bisbee city directory.³

But putting the motivation for the Bisbee Deportation down to anti-radicalism, to defense of corporate profits, to the ways of the Old West, though all true, as we have seen, doesn't go far enough. The impulse to take the law into one's own hands, to humiliate, to expel, and even kill those who think differently, or look different, or whose actions can be ascribed to some enemy, has deep roots in the American psyche, in American history, in the American way of life.

Tarring and feathering, which went on in the fight against the miners' unions, was famously used as a weapon against Americans who supported the British in the American Revolution. Mob attacks on those they disliked are as American as apple pie, and have little necessarily to do with the Old West: think of the killing of the abolitionist publisher Elijah Lovejoy in Alton, Illinois, in 1837, or of the founder of Mormonism, Joseph Smith, in 1844 in Carthage, Illinois.

When justice was not seen to be done, or was judged to be insufficient, America has a long history of the crowd taking justice into its own hands in the form of lynch law, a notorious case of it involving Bisbee itself in 1884, when, after the robbery of a general store during which four people were killed, one of the six thieves was not sentenced to hang. A mob made up largely of miners stormed the prison in Tombstone where the thief was being held, seized the prisoner, and hung him from an electric pole. Photos, of course, were taken.

That mob violence continued and was even countenanced in Arizona is proved by the lynching in Phoenix on May 7, 1917, of Star Daley, accused of murdering a man and forcing his wife "to submit to his whims." After Daley was seized by fifty masked men from the deputy sheriffs and hung, the coroner's jury returned a verdict of "justifiable homicide at the hands of persons unknown."⁴

Vigilante justice reached its height in the South, with the post–Civil War reign of terror of the Klan and its ilk, and the nearly hundred-year history of lynching of Black people—yet another form of the mob determining who is guilty and who is not, even deciding what crimes merit punishment, and meting out its form of justice.

The murder of Black men by mobs was the predominant form of mob action, but it should be remembered that the single largest group lynching was of Italians in New Orleans in 1891, one of the subjects dealt with in E. Annie Proulx's novel *Accordion Crimes*.

Lynchings occurred around the time of the Bisbee Deportation for reasons directly related to the ostensible cause of the mob actions in Arizona: in 1918 the German-American coal miner Robert Prager was lynched in an outburst of war-induced xenophobia.[5] And most directly, in November 1917 a group of hooded men dressed in black seized seventeen Wobblies in Tulsa, whipped them and tarred and feathered them, accompanying each stroke of the brush with, "This is for the outraged women and children of Tulsa."[6] Then there was the lynching in Butte of IWW organizer Frank Little.

It would be wrong, then, to view the Bisbee Deportation as a product of a regional quirk. There exists a continuum upon which acts of mob violence occur in American life, and the act executed is the one that best matches the circumstances. It can be tarring and feathering, or lynching, or driving out of town, or murder. The causes, as well, are widely varied. The mob can view the victim or victims as unpatriotic, as red, as an enemy alien, as guilty of having the wrong skin color or religion. But in all cases the mob feels that it is the defender of justice, of the right, a justice and right whose definition it has the right to determine.

In Bisbee the mob was organized and led by corporate interests working in conjunction with the forces of law and order, but there's no reason to think that the presence of the sheriff made the act less than classic mob justice. The kidnapping and expulsion of the deportees was carried out in contravention of existing law, willfully and gladly, by a posse of citizens who felt it was their right to threaten and expel their fellow townsmen simply because they viewed class relations differently.

There being no law on the statute books that could be used against the strikers—though they later came up with specious excuses like "the law of necessity"—the mob in Bisbee fell back on American instincts.

Acknowledgments

I would first like to thank my brother Bob in Phoenix for his invaluable assistance in researching this book and his willingness to return to archives to help me fill in gaps in my research. He and his wife Selena were also generous in their hospitality.

Wendi Goen at the Arizona State Library and Archives provided helpful tips and assistance in tracking down sources.

Fellow Worker Mike Anderson in Bisbee was generous with his time and encyclopedic knowledge of the deportation.

Amanda Hetro of the Bisbee Mining and Historical Museum helped with sources, local experts, and copies.

Tim Davenport, my comrade at the Marxists Internet Archive and an indefatigable expert in all things early-American Marxist and radical, provided me with countless documents when I informed him of my project.

Katherine Benton-Cohen, one of the great experts on the topic and region, was touchingly generous in sharing her research.

Finally, my wife, Joan Levinson, with whom I first discovered Bisbee many years ago, was, as always, my main support.

NOTES

CHAPTER ONE: BISBEE'S BEGINNINGS

1. Robert Glass Cleland, *A History of Phelps Dodge, 1834–1950* (New York: Knopf, 1952), 84–86.
2. Katherine Benton-Cohen, *Borderline Americans: Radical Division and Labor War in the Arizona Borderlands* (Cambridge, MA: Harvard University Press, 2009), 80–81.
3. Cleland, *A History of Phelps Dodge*, 89.
4. Ibid., 98.
5. Ibid., 109–10.
6. Benton-Cohen, *Borderline Americans*, 92.
7. Cleland, *A History of Phelps Dodge*, 125.
8. Ibid., 169–70.
9. James W. Byrkit, *Forging the Copper Collar: Arizona's Labor-Management War, 1901–1921* (Tucson: University of Arizona, 1982), 28–29.
10. Ibid., 30.
11. Testimony of J.C. Ryan at Presidential Mediation Commission, 241. RG 101 Cochise County, SG 8, Superior Court Civil Division, 1917, Arizona State Library, Archives, and Public Records (ASLAPR).
12. Byrkit, *Forging the Copper Collar*, 31–32.
13. Benton-Cohen, *Borderline Americans*, 82–83.
14. Katherine Benton-Cohen, "Docile Children and Dangerous Revolutionaries," *Frontiers* 24, nos. 2 and 3 (2003): 32–33.
15. Benton-Cohen, *Borderline Americans*, 90.
16. Ibid., 91.
17. Benton-Cohen, "Docile Children and Dangerous Revolutionaries," 32.
18. Ibid., 35.
19. Samuel Truett, *Fugitive Landscapes: The Forgotten History of the U.S.-Mexico Borderlands* (New Haven: Yale, 2006), 87–98 passim.
20. Claudio Lomnitz, *The Return of Ricardo Flores Magón* (New York: Zone, 2014), 132–33.
21. Truitt, *Fugitive Landscapes*, 138–41.
22. *Los Angeles Herald*, June 3, 1906.

23. *Bisbee Daily Review*, June 2, 1906.

24. Truitt, *Fugitive Landscapes*, 138–41; *Bisbee Daily Review*, June 5, 1906.

25. AHS photograph #4355, Arizona Historical Society, Tucson.

26. *Bisbee Daily Review*, June 3, 1906.

27. AHS photograph #4362, Arizona Historical Society, Tucson.

28. Truitt, *Fugitive Landscapes*, 144–49 passim.

29. *Bisbee Daily Review*, June 5, 1906.

30. *Bisbee Daily Review*, June 3, 1906.

31. *Bisbee Daily Review*, June 5, 1906.

32. Allen A. Erwin, *The Southwest of John H. Slaughter* (Spokane: Arthur Clarke, 1997), 275–76.

33. *Bisbee Daily Review*, June 7, 1917.

34. *Bisbee Daily Review*, June 24, 1917.

35. Except where otherwise noted, this account of the trial of Flores Magón is drawn from John W. Sherman, "Revolution on Trial: The 1909 Tombstone Proceedings Against Ricardo Flores Magón," *Journal of Arizona History* 32, no. 2 (1991): 173–94.

36. University of Arizona Special Collections, State of Arizona v Harry Walters, AZ 114, box 2, folder 4.

37. Byrkit, *Forging the Copper Collar*, 21–23.

38. *Mining and Engineering World*, September 3, 1916, 545.

39. Standard Statistics Co., "Standard Daily Revised, January–April 1917," 295.

CHAPTER TWO: THE INDUSTRIAL WORKERS OF THE WORLD

1. Paul F. Brissenden, "The Launching of the Industrial Workers of the World," *University of California Publications in Economics* 4, no. 1 (1913): 4–6.

2. *Proceedings of the First Convention of the Industrial Workers of the World* (New York Labor News Company, 1905), 609–16.

3. Brissenden, "The Launching of the Industrial Workers of the World," 15–16. Brissenden points out that the Railway Employees were members of the ALU, and so there is a certain amount of double counting here.

4. *Proceedings of the First Convention of the Industrial Workers of the World,* 194–95.

5. Ibid., 575.

6. Ibid., 247.

7. Ibid., 223–24.

8. Ibid., 222.

9. Brissenden, "The Launching of the Industrial Workers of the World," 40.

10. Melvyn Dubofsky, *We Shall Be All: A History of the Industrial Workers of the World* (Chicago: University of Illinois, 1969), 110–12.

11. Dubofsky, *We Shall Be All*, 126.

12. Patrick Renshaw, *The Wobblies: The Story of the IWW and Syndicalism in the United States* (New York: Anchor Books, 1967), 99–100.

13. Dubofsky, *We Shall Be All*, 251.

14. Renshaw, *The Wobblies*, 109–11; Ralph Chaplin, *Wobbly: The Rough-and-Tumble Story of an American Radical* (Chicago: University of Illinois, 1948), 135–36.

15. Dubofsky, *We Shall Be All*, 263, 267.

16. Ibid., 269–70.

17. John Reed, "The War in Paterson," *Masses*, June 1913, 14, 16.

18. Dubofsky, *We Shall Be All*, 271, 274–76; William D. Haywood, *Big Bill Haywood's Book* (New York: International Publishers, 1929), 262.

19. Dubofsky, *We Shall Be All*, 279–80; Haywood, *Big Bill Haywood's Book*, 263.

20. Joyce Kornbluh, *Rebel Voices: An IWW Anthology* (Ann Arbor, MI: University of Michigan Press, 1968), 210–12.

21. Dubofsky, *We Shall Be All*, 280.

22. Ibid., 283.

23. Ibid., 285.

24. Kornbluh, *Rebel Voices*, 94–95.

25. Ibid., 97–98.

26. Dubofsky, *We Shall Be All*, 302.

27. Ibid., 302–303.

28. Ibid., 307.

29. David R. Berman, *George Hunt: Arizona's Crusading Seven-Term Governor* (Tucson: University of Arizona Press, 2015) 104–111.

30. David R. Berman, *Radicalism in the Mountain West, 1890–1920: Socialists, Populists, Miners, and Wobblies* (Boulder: University Press of Colorado, 2007), 244–47.

31. Ibid., 272.

32. Letter to William Haywood from Grover Perry, University of Arizona Special Collections (UASC), AZ 114 box 1, folder 1, exhibit 31.

33. Letter from General Secretary-Treasurer to A.C. Christ, April 28, 1916, BMHM, Bisbee Deportation Files.

34. Statement of Work, Frank Little; El Paso and Southwestern Railroad Exhibits, University of Arizona Special Collections (UASC), AZ 114, box 1, folder 2.

35. IWW, *Songs of the Workers: To Fan the Flames of Discontent* (Chicago: IWW, [n.d]), 60.

36. Renshaw, *The Wobblies*, 162.

37. Correspondence between Bill Haywood and John Pancner, UASC, AZ 114 box 1, folder 1, exhibit 43.

38. Kornbluh, *Rebel Voices*, 329–30.

39. UASC, AZ 114 box 1, folder 1, exhibit 35.

40. Dubofsky, *We Shall Be All*, 356.

41. Grover Perry to William Haywood, UASC, AZ 114 box 1, folder 1, exhibit 48.

42. Chaplin, *Wobbly*, 208–209.

43. Dubofsky, *We Shall Be All*, 357–58.

44. Quoted in Joseph Robert Conlin, *Bread and Roses Too: Studies of the Wobblies* (Westport, CT: Greenwood, 1969), 97.

45. Renshaw, *Wobblies*, 130.

46. Dubofsky, *We Shall Be All*, 24–25; Haywood, *Big Bill Haywood's Book*, 7.

47. Conlin, *Bread and Roses Too*, 102.

48. Letter from General Secretary-Treasurer to Hugh P. Gallagher, July 13, 1915, Bisbee

Mining and Historical Museum (BMHM), Bisbee Deportation.

49. Letter to Grover H. Perry from Roger S. Culver, April 28, 1917; UASC, AZ 114, box 1, folder 2.

50. Conlin, *Bread and Roses Too*, 87.

51. William Preston, Jr., *Aliens and Dissenters: Federal Suppression of Radicals, 1903–1933* (Chicago: University of Illinois Press, 1994), 101.

52. Chaplin, *Wobbly*, 206.

53. Conlin, *Bread and Roses Too*, 104.

54. Elizabeth Gurley Flynn, *Sabotage: The Conscious Withdrawal of the Workers' Industrial Efficiency* (Chicago: IWW Publishing Bureau, October 1916), 5.

55. Conlin, *Bread and Roses Too*, 105–106.

56. Ibid., 107.

57. John Spargo, *Syndicalism*, cited in Conlin, *Bread and Roses Too,* 112.

58. The main defendant, Bill Haywood, jumped bail after his conviction and fled to Soviet Russia.

59. Chaplin, *Wobbly*, 207.

60. Eldridge Foster Dowell, *A History of Criminal Syndicalism Legislation in the United States* (Baltimore: Johns Hopkins University Press, 1939), 36.

61. Richard C. Cortner, "The Wobblies and Fiske v. Kansas: Victory Amid Disintegration," *Kansas History* 4 (Spring 1981): 30–38.

CHAPTER THREE: THE STRIKE

1. Byrkit, *Forging the Copper Collar*, 27–29.

2. Ibid., 30.

3. Ibid.

4. Minutes of First Convention of MMWIU Union 800, June 15–17, 1917, University of Arizona Special Collections (UASC) AZ 114, box 1 folder 3.

5. Byrkit, *Forging the Copper Collar*, 163.

6. *Butte Daily Post*, June 9, 1917.

7. *Solidarity*, June 30, 1917.

8. *Butte Daily Post,* June 12, 1917

9. *Butte Daily Post*, June 12, 1917.

10. Jeannette Rankin and Mrs. Rosa McKay, "Butte and Bisbee Outrages Scored by Brave Woman Representatives," *Appeal to Reason*, August 18, 1917.

11. *Bisbee Daily Review*, June 26, 1917.

12. Telegram from A. S. Embree to Bill Haywood, UASC, AZ 114, box 1, folder 1.

13. Telegram from A. S. Embree to Bill Haywood, UASC, AZ 114, box 1, folder 2, exhibit 83.

14. Letter from A.S. Embree to Grover Perry, June 26, 1917; Bisbee Mining and Historical Museum (BMHM), Bisbee Deportation.

15. Benton-Cohen, *Borderland Americans*, 218–21.

16. Benton-Cohen, "Docile Children and Dangerous Revolutionaries," 31.

17. John MacDonald, "From Butte to Bisbee," *International Socialist Review* XVII, no. 2 (August 1917): 71.

18. *Bisbee Daily Review*, June 17, 1917.

19. Minutes of First Convention of MMIU Union 800, June 15–17, 197, UASC, *Simmons vs. El Paso and Southwestern RR* exhibits, AZ 114, box 1, folder 3.

20. MacDonald, "From Butte to Bisbee," 69–71.

21. Benton-Cohen, "Docile Children and Dangerous Revolutionaries," 38.

22. *Solidarity*, June 30, 1917.

23. Letter from Press Committee to Grover Perry, July 5, 1917; UASC, AZ 114, box 1, folder 2.

24. Letter from Secretary-Treasurer to Executive Committee, July 10, 1917; UASC, box 1, folder 2.

25. *Bisbee Daily Review*, June 20, 1917.

26. *Bisbee Daily Review*, June 21, 1917.

27. *New York Times*, July 13, 1917.

28. *New York Times*, July 17, 1917.

29. *Sixth Annual Report of the Secretary of Labor for the Fiscal Year Ended June 30, 1918* (Washington, DC.: Government Printing Office, 1918), 12.

30. John D. Lawson, ed., *American State Trials, Volume XVII* (Saint Louis: Thomas Law Book Co., 1936), 139.

31. Address of Senator Sutter at Third Legislature, First Special Session, June 4, 1918; BMHM, Bisbee Deportation.

32. Minutes of IWW Meeting of June 23, 1917, Deposition of John Hughes in the case of *Michael Simmons v. the El Paso and Southwestern Railroad Co.*, in UASC, AZ 114 box 1, folder 2, exhibit 116.

33. Testimony of Charles Ward at Presidential Mediation Commission, ASLAPR, RG 101, Cochise County, SG8, Superior Court, Civil Division, 1917, 115.

34. Testimony of Frank Vaughn at Presidential Mediation Commission, ASLAPR, RG 101, Cochise County, SG8, Superior Court, Civil Division, 1917, 47.

35. Testimony of Fred Brown at Presidential Mediation Commission, ASLAPR, RG 101, Cochise County, SG8, Superior Court, Civil Division, 1917, 26–27.

36. "To the Members of the Citizens Protective League and Loyalty League," Arizona Historical Society Library MS 0154, folder F2.

37. Letter from A. C. Embree to Grover Perry, June 26, 1917; BMHM, Bisbee Deportation.

38. Fred Watson, "Still on Strike! Recollections of a Bisbee Deportee," *Journal of Arizona History*, 18, no. 2 (Summer 1977): 172.

39. Fred Brown, Testimony at Federal Mediation Commission, ASLAPR, RG 101, Cochise County, SG8, Superior Court, Civil Division, 1917, 29.

40. Watson, "Still on Strike! Recollections of a Bisbee Deportee," 172.

41. Testimony of Edward Massey, Presidential Mediation Commission, ASLAPR, RG 101, Cochise County, SG, Superior Court, Civil Division, Bisbee Deportation, 51.

42. "Butte and Bisbee Outrages Scored by Brave Woman Representatives," *Appeal to Reason*, August 18, 1917.

43. *Bisbee Daily Review*, June 29, 1917

44. Database of deputies compiled and provided by Katherine Benton-Cohen, private

communication.

45. *Bisbee Daily Review*, June 29, 1917.

46. MG 25, George W. P. Hunt Papers, ASLAPR, series 3, box 16, file 345.

47. *Bisbee Daily Review*, June 29, 1917.

48. *Bisbee Daily Review*, June 30, 1917.

49. UASC, State of Arizona v. Harry Walters, AZ 114, box 2, folder 4.

50. J. F. McDonald, testimony at the Presidential Mediation Commission, ASLAPR, RG101, Cochise County, SG8, Superior Court, Civil Division, 1917, 21.

51. *Bisbee Daily Review*, July 3, 1917.

52. MG 25, George W.P. Hunt Papers, ASLAPR, series 3, box 16, file 345.

53. See "Authority to Travel" and instructions from Division of Conciliation dated July 5, 1917, in MG 25, George W.P. Hunt, 1859–1940, ASLAPR, series 3, box 16, file 345.

54. *Bisbee Daily Review*, July 4, 1917.

55. Testimony of Frank A. Thomas, Presidential Mediation Commission, ASLAPR, RG101, Cochise County, SG8, Superior Court, Civil Division, 1917, 64–65.

56. Testimony of M. W. Merrill, Presidential Mediation Commission, ASLAPR, RG101, Cochise County, SG8, Superior Court, Civil Division, 1917, 223.

57. *Ajo Copper News*, July 6, 1917.

58. *Bisbee Daily Review*, July 5, 1917.

59. *Bisbee Daily Review*, July 4, 1917.

60. Testimony of M. W. Merrill, Presidential Mediation Commission, ASLAPR, RG101, Cochise County, SG8, Superior Court, Civil Division, 1917, 227.

61. Letter to Grover Perry from Press Committee, July 4, 1917, University of Arizona Special Collections, AZ 114, box 1, folder 2.

62. Letter from Press Committee to Grover Perry, July 5, 1917, University of Arizona Special Collections, AZ 114, box 1, folder 2.

63. Letter dated July 25, 1917, of Frank Vaughan to Governor Hunt, MG 35, Series 3, box 17, folder 388.

64. Harry Wheeler, testimony at Presidential Mediation Commission, ASLAPR, RG101, Cochise County, SG8, Superior Court, Civil Division, 1917, 139.

65. *Bisbee Daily Review*, July 6, 1917.

66. "Strike in Bisbee is practically at end," *Miner's Magazine*, July 1917, 3.

67. *Bisbee Daily Review*, July 6, 1917.

68. David R. Berman, *George Hunt: Arizona's Crusading Seven-Term Governor*. This volume is the source for the biographical information on Hunt that follows.

69. Berman, *George Hunt,* 32–33.

70. Ibid., 8.

71. Ibid., 93.

72. MG 25, George W.P. Hunt, 1859–1940, Series 3, box 16, File 345, ASLAPR.

73. Bassett Watkins, Testimony at the Presidential Mediation Commission, RG 101, Cochise County, SG8, Superior Court Civil Division, 1917, 231–32.

74. Harry Wheeler, Testimony at Presidential Mediation Commission, RG 101, Cochise County, SG8, Superior Court Civil Division, 1917, 140–41, ASLAPR.

75. Testimony of J. C. Ryan at Presidential Mediation Commission, RG 101 Cochise

County SG 8 Superior Court Civil Division, 1917, 253, ASLAPR.

76. Testimony of Harry Wheeler at Presidential Mediation Commission, RG 101 Cochise County SG 8 Superior Court Civil Division, 1917, 151, ASLAPR.

77. Testimony of Harry Wheeler at Presidential Mediation Commission, RG 101 Cochise County SG 8 Superior Court Civil Division, 1917, 151, ASLAPR.

78. Testimony of Harry Wheeler at Presidential Mediation Commission, RG 101 Cochise County SG 8 Superior Court Civil Division, 1917, 151, 147–49 passim.

79. *Bisbee Daily Review*, July 7, 1917.

80. Harry Wheeler, Testimony at Presidential Mediation Commission, RG 101 Cochise County SG 8 Superior Court Civil Division, 1917, 141, ASLAPR.

81. Telegram from Little and Haywood, July 6, 1917, UASC, Az 114, box 1, folder 1.

82. *Bisbee Daily Review*, July 7, 1917.

83. *Bisbee Daily Review*, July 8, 1917.

84. Testimony of Frank A. Thomas, Presidential Mediation Commission, RG 101 Cochise County SG 8 Superior Court Civil Division 1917 Bisbee Deportation, 62–64, ASLAPR.

85. *Bisbee Daily Review*, July 10, 1917.

86. Watson, "Still on Strike! Recollections of a Bisbee Deportee," 174.

87. Letter from Secretary-Treasurer to Executive Committee, July 10, 1917, UASC, AZ 114, box 1, folder 2.

88. *Bisbee Daily Review*, July 11, 1917.

89. W. T. Merrill, Testimony at Presidential Mediation Commission, RG 101 Cochise County SG 8 Superior Court Civil Division 1917, 194, ASLAPR.

90. W. T. Merrill, Testimony at Presidential Mediation Commission, RG 101 Cochise County SG 8 Superior Court Civil Division 1917, 208, ASLAPR.

91. J. F. McDonald, Testimony at Presidential Mediation Commission, RG 101 Cochise County SG 8 Superior Court Civil Division 1917, 23–24, ASLAPR.

92. *Bisbee Daily Review*, July 11, 1917.

93. *Verde Copper News*, July 10, 1917.

94. *Jerome Sun*, July 10, 1917.

95. *Prescott Journal Miner*, July 11, 1917.

96. *Verde Copper News*, July 12, 1917.

97. *Verde Copper News*, July 15, 101.

98. *Verde Copper News*, July 11, 1917.

99. *Prescott Journal Miner*, July 12, 1917.

100. *Verde Copper News*, July 17, 1917.

101. Jeannette Rankin and Mrs. Rosa McKay, "Butte and Bisbee Outrages Scored by Brave Woman Representatives," *Appeal to Reason*, August 18, 1917.

102. W. T. Merrill, Testimony at Presidential Mediation Commission, ASLAPR, RG 101 Cochise County SG 8 Superior Court Civil Division 1917, 193.

103. *Bisbee Daily Review*, July 12, 1917.

104. Affidavit of Frederick Watson, August 31, 1970, John Pintek Papers, MG112, series 1, folder 23.

105. Bassett Watkins, Testimony at Presidential Mediation Commission, RG 101

Cochise County SG 8 Superior Court Civil Division 1917, 233, ASLAPR, George Kellogg Testimony at Presidential Mediation Commission, RG 101 Cochise County SG 8 Superior Court Civil Division 1917, 5, ASLAPR.

106. Testimony of W. T. Merrill at Presidential Mediation Commission, RG 101 Cochise County SG 8 Superior Court Civil Division 1917, 204, ASLAPR.

107. Testimony of Bassett Watkins at Presidential Mediation Commission, RG 101 Cochise County SG 8 Superior Court Civil Division 1917, 232, ASLAPR.

108. Testimony of W. T. Merrill at Presidential Mediation Commission, RG 101 Cochise County SG 8 Superior Court Civil Division 1917, 221, ASLAPR.

109. Oral History interview dated February 18, 1971, Bisbee Mining and Historical Museum.

110. Except where noted elsewhere, what follows can be found in [William Beeman] "History of the Bisbee Deportation," John Pintek Papers, MG112, box 1, folder 26, ASLAPR.

111. J. F. McDonald, Testimony at Presidential Mediation Commission, RG 101, Cochise County, SG8, Superior Court, Civil Division, 1917, 24, ASLAPR.

112. Cleland, *A History of Phelps Dodge,* 188

113. George Kellogg, Testimony at Presidential Mediation Commission, RG 101, Cochise County, SG8, Superior Court, Civil Division, 1917, ASLAPR, 5.

114. George Kellogg, Testimony at Presidential Mediation Commission, RG 101, Cochise County, SG8, Superior Court, Civil Division, 1917, ASLAP, 5–6.

115. [William Beeman] "History of the Bisbee Deportation," John Pintek Papers, MG112, box 1, folder 26.

CHAPTER FOUR: THE ROUNDUP

1. Frank Martin, Testimony at Presidential Mediation Commission, RG 101 Cochise County SG 8 Superior Court Civil Division 1917, 72, ASLAPR.

2. Letter of Frank Vaughan to Governor Hunt, MG 25, George Hunt Papers, box 17, Series 3, folder 388.

3. *Jerome Sun,* July 12, 1917, ASLAPR.

4. George E. Kellogg, Testimony at Presidential Mediation Commission, RG 101 Cochise County SG 8 Superior Court Civil Division 1917, 12–13, 16, ASLAPR.

5. *Los Angeles Times,* July 13, 1917.

6. *New York Times,* July 14, 1917.

7. Mr. Gehringer, Testimony at the Presidential Mediation Commission, RG 101 Cochise County SG 8 Superior Court Civil Division 1917, 479, ASLAPR.

8. *Bisbee Daily Review,* July 13, 1917.

9. Oral History interview conducted August 22, 1995; Bisbee Mining and Historical Museum (BMHM).

10. George Kellogg, Testimony at Presidential Mediation Commission, RG 101 Cochise County SG 8 Superior Court Civil Division 1917, ASLAPR, 10–11; *Bisbee Daily Review,* July 13, 1917; *New York Times,* July 13, 1917.

11. R. E. Thompson to Governor Hunt, August 11, 1917, MG 26, George Hunt Papers, series 3, box 17, file 388, ASLAPR.

12. Fred Watson, "Still on Strike! Recollections of a Bisbee Deportee," *New York Times*, July 13, 1917, 176.

13. Mr. Gehringer, Testimony at the Presidential Mediation Commission, RG 101 Cochise County SG 8 Superior Court Civil Division 1917, 438–39, ASLAPR.

14. Letter from Mrs. O. Snyder to Mrs. M.E. Rieter, July 21, 1917; Bisbee Mining Museum, Bisbee Deportation.

15. George P. Hunt Papers, MG 25, Series 3, box 17, folder 288, ASLAPR.

16. Fred Brown, Testimony at the Presidential Mediation Commission, RG 101 Cochise County SG 8 Superior Court Civil Division 1917, 29–30, ASLAPR.

17. Thomas English, Testimony at Presidential Mediation Commission, RG 101 Cochise County SG 8 Superior Court Civil Division 1917, 81, ASLAPR.

18. George P. Hunt Papers, MG 25, Series 3, box 17, folder 288, ASLAPR.

19. Undated oral history interview, BMHM.

20. Testimony of Rosa McKay, Presidential Mediation Commission, RG 101, Cochise County, SG8, Superior Court, Civil Division, 1917, Bisbee Deportation files, 127–128, ASLAPR; Harry Wheeler, Testimony at the Presidential Mediation Commission, RG 101 Cochise County SG 8 Superior Court Civil Division 1917, 174, ASLAPR.

21. Oral history interview conducted January 15, 1981, BMHM.

22. Bassett Watkins, Testimony at Presidential Mediation Commission, 235, ASLAPR.

23. Affidavit of Frederick Watson, August 31, 1970, ASLAPR, John Pintek Papers, MG112, Series 1, folder 23, ASLAPR.

24. Fred Watson, "Still on Strike! Recollections of a Bisbee Deportee," 178.

25. Oral History interview conducted March 27, 1992; Bisbee Mining and History Museum.

26. Undated oral History interview; Bisbee Mining and Historical Museum.

27. Letter to Governor Hunt, July 16, 1917, MG 25, George Hunt Papers, Series 3, box 17, folder 388, ASLAPR.

28. Rosa McKay, Testimony at the Presidential Mediation Commission, 129–30.

29. Affidavit of Fred Watson, August 31, 1970, MG 112, Series 1, folder 23, Fred Watson, "Still on Strike! Recollections of a Bisbee Deportee," 177.

30. Undated oral history, Bisbee Mining and Historical Museum.

31. 1910 Census, ancestry.com.

32. Affidavit of Fred Watson, August 31, 1970, ASLAPR, MG 112, Series 1, folder 23.

33. Superior Court of the County of Cochise, inquest held on the body of O.P. McRae and James Brew, ancestry.com.

34. George Hunt Papers, MG 25, Series 3 box 17, folder 288.

35. Oral History interview conducted April 6, 1990; Bisbee Mining and Historical Museum.

36. Jeannette Rankin and Mrs. Rosa McKay, "Butte and Bisbee Outrages Scored by Brave Woman Representatives."

37. Oral History interview conducted September 10, 1978; Bisbee Mining and Historical Museum.

38. Statements of Blagoje Gjurovich and Carl Thomas, MG25, George Hunt Papers, Series 3, box 17, folder 288, Renio Merilo MG25, Series 3, box 17, folder 289, ASLAPR.

39. J. F. McDonald, Testimony at Presidential Mediation Commission, ASLAPR, RG101, Cochise County, SG8, Superior Court, Civil Division, 1917, 22–23.

40. Fred Watson, "Still on Strike! Recollections of a Bisbee Deportee," 177.

41. George Hunt Papers, MG25, Series 3, box 187, folder 289.

42. Merrill, Testimony at Presidential Mediation Commission, 203.

43. Statement of Louis Asic, George Hunt Papers, MSG 25, Series 3, box 17, folder 288, ASLAPR.

44. Statement of Steven Switish, George Hunt Papers, MG25, Series 3, box 17, folder 289, ASLAPR.

45. Letter dated July 25, 1917, of Frank Vaughan to Governor Hunt, George Hunt Papers, MG 35, Series 3, box 17, folder 388, ASLAPR.

46. Statements of Isaac Conky and Frank Wheeler, George Hunt Papers, MG 25, Series 3, box 17 folder 288, ASLAPR.

47. John Pintek Papers, MG 112, Series 1, folder 23, ASLAPR.

48. Testimony of George Kellogg, Presidential Mediation Commission, 13.

49. Telegram, Edw. Stanigan, Alexander Murry, and E.P. Dupen to Governor Hunt, July 12, 1917, George Hunt Papers, MG 25, box 17, Series 3, folder 388, ASLAPR.

50. *New York Times*, July 13, 1917.

51. Fred Brown, Testimony at Presidential Mediation Commission, 32; Testimony of Harry Wheeler, 170.

52. Oral history interview conducted September 16, 1974, Bisbee Mining and Historical Museum.

53. Affidavit of Frederick Watson, John Pintek Papers, MG112, Series 1, folder 23.

54. John Wilson, Testimony at Presidential Mediation commission, 121.

55. Oral history interview conducted Feb 20, 1991, Bisbee Mining and Historical Museum.

56. John Pintek Papers, MG 112, Series 1, folder 23, ASLAPR.

57. Letter to Governor Hunt, July 16, 1917, MG 25, George Hunt Papers, Series 3, box 17, folder 388, ASLAPR.

58. Statement of Milos Vukotich, George Hunt Papers, MG 25, Series 3, box 17, folder 288.

59. Fred Watson, "Still on Strike! Recollections of a Bisbee Deportee," 180.

60. Oral History interview, November 10, 1944, Bisbee Mining and Historical Museum.

61. Undated oral History interview, Bisbee Mining and Historical Museum.

62. Stewart Bird, Dan Georgakas, and Deborah Shaffer, *Solidarity Forever: An Oral History of the IWW* (Chicago: Lake View Press, 1985), 133.

63. Letter dated July 25, 1917, of Frank Vaughan to Governor Hunt, George Hunt Papers, MG 35, Series 3, box 17, folder 388. A close examination of photos of the round-up does indeed seem to show a man and sandbags on the roof of that building, but the presence of machine guns there cannot be proved definitively.

64. *New York Times*, July 14, 1917.

65. Letter from Mrs. O. Snyder to Mrs. M.E. Rieter, July 21, 1917; BMHM, Bisbee Deportation.

66. Letter to Governor Hunt, July 16, 1917, MG 25, George Hunt Papers, Series 3, box 17, folder 388, ASLAPR.

67. Bulletin of Metal Mine Workers Industrial Union 88, July 13, 1917, *Simmons v. El Paso and Southwestern Railroad* exhibits, AZ 114, box 1, folder 3, UASC.

68. *Bisbee Daily Review*, October 4, 1917.

69. Commissioner Walker at the Presidential Mediation Commission, ASLAPR, RG 101 Cochise County SG 8 Superior Court Civil Division 1917, 461.

70. *Solidarity*, July 21, 1917; *New York Times*, July 13, 1917.

71. *New York Times*, July 14, 1917.

CHAPTER FIVE: THE DEPORTEES IN NEW MEXICO

1. Fred Brown, Testimony at Presidential Mediation Commission, RG101, Cochise County, SG8, Superior Court, Civil Division, 1917, 37, ASLAPR.

2. Fred Brown, Testimony at Presidential Mediation Commission, 38.

3. Fred Brown, Testimony at Presidential Mediation Commission, 39.

4. Affidavit of Owen Jones, George Hunt Papers, MG 25, Series 3, box 17, folder 289.

5. *New York Times*, July 14, 1917.

6. Deposition of Ilja Luka Gabovich, George Hunt Papers, MG 25 Series 3, box 17, Fred Brown, Testimony at Presidential Mediation Commission, 39–40.

7. *New York Times*, July 14, 1917.

8. *Verde Copper News*, July 13, 1917.

9. *Bisbee Daily Review*, July 14, 1917.

10. *Milwaukee Leader*, July 13, 1917.

11. J. Oates, "Globe-Miami District," *International Socialist Review* XVII, no. 2, August 1917, 73.

12. Telegram from William Cleary to Governor Hunt, July 13, 1917, George Hunt Papers, MG25, Series 3, box 17, folder 388.

13. *Weekly Journal* (Prescott, Arizona), July 18, 1917.

14. *Columbus (NM) Courier*, July 13, 1917.

15. *Bisbee Daily Review*, July 14, 1917.

16. *Bisbee Daily Review*, July 15, 1917.

17. *New York Times*, July 15, 1917.

18. *Bisbee Daily Review*, July 18, 1917.

19. *New York Times*, July 16, 1917.

20. Address of Senator Sutter at the first special session of the third legislature of the state of Arizona, June 4, 1918, BMHM, Bisbee Deportation.

21. Bisbee Mining and Historical Museum, Bisbee Deportation.

22. Fred Brown, Testimony at Presidential Mediation Commission, 36.

23. Speech of Senator Sutter, BMHM, Bisbee Deportation.

24. Mike Anderson, "Forgotten Men: The Odyssey of the Bisbee Deportees." *Cochise County Historical Journal*, 47, no. 1 (Spring/Summer 2017): 62.

25. Anderson, "Forgotten Men: The Odyssey of the Bisbee Deportees," 64–72 passim.

26. Article on Liberty Bonds, found at https://www.federalreservehistory.org/essays/liberty_bonds.

27. Speech of State Senator Sutter, BMHM, Bisbee Deportation Files.

28. *Bisbee Daily Review*, July 22, 1917.

29. Affidavit of Frederick Watson, John Pintek Papers, MG112, Series 1, folder 23, ASLAPR.

30. Letter from J. MacDonald to Grover Perry, July 23, 1917. BMHM, Bisbee Deportation Files.

31. Telegram from Ben K. Webb, A.S. Embree, and A.D. Kimball to Governor Hunt, July 24, 1917, George P. Hunt Papers, MG 25, Series 3, box 17, folder 388, ASLAPR.

32. *Bisbee Daily Review*, July 27, 1917.

33. Letter of A.S. Embree to Grover H. Perry, July 26, 1917, Bisbee Mining and Historical Museum, Bisbee Deportation Files.

34. *Bisbee Daily Review*, August 4, 1917.

35. Letter from Jack Norman to Grover Perry, July 30, 1917, UASC, AZ 114, box 1, folder 2, Simmons v. El Paso and Southwestern Railroad exhibits.

36. Letter from M. C. Sullivan to Grover Perry, UASC, AZ 114, box 1, Simmons vs. EL Paso and Southwestern Railroad exhibits.

37. Watson, "Still on Strike! Recollections of a Bisbee Deportee," 181.

38. Letter of Jack Norman to V. V. O'Hair dated August 18, 1917, BMHM, Bisbee Deportation.

39. Letter [from Grover Perry] to Jack Norman, August 24, 1917, BMHM, Bisbee Deportation.

40. *Bisbee Daily Review*, August 21, 1917.

41. Unsigned letter [George Hunt?], August 21, 1917, George P. Hunt Papers, MG 25, Series 3, box 16, file 345.

42. *Bisbee Daily Review*, August 22, 1917.

43. *Bisbee Daily Review*, June 19, 1917.

44. *Bisbee Daily Review*, August 22, 1917.

45. Quoted in letter to President Wilson from George Hunt dated September 3, 1917. George Hunt Papers, MG25Series 3, box 16, file 345, ASLAPR.

46. Frank Vaughan to Governor Hunt, July 25, 1917, George P. Hunt Papers, MG 25, Series 3, box 16, ASLAPR.

47. Fred Brown, Testimony at Presidential Mediation Commission, 36.

48. Quoted in letter to President Wilson from George Hunt dated September 3, 1917, George Hunt Papers, MG25, Series 3, box 16, file 345, ASLAPR. Frank Vaughan to Governor Hunt, July 25, 1917, George Hunt Papers, MG 25, Series 3, box 16, ASLAPR.

49. *Bisbee Daily Review*, September 12, 1917.

50. V. V. O'Hair, letter to Jack Norman, August 8, 1917, AZ 114, box 1, folder 2, UASC.

51. Letter from Jack Shean to Bill Haywood, August 28, 1917, AZ 114, box 1, folder 1, UASC.

52. *Bisbee Daily Review*, September 13, 1917.

53. *Bisbee Daily Review*, September 15, 1917.

54. *Bisbee Daily Review*, September 18, 1917.

CHAPTER SIX: BISBEE AFTER THE DEPORTATION

1. *Bisbee Daily Review*, July 13, 1917.
2. M. W. Merrill, Testimony at Presidential Mediation Commission, 214, Harry Wheeler, Testimony, 157.
3. *Bisbee Daily Review*, July 14, 1917.
4. *Bisbee Daily Review*, July 15, 1917.
5. Frank Vaughan, Testimony at Presidential Mediation Commission, 47.
6. S. W. White to Governor Hunt, July 13, 1917, MG 25, George P. Hunt Papers, box 17, series 3, file 388, ASLAPR.
7. *Bisbee Daily Review*, July 15, 1917.
8. Oral history interview with Dan Kitchell, BMHM.
9. Watson, "Still on Strike! Recollections of a Bisbee Deportee," 177.
10. *Bisbee Daily Review*, July 17, 1917.
11. *Bisbee Daily Review*, July 18, 1917.
12. Ibid.
13. Watson, "Still on Strike! Recollections of a Bisbee Deportee," 184.
14. M. W. Merrill et al., "Mining Condition in Bisbee, Arizona," UASC L9791 B62 pam. 15.
15. Testimony of Frank A. Thomas, Presidential Mediation Commission, 67–68.
16. *Bisbee Daily Review*, July 18, 1917.
17. Fred Brown, Testimony at Presidential Mediation Commission, 31–34.
18. Letter from Rowan to Governor Hunt, George Hunt Papers, Arizona State Library and Archives, MG 25, Series 3, box 16, File 345, ASLAPR.
19. *Bisbee Daily Review*, July 18, 1917.
20. *Los Angeles Times*, July 15, 1917.
21. Personal communication from D.D. Guttenplan.
22. [Oswald Garrison Villard] "The Week," *Nation* 105, no. 2716, July 19, 1917, 57.
23. [Oswald Garrison Villard] "The Week," *Nation*, 105, no. 2721, August 23, 1917, 191.
24. George P. Hunt Papers, MG 25 Series 3, box 17, folder 388, ASLAPR.
25. *New York Times*, July 22, 1917.
26. *Bisbee Daily Review*, July 19, 1917.
27. *Bisbee Daily Review*, July 24, 1917.
28. *Bisbee Daily Review*, July 27, 1917.
29. Letter dated July 25, 1917, Frank Vaughan to Governor Hunt, MG 35, Series 3, box 17, folder 388, ASLAPR.
30. *Bisbee Daily Review*, July 28, 1917.
31. Oral history interview, BMHM.
32. Letter from John T. Hughes to George Hunt, August 3, 1917, George Hunt Papers, MG 25, Series 3, box 17, folder 389, ASLAPR.
33. *Bisbee Daily Review* July 31, 1917.
34. *International Socialist Review*, XVIII, no. 3, September 1917, 142.
35. *New York Times*, August 8, 1917.
36. Chaplin, *Wobbly*, 210.

37. *Butte Daily Post*, August 1, 1917, 1.

38. Arnold Stead, *Always on Strike* (Chicago: Haymarket, 2014), 3.

39. *Bisbee Daily Review*, August 14, 1917.

40. *Bisbee Daily Review*, August 17, 1917.

41. *New York Times*, August 10, 1917.

42. *Bisbee Daily Review*, August 21, 1917.

43. *Bisbee Daily Review*, August 21, 1917.

44. Testimony of Frank A. Martin, Presidential Mediation Commission, 71.

45. *Bisbee Daily Review*, July 12, 1917.

46. *Bisbee Daily Review*, August 24, 1917.

47. *Bisbee Daily Review*, August 28, 1917.

48. *Bisbee Daily Review*, August 25, 1917.

49. *Bisbee Daily Review*, August 26, 1917.

50. *Solidarity*, September 1, 1917.

51. *Bisbee Daily Review*, September 1, 1917.

52. *Appeal to Reason*, October 6, 1917.

53. Letter from Adjutant General, Arizona, to Chief Military Bureau, Washington, DC., November 27, 1917. MG25 George Hunt Papers, Series 3, box 16, file 345, ASLAPR.

54. Fred Brown, Testimony at Presidential Mediation Commission, 42.

55. Letter from International Union of Mine, Mill & Smelter Workers to Secretary of Labor William B. Wilson's Mediation Commission et al., dated Miami, Arizona, November 30, 1917. George Hunt Papers, MG 25, box 16, file 345, ASLAPR.

56. *Bisbee Daily Review*, September 6, 1917.

57. Bureau of Investigation case files, NARA M-1085 collection, reel 57. (Thanks to Tim Davenport for locating and sharing this record.)

58. *Bisbee Daily Review*, March 21, 1920.

CHAPTER SEVEN: THE PRESIDENTIAL MEDIATION COMMISSION

1. Meyer H. Fishbein, "The President's Mediation Commission and the Arizona Copper Strike, 1917," *Southwestern Social Science Quarterly* 30, no. 3 (December 1949): 179–180.

2. *Bisbee Daily Review*, September 28, 1917.

3. William B. Wilson, Testimony at Presidential Mediation Commission, 317.

4. *Bisbee Daily Review*, November 4, 1917.

5. Letter from the Warren Trades Assembly, MG 25, George Hunt Papers, series 3, box 16, file 345, ASLAPR.

6. *Bisbee Daily Review*, November 2, 1917.

7. *Bisbee Daily Review*, November 3, 1917.

8. Testimony of Secretary Wilson, Presidential Mediation Commission, 77.

9. Testimony of Harry Wheeler, Presidential Mediation Commission, 153.

10. Testimony of Harry Wheeler, Presidential Mediation Commission, 163.

11. Testimony of Harry Wheeler, Presidential Mediation Commission, 158–59.

12. Testimony of J. C. Ryan at Presidential Mediation Commission, 242.

13. Testimony of J. C. Ryan at Presidential Mediation Commission, 253.
14. Testimony of J. C. Ryan at Presidential Mediation Commission, 329.
15. Testimony of J. C. Ryan at Presidential Mediation Commission, 259–60.
16. Testimony of J. C. Ryan at Presidential Mediation Commission, 171–72.
17. Secretary Wilson at Presidential Mediation Commission, 260–61.
18. Testimony of J. C. Ryan at Presidential Mediation Commission, 262.
19. Testimony of J. C. Ryan at Presidential Mediation Commission, 330.
20. Testimony of Secretary Wilson at Presidential Mediation Commission, 333–34.
21. Testimony of E. E. Ellinwood at Presidential Mediation Commission, 407–408.
22. Testimony of Arthur Houle at Presidential Mediation Commission, 451.
23. Testimony of Arthur Hole at Presidential Mediation Commission, 453.
24. Testimony of Commissioner J. H. Walker at Presidential Mediation Commission, 459–60.
25. "Correspondence and Agreement at Bisbee," *Miner's Magazine*, December 1917.
26. *Bisbee Daily Review*, November 24, 1917.
27. President's Mediation Commission, *Report on the Bisbee Deportation* (Washington, Government Printing Office, 1918), 3 University of Arizona Special Collections, H9791, B621, U58r.
28. President's Mediation Commission, *Report on the Bisbee Deportations*, 4.
29. President's Mediation Commission, *Report on the Bisbee Deportations*.
30. "Sixth Annual Report of the Secretary of Labor for the Fiscal Year Ended June 30, 1918" (Washington, Government Printing Office), University of Arizona Special Collections, H9791, B621, U58.
31. Letter from Theodore Roosevelt to Felix Frankfurter, December 19, 1917, BMHM, Bisbee Deportation.

Chapter Eight: The Deportation on Trial

1. *Bisbee Daily Review*, December 2, 1917.
2. [Oswald Garrison Villard] "The Week," *Nation*, 107, no. 2789, December 14, 1918, 717.
3. Byrkit, *Forging the Copper Collar*, 288–91 passim, *New York Times*, May 29, 1918; *Bisbee Daily Review*, December 3, 1918. Isabel Shattuck Fathauer, *Lemuel Shattuck* (Tucson: Westernlore Press, 1991), 197.
4. RG101 Cochise County, SG8, Superior Court, box 1, Bisbee Deportation, ASLAPR.
5. RG101 Cochise County, SG8, Superior Court, box 1, Bisbee Deportation, ASLAPR.
6. Byrkit, *Forging the Copper Collar*, 291.
7. Arizona State Library and Archives, John Pintek Papers, MG 112, Bx 1, folder 26.
8. *New York Times*, February 3, 1920.
9. *Bisbee Daily Review*, February 3, 1920.
10. Lawson, *American State Trials*, 6.
11. *Bisbee Daily Review*, February 4, 1920.
12. *Bisbee Daily Review*, February 5, 1920.
13. *Bisbee Daily Review*, February 6, 1920.
14. *Bisbee Daily Review*, Feb 12, 1920; February 20, 1920.

15. *Bisbee Daily Review*, February 8, 1920.

16. *Bisbee Daily Review*, February 15, 1920.

17. *Bisbee Daily Review*, February 27, 1920.

18. *Bisbee Daily Review*, February 28, 1920.

19. *Bisbee Daily Review*, March 2, 1920.

20. *Bisbee Daily Review*, March 5, 1920.

21. *Bisbee Daily Review*, March 6, 1920; March 7, 1920.

22. *Bisbee Daily Review*, March 9, 1920.

23. *Bisbee Daily Review*, March 11, 1920.

24. Lawson, *American State Trials*, 8.

25. Ibid., 9–11 passim.

26. Ibid., 11

27. Ibid., 16.

28. Ibid., 43.

29. The *Law of Necessity as Applied in the State of Arizona, Bisbee I.W.W. vs. Deportation Case H. E. Wootton*, Star Publishing, 94–95, H9791 B621 L41, UASC.

30. Lawson, *American State Trials*, 49–50.

31. Ibid., 50.

32. Ibid., 50.

33. Ibid., 64–67 passim.

34. *Bisbee Daily Review*, May 1, 1920.

35. John D. Lawson, *American State Trials*, 69.

36. Lawson, *American State Trials*, 67.

37. Ibid., 76.

38. Ibid., 77–90 passim.

39. Ibid., 90.

40. Ibid., 92–93.

41. Ibid., 97–98.

42. Ibid., 100.

43. George Soule, "The Law of Necessity in Bisbee," *Nation* 113, no. 2930, August 31, 1921, 226–27.

44. Lawson, *American State Trials*, 106–107.

45. Ibid., 109–10.

46. Ibid., 127.

47. Ibid., 130.

48. Ibid., 136.

49. Ibid., 143–44.

50. Ibid., 153.

51. Ibid., 157.

52. Ibid., 162–64.

53. Ibid., 168.

54. *Bisbee Daily Review*, May 1, 1920.

NOTES

CHAPTER NINE: THE AFTERMATH

1. Samuel Truett, *Fugitive Landscapes* (New Haven: Yale University Press, 2006), 183.
2. Interview with Charles Bethea, March 15, 2019.
3. Watson, "Still on Strike! Recollections of a Bisbee Deportee," 184.
4. Undated interview with Ralph Hargis, BMHM.
5. Personal communication, Ruben Gomez, March 24, 2019.
6. Personal communication, Steve Ray.
7. Anderson, "Forgotten Men: The Odyssey of the Bisbee Deportees," 74.
8. John Pintek Papers, Arizona State Library and Archives, MG 112, box 1, File 26.
9. Letter from Todd Bogatay to Mayor Ron Oertle, May 30, 2005, John Pintek Papers, MG 112, box 1, File 26, ASLAPR.

CONCLUSION

1. Byrkit, *Forging the Copper Collar*, 326–27.
2. Ibid., 327.
3. *McKinney's Bisbee and Warren District Directory, 1917–1918* (Bisbee, AZ: Walsh & Fitzgerald, 1917); Interview with Mike Anderson, Bisbee Mining Museum, March 15, 2019.
4. *Bisbee Daily Review*, May 8, 1917.
5. Christopher Capozzola, "The Only Badge Needed Is Your Patriotic Fervor: Vigilance, Coercion, and the Law in World War I America," *Journal of American History* 88, no. 4 (2002): 1354.
6. *Bisbee Daily Review*, November 10, 1917.

INDEX